DARE

The transformational journey of a woman who dared to be more

DIANE DEMETRE

The author of this book does not dispense medical advice or prescribe the use of any technique as a form of treatment for physical, emotional or medical problems without the advice of a physician, either directly or indirectly. The intent of the author is only to offer information of a general nature to help you in your quest for physical, emotional, mental and spiritual well-being. In the event you use any of the information in this book for yourself, the author and the publisher assume no responsibility for your actions.

The events related in this memoir, including conversations that occurred, have been recreated to the best recollection of the author. Some situations have been modified, compressed or expanded; and names and identifying details of certain individuals have been changed for confidentiality purposes.

DARE
the transformational journey of a woman who dared to be more
© Diane Demetre 2021
This edition January 2024

All rights reserved. No part of this publication may be reproduced, stored in a retrieval system, or transmitted in any form or by any means, electronic, mechanical, photocopying, recording or otherwise, without the prior written permission of the author.

ISBN: 978-1-7384979-0-4

Cover Design: by Asya blue

Published by Diane Demetre

ABOUT THE AUTHOR

Diane Demetre has helped countless people dare to create their own success stories. Spanning 40+ years, her successful career in education, entertainment and entrepreneurship is testament to the philosophy she advocates.

An award-winning business leader, keynote speaker, and author of over a dozen books, Diane believes that life is either a daring adventure or nothing at all. She knows that when we fear less and dare more, the best of us shines through and the leader within is revealed.

In DARE, she writes with her trademark honesty, courage, and inspiration giving a frank, no-holds-barred account of her life as she guides the reader through her most heart-warming and heart-breaking moments, sharing the 50 life-affirming insights she learned along the way.

In recognition of her exceptional contributions to the Entertainment, Creative Arts, and Media Industry, Diane was awarded the prestigious SBAA International Women's Day Leader Award for her unwavering leadership, pioneering spirit, and women's advocacy.

She lives on the Gold Coast in Australia with her husband, eagerly anticipating and appreciating the next daring adventure that is yet to unfold.

CONNECT WITH DIANE:

dianedemetre.com
Facebook @DianeDemetreOfficial
Instagram @dianedemetreofficial
Linkedin @dianedemetrespeaks
Twitter @DianeDemetre

DEDICATION

To my wonderful parents, Max and Beryl Bowman.
Until we meet again.

CONTENTS

About the Author iii
Foreword ix
Praise xi
Overture xvii

Act One: The Making and Breaking
of a Woman 1
   Chapter One: The beginning of the dream 3
      And so, it begins 13
   Chapter Two: Cultivating the dream 17
      Laying the cornerstone 23
   Chapter Three: Dreams do come true 25
      Game on 31
   Chapter Four: Tipping point 33
      Everything is energy 40
   Chapter Five: The gauntlet is thrown 43
      We choose the life we live 45
   Chapter Six: Do the good guys win? 49
      The power of practice and persistence 54
   Chapter Seven: Crash and burn 57
      Destiny is repeated experience 61

Act Two: The Awakening of a Woman 63
   Chapter Eight: Let go and lean in 65
      Insights…Be decisive, Be playful,
      Be Spontaneous, Be joyous 73
   Chapter Nine: Listen and look for the omens 77
      Insights…Be willing, Be responsible, Be perceptive .. 80
   Chapter Ten: Stirrings of the soul 83
      Insights…Be centered, Be curious, Be receptive, Be in
communion 90

Chapter Eleven: Releasing my emotional past 91
    Insights…Be love, Be forgiving, Be present 98
Chapter Twelve: Fire of desire 101
    Insights…Be focused,
    Be committed, Be purposeful 107
Chapter Thirteen: Passion is power 111
    Insights…Be passionate, Be powerful,
    Be patient, Be fearless 116
Chapter Fourteen: Creating a brighter future 121
    Insights…Be peaceful, Be healthy,
    Be disciplined, Be driven, Be determined 129
    Chapter Fifteen: Reaping the rewards 131
    Insights…Be persistent, Be strong, Be thankful 135
Chapter Sixteen: Attention and intention 137
Insights…Be Intentional, Be generous,
    Be undefended, Be courageous 142
Chapter Seventeen: Magic and miracles 145
    Insights…Be Optimistic, Be Open, Be Bold 152
Chapter Eighteen: A new role 153
    Insights…Be Kind, Be Intuitive, Be Flexible 158
Chapter Nineteen: Fulfillment and success. 161
    Insights…Be inspired, Be valuable,
    Be intelligent 165
Chapter Twenty: Setting the trap 169
    Insights…Be creative, Be gentle,
    Be intimate, Be Balanced 179
Chapter Twenty-One: Let it be 183
    Insights…Be yielding, Be humble,
    Be honest, Be in a state of grace 198
    Encore 203

50 Insights to Being and Their Meanings. 207
Award Winning Author 211
Also by Diane Demetre. 213

FOREWORD

Imagine, if you can, being given up at birth and spending the first two weeks of your formative and curious life without the warmth of human contact except for the basic necessities to keep you alive.

Imagine, if you can, being born with a zest for life and an exuberance of spirit that nourishes your soul with endless ideas and visions of conquests that lay ahead.

At two weeks of age, Diane Demetre was blessed by being adopted by loving parents who supported and encouraged her boundless hopes, dreams, and desires. Although their material wealth was modest their devotion to and delight with their bouncing baby girl was endless.

From an early age, Diane exhibited qualities that would sustain her through her rollercoaster life. She was creative, questioning, and filled with ideas and goals as she looked forward to the life she imagined would unfold.

During her six decades, so far, on earth, Diane has been the catalyst for major legislative change in industrial relations concerning an important social issue, she has plummeted to the depths of despair and she has risen like a Phoenix from the ashes to become a glamorous, competent and respected business woman whose projects and endeavors span the globe. Her innate warrior spirit combined with her intuitive spiritual insights have held her in good stead, even when those around her strove to see her professionally and psychologically destroyed. It is, perhaps, that warrior spirit which rose in her darkest of hours that has drawn my admiration for this remarkable woman, to say nothing of her lifelong passion and devotion towards animal welfare, yet another facet of this rare diamond which shone like a light in the darkness for me.

Her experiences in life, the triumphs and the tragedies, have led her down one path after another not like a moth to a flame but like an Amazon into glorious battle. Along the way, both by accident and by design she has acquired a wealth of knowledge and insights which she shares as whispered words of wisdom in this compelling memoir. The page-turning narrative evokes both laughter and tears as each chapter wraps up with a summation offering insights and lessons that many will benefit from on their own life's journey as they join Diane vicariously on hers.

Think big, be bold and at times be brazen! Fortune favors the bold and this has certainly proven true in the life story of Diane Demetre. Join this fiery redhead as she dances up the stairway to paradise, occasionally missing her footing, and sometimes even sliding back a few stairs, but never erring in her quest or thirst for life as she knows it can be. As she says so eloquently and correctly, "If it's meant to be, it's up to me". These are words I have not only lived by myself but sound advice that many others should heed.

When we reach an age of maturity and accomplishment appropriate to pen a memoir, it should be with the thought in mind not only of sharing our lives with the world but in leaving a footprint that might help direct another on their own path. As the 19th century philosopher and poet, Ralph Waldo Emerson, so eruditely and correctly said, "If one life has breathed easier because you have lived, this is to have succeeded."

A dancer, a choreographer, a speaker, an author of contemporary fiction, a wife, a fur baby mother, a daughter, an adopted daughter, a step parent to a large and growing Greek family, an entrepreneur and a visionary, Diane is as prolific as she is passionate, and her effervescence is infectious.

She is a woman to be admired with a life story you can't afford to miss.

Hollywood Actress and Animal Rights Activist

PRAISE

Demetre is a strong, determined, successful woman who has self-actualized more than most. This is evident in this engaging memoir. She is clearly a passionate and experienced writer, her prose sophisticated, her narrative moving. Her spiritual experiences are compelling, unique, and very readable making this book a strong, fascinating addition to the memoir/spiritual journey genre.

—Book Life Review

DARE is an incredibly beautiful and challenging journey, Diane, and I cherished every page. Your story of overcoming wildly inappropriate advances in your career provided me with a chance to reflect on my own experiences and imagine a world where women aren't burdened by exploitation and domination. I'm truly in awe of you.

On behalf of women in Australia and around the globe, I extend my heartfelt gratitude. Thank you, Diane, for being a pioneer in the #MeToo movement, creating space for women to be bold and strong enough to say no.

Together, your readers can now rise and change the world!

—Annie Gibbons
Founder & CEO – Women's Biz Global

DARE has solid grounds to become a relevant film drama with a satisfactory resolution to the crime of harassment committed against a woman. Diane is a woman who, despite being tormented by childhood traumas, has a strength that leads her to follow her rights and dreams. This is very inspiring and engaging at this time when discussions are abundant about the feminist movement.

—Taleflick Pick

Have you recently read a book that you resonated with so strongly, it made your heart do little leaps of joy? This is what happened to me when I devoured DARE.

I started reading and couldn't put it down. Diane's crisis led to her exploration of the nature of consciousness, energy, and intuition. As she tunes into her inner world to consciously create her outer world, Diane transforms herself, leading her to live a big, courageous life that is as fulfilling as it is exciting.

Alongside the gripping story, there are lessons to be taken away from each chapter, each one outlined at the back of the book. This book is one of the most inspirational and important books I have read...and I read a lot!

—Moncia Rosenfeld
Founder – The Global Stories that Stir Movement

Diane Demetre is a fiercely vibrant, brilliant, dynamic, and professional leader who has laid her life bare in DARE. Much more than a memoir, DARE is a handbook on life and one that should sit on the self-help shelves of reader's library (sic). Not only is DARE required reading for every woman, it awakened something in me which has made a lasting impact on my life. An extraordinary woman, with extraordinary gifts and an extraordinary story to share.

—Amy Rose Gilltrap

DARE is a very powerful memoir and self-help book all rolled into one. It challenges the reader to confront their personal and professional reality and through the brave showcasing of Diane's own very personal and difficult journey through life, they will be inspired. The author has shown that every obstacle in life can be overcome if you follow your truth.

—Cynthia Dutton

Diane writes from her deep internal well; her journey is both inspiring and nurturing for all of us. The world is a better place for the "Being of Diane" which I am certain all she touches would agree. A must read!

—The Law Lady

DARE is a perfectly balanced book that should take its rightful place among the non-fiction shelves, but especially in the Self-Help section, for here is where its true value lies. I particularly enjoyed the structure of DARE; of how Diane tells her story then writes the life lessons and guidance she received at the end of the chapters. This book is a very humbling and profound gift.

—*Elizabeth Townsend*

The balance of Diane's personal stories; both painful and joyous, with the wise, hard-earned lessons that she shares is rich in its teaching. There are so many self-help books out on the shelves but this one is a teaching tool, a healing tool and a life-meaning tool. Diane has broken down and rebuilt her life so many times and in DARE she shares her thoughts, wisdom gained, and life lessons, so that we may know we're not alone when bad things happen, and that by changing our thoughts, we change our behaviours without losing who we are and what our innate spirit and purpose on this earth is.

—*Robyn Powers*

Diane has laid her life and soul bare on every page and exposed the rawness and challenge that is life. It felt as if the author had cut open her veins and let the blood flow, not so much a loss of blood but a transfusion of the blood of a courageous woman to others. A woman who would not allow anything or anyone get in her way of being the very best she could be as was her destiny. Unstoppable. Unmoveable. Unlimited.

—*Wendy Branks*

Life is either a daring adventure, or nothing at all.
　　　—Helen Keller

OVERTURE

"Look, Disy. A shooting star. Make a wish." My father pointed high into the night sky while his other hand clung to mine with a reassuring squeeze. I was about three years old and filled with wonder at the brilliance of the dying star as it arced across the constellations. That Disneyesque luminescence stirred my soul, beckoning me to reach for the stars and believe dreams do come true—and I did just that. I dared to make a wish and dream bigger dreams.

And those dreams became my reality when I scored the top job in the live entertainment industry in Australia twenty-five years later. That was when I dared to refuse my producer's sexual advances only to have my world come crashing down. Dramatically and unfairly sacked, I became the first public #metoo case in Australia long before the social movement began. My court cases received national front-page news coverage and were instrumental in eventually changing the anti-discrimination laws in the country. But I lost everything. Battered, broken and stripped of my worth, my identity, my career and my future, I teetered on the brink of suicide. My choice was painfully clear, either die or dare.

So, I dared to dream bigger dreams, to challenge my conditioned thinking, to ignore my past limitations and press on until those dreams or something better manifested. As tough as it was, I dared to believe in a new destiny. Year after year, I pressed on until I manifested a remarkable life brimming with love, fulfillment and success. I'm not going to lie and say it was easy. It wasn't. But it was simple. And what I found is that it only requires one quantum shift of perspective to live a wonderful life.

I believe we inherently know that it's possible for life to be wonderful. We just need to search for it. The real challenge is where will our search lead and do we dare make the journey along the road less traveled to find it? I decided to make that journey and discovered it's not about what I do or have. It's about who I am that defines my life. It's about who I'm *being*.

Throughout life, most of us focus our attention on ourselves, on our personality. We're obsessed with doing things to give meaning to our personality—doing a job, doing the chores, doing the family commitments, and the to-do list gets longer. We do our lives in order to have things—have a better job, have more money, have a bigger house, have more loving relationships. Our personality craves to have things, seducing us into doing more so it can have more. *Doing* and *having* cannibalize our time, peace and sanity. This addiction to doing and having is now endemic in Western civilization, as evidenced by society's chronic levels of stress, fear and depression.

Despite everything we're conditioned to believe, an abundant, loving, successful and healthy life is *not* about doing and having. It's about *being* the fullest expression of who we are, of demonstrating our inherent goodness. When we shift our attention away from the personality 'me' to the universal 'I am' and come from *being*, the doing and the having naturally unfold in perfect alignment. Contrary to popular belief, *being* comes before doing and having. We must first *be* the person who can *do* what it takes to *have* our big dreams manifest. Who we are *being* sets the benchmark for our health, wealth and happiness.

Being is the undistorted experience of Life. It's the conscious experience of self-knowing. When we come from *being*, magic and miracles happen. The universal cogs click into place and our dreams become reality, seemingly without effort.

But what if we can create this on a daily basis? What if life is enchanted? What if we are the conduit for such magic and miracles? My search for these answers uncovered a truth which spans the spectrum of sciences, philosophy and religion. Time and again the answer pointed to one fact. The power to live an enchanted life of magic and miracles lies within us. We must dare to *be* that one who aligns with *being*, claims that power and uses it in service for the highest good.

Like the knights in search of the Holy Grail, we must begin our quest with the clear intention of finding that which we seek. We must visualize victorious success, while living our life on purpose and with purpose. During our journey, and with passionate heart, we must dare to challenge our conditioned thinking and ignore our past limitations. Trusting in our vision, we must press on through our ordeals, daring to keep the faith, even when all seems lost. For those who dare will triumph in the end.

In this book, I condense my decades of intensive study and critical practice as a performer, teacher, speaker, stress and life-skills therapist and business leader, describing the experiences, some ordinary and some extraordinary, which inspired me on my quest. I've blended memoir with the practical insights I've gleaned along the way which I summarize at the end of each chapter. In reading how my experiences impacted me, you may find answers to some of the questions in your life and reap the rich rewards destined to be yours. I can't tell you anything you don't already know. I'm not sharing a secret. The truth and its laws have always expressed themselves in our lives, except most of us live in ignorance or denial of this fact. I know I did.

The evolution of human consciousness stirs within each of us. Like luminescent fireflies in spring, shimmering in the moonlight, the dance of life is eternal and everlasting. We may hinder its radiant expression, but we can never halt it. If any of this resonates with you, it's because you're ready. I am no more than a tinkling bell, a messenger of good news and a storyteller of love. Dare to come with me.

You are the Master of your Destiny, the Captain of your Soul…Let me be your guide.

ACT ONE
The Making and Breaking of a Woman

CHAPTER ONE
The beginning of the dream

Born an illegitimate child in the winter of 1957, I was given up for adoption at birth. The lovechild of a teenage mother, I was held by her but once. Distraught at being forced by her own mother to give up her first-born baby, she named me Michelle before she was whisked back to her country hometown with a fabricated story of having spent the last seven months with relatives. In fact, she spent her pregnancy disgraced and isolated, awaiting the arrival of her mistake. I hurtled into this lifetime full of spirit and chutzpah only to spend the first two weeks disconnected, alone and unwanted in a hospital crib, where the only touch I received was from the busy nurses who cared for me.

My heartbroken, biological mother returned to her prior life, while I lay unseen and unwelcome as her shameful secret. Little wonder I dreamed of stardom, wealth and success from an early age. How else does an unloved, illegitimate kid with a fierce, energetic nature get noticed? And what better way for me to learn the necessary character traits of courage, independence and self-reliance than to be exposed to abandonment and rejection at the moment of my incarnation.

Reflecting the twin-like nature of my Gemini zodiac sign, I began my journey. Witty, generous and naturally communicative, I arrived with the blithe spirit of the divine feminine, eager to enjoy the effervescence of life. The other side of me exuded a warrior spirit, a strong masculine energy prepared to uphold the virtues of truth, loyalty and fairness. Thus, ready for the quest, I settled into my new body at a most auspicious time on the planet, the post-war boom. With its growing middle class, it was a buoyant era of enormous economic growth and productivity. For those of us baby boomers born between 1946 and 1964, we took up residence in this new world like a wildebeest migration on the Serengeti. We arrived in the millions.

As an only child, adopted by an older, loving couple, Max and Beryl Bowman, I lived in a small weatherboard house that my father qualified for as a returned World War II veteran. Modest and unassuming, our shoebox house was more like an oversized doll's house compared to homes of today. Though the mortgage was nominal, it took my parents thirty years to pay it off with the meagre income they earned. Humble and hard-working, they perceived life with a grateful, happy heart, particularly after enduring and surviving the second world war.

With a faint resemblance to the movie star of the day, Errol Flynn, my father was a quiet, kind man who grew up on a wheat farm in Ardrossan, South Australia, as the youngest of seven children. His childhood reflected the tough rural life of the early twentieth century—walking barefoot or riding the horse and cart to school with his siblings, helping his parents with the chores and being the object of affection for his older sisters. At the age of twenty-six, he moved to Queensland, where he worked as a labourer on the cane fields and cotton farms before enlisting in the Australian army. At thirty-one, he was shipped off to war to serve as a military medic in the Middle East and Papua New Guinea for four, long years.

I'm certain the horrors he witnessed while carrying his dismembered mates on canvas stretchers or trying to control their pain as they faced death, impacted him greatly. No matter how much I questioned him when I grew older, he remained stoically silent and refused to speak of his war days, except to tell me of the pranks he'd played on his mates. My father was always a private man.

On his return home, he wanted to continue in medical services, but failed the exam to become a civilian ambulance medic. In retrospect, I suspect that failure became a critical turning point in his life. Instead of re-sitting the test until he succeeded, he chose to accept a lesser lot in life. Perhaps his commitment to and pride in my later successes compensated for his own perceived failures. As far as I was concerned, he was a great dad because he supported me in my dreams and did whatever was in his power to help me realize them.

Ten years his junior, my mother worked as a part-time fashion model and retail assistant, aspiring for nothing more than a happy family. Frequently over-anxious, she was a pretty, stylish young woman with a kind heart. As the eldest of two girls, her childhood and teenage years were fraught with difficulties because of her bipolar mother's unpredictability which wreaked havoc in her daughters' lives. The nervous disposition my mother inherited from her own mother played vicious games with her confidence, and she fluctuated between not feeling good enough and fits of frustration.

Due to teenage peritonitis and subsequent surgery at seventeen, my mother couldn't bear children. Therefore, adoption was my parents' only option. After waiting twelve, long years in the adoption queue and at forty-six and thirty-six years of age respectively, my father and mother welcomed me with unrestrained delight as an unexpected miracle. Unable to afford a telephone, they received the long-awaited call via a neighbor. Mum jumped the fence and rushed to pick up the neighbor's phone. She retold this moment as being the happiest in her life, when the nurse said, "Mrs. Bowman, your baby daughter is waiting here for you."

Overjoyed, they piled into the neighbor's car and drove the trip they'd long prayed for. There at two weeks of age, bundled up and ready to go, I waited, probably with an impatient scowl. Even to this day I dislike being kept waiting. My father looked down at me and in his usual casual manner, said "She'll do." And everyone's lives changed.

Since Dad's favorite song of that year was Paul Anka's "Diana," they ignored my given name of Michelle listed on my birth certificate, and called me Diane, a derivation they both preferred. In my first week home, my mother was so stricken with inadequacy and fear that she'd drop such a tiny baby, she was unable to function and took to her bed. Calling on the assistance of her cousin who duly fed, bathed and cared for me, Mum watched on, learning how to deal with the new family addition. Over time, her confidence grew and with it a loving mother-daughter relationship that enriched us both.

With my Shirley Temple curls, bright eyes and sunny disposition, I launched myself into this working-class couple's lives, wrapping us all in hope and joy. Possessing an unrelenting drive to prove that I was worthy, I somehow knew I was to shine brightly like the stars in the sky. Within me burned a flaming desire to be all I came here to be.

Although we had little disposable income, I considered myself a lucky kid. Not only did my parents adore me, my good-natured, childless godparents, Aunty Nell and Uncle George lived just a jump over the back fence. Given lots of cuddles and patient answers to my many questions, I thrived in the company of the four caring adults who surrounded me. My father and godfather were attentive, calm men, appreciative of the sunshine I added to their lives. I was fortunate to have them as such positive male role models. My mother and godmother taught me about quiet strength and hard work, instilling in me values of compassion and perseverance. The image of Aunty Nell toiling over the steaming copper washing clothes with a gigantic wooden paddle, perspiration dripping from her brow, still speaks to me of the formidable power of women.

As my young mind filed away these new, thrilling experiences, my little heart filled with joy during these happy early years, giving rise to my effervescent spirit. An adventurous spirit which delighted, yet frightened Mum. She often voiced her concerns that something unfortunate might befall me if I climbed a tree, played too roughly or rode a bicycle. Activities I rarely engaged in because of her fears, and only in her absence. She was an incessant worrier. Whenever we went shopping together, she'd leash me to her with a toddler's walking lead, securing me against possible disaster. Like a dog on point, I'd pull ahead, straining at the lead, keen to explore and talk to people or share my ice-cream with stray dogs. Unaware that her anxieties pricked like arrows at my soul, she held firm. My campaign for freedom from her loving over-protection began at an early age, fueling me with a strong drive to break out, succeed and live life to the fullest.

To make ends meet, Dad grew our own vegetables and raised chickens in the backyard patch he cultivated. A ramshackle plot of vines fruiting with pumpkins, passionfruit and tomatoes took over like marauding invaders, advancing toward the Hills Hoist clothesline until Dad thwarted their attack with a machete every few months. He spent many happy hours picking his harvest and mucking out the chicken coop, while I talked to the fairies, elves and my invisible friends in my own secret corner of the garden. Like a fairy incarnate, I was drawn to all things magical, the elfin kingdom and the majesty of the natural world. Luckily, my parents never discouraged my connection to the unseen realms.

Prior to my arrival, the chickens systematically found their way to Sunday's dining table. It was when I was about three years of age and learned in horror of the fate of my feathered friends, that the practice stopped. Due to my sobbing and refusal to eat my now roasted pal, my parents discovered a new appreciation for the birds which joined our growing menagerie of stray dogs and cats I adopted when, as if by unspoken invitation, they arrived on our doorstep. It was as if the

Bowman residence had an invisible sign that read, "Free home and board for all unwanted cats and dogs."

I felt a kindred spirit toward their unfortunate abandonment and wanted to save them all. My parents were likewise sympathetic, and the animals who decided to stay returned the favor, becoming steadfast, loving and trusted companions. This love of animals and my relationship with them carried forward throughout my life, sustaining me in both my brightest and darkest hours.

Before the advent of television, our home was filled with music. Either my father whistled tunes and played records, or my mother tested her singing voice with songs sung by Deanna Durbin or Jeanette MacDonald. She was pretty good, too. With all this music in the house, it was little wonder that as a toddler, I danced my night-time nappy off in front of the radiogram. When I stepped clean out of it to dance around the room, my parents pledged to find the extra money to send me to ballet classes. This was an inspired decision on their part and set me on the path to my destiny. Even though Dad worked fulltime as a storeman and packer, he took a second job as a postman delivering the mail on Saturdays on his pushbike, and Mum returned to retail work as soon as I started kindergarten to fund my future lessons.

I never missed having siblings, nor did I want them. As an only child, I explored within to find my playmates, which gave me a rich and inventive imagination. Rarely lonely, I spent hours conversing and playing with Sheena. She was a jungle princess only I could see and who my parents accepted with good humor. Whenever Mum brought me a glass of milk and a biscuit, there'd always be one for Sheena, which I promptly ate because Sheena didn't like biscuits. Whenever my human friends visited, I'd sit them down, and with my favorite chicken in my arms, tell them colorful stories or pretend to be a teacher giving lessons and advice. Perhaps the stirrings of my soul were already in motion as I gathered around me those I could entertain and educate with my performance.

Although my parents' faith was Christian, they hadn't practiced for years. Aside from celebrating Christmas and Easter, we had little religious discussion or education in the home. So, they were surprised, when at the age of four, I walked into our kitchen and said, "I want to go to church."

Since we couldn't afford a car, Dad propped me on the crossbar of his pushbike and cycled me to Sunday school each week. Even through the heat of summer, my father, who at the time was close to fifty years of age, struggled up the hills with his golden-haired daughter perched like a princess atop his bike.

Despite my young age, I experienced a strong, emotional connection to Jesus. I admired his example, not of martyrdom as the church extolled, but as someone who dared to stand for truth. Whenever I heard the teachings and stories of Jesus, I listened intently, reacquainting myself with a long-lost friend I'd known before. At least, that's how it felt to me.

Meanwhile, Dad waited under a tree rolling a cigarette and contemplating his own form of God. I remember the gentle smile on his face on our way home as I prattled about Jesus and his good works, trying to convince Dad to come to church with me. He never did. I wonder if the atrocities he'd witnessed at war tainted his notion of any sort of merciful God.

By the time I was old enough to go to school, I'd been studying ballet for over a year. Dressed in my black leotard, pink tights and ballet slippers, I loved the freedom that coursed through my body when I danced. I was a hard-working student, an instinctive learner and easily absorbed the elements of ballet. With the dance school only a block away, I skipped home from my bi-weekly classes, practicing my newly learned steps. Because Mum worried that I might dehydrate after class, she packed a Tupperware tumbler of fresh orange juice for me to drink on my way home. It was warm and tasteless, but I drank it to please her.

With the arrival of 1963, Mum sniffled back her well-entrenched anxiety and tears, as she readied herself for my primary school days. I'd long outgrown kindergarten and was dressed, ready and waiting at the gate to get the show on the road. Holding my hand, she walked me to the school bus stop, where I turned and told her not to worry. Even then I realized my words fell on deaf ears, because she worried about everything.

Filled with a bubbling enthusiasm and the confidence of a child older than my six years, I climbed aboard, took my seat and waved goodbye to my somewhat bewildered mother, who I'm sure, often wondered where I'd come from. We were so different, my mother and me. But despite our differences, I knew we shared a deep respect and love for each other, not just as mother and daughter, but as women. In many ways, I felt responsible for her, to guide and empower her to be more daring in her life.

I relished school, its discipline, its systems and the opportunity it gave me to shine and sit in the top percentage of the class. With a natural fierceness to excel, I tried hard to please my teachers and be the first one with my hand up to answer the question correctly. I was a cooperative, conscientious student, which meant my teachers liked me and trusted me to get the job done. Gaining constant approval was important to an abandoned kid, and interacting with adults who appreciated me, fed my need for acceptance.

Although my early to middle primary school years were generally happy, I knew I was somehow different. Wanting to be liked and accepted, I tried to fit in with my class peers, but following a herd mentality of complying with stupid, factional rules was something I wouldn't do. Nor would I cave in to peer pressure. Putting distance between myself and others was an effective, short-term solution, particularly if their behavior was petty and nasty. The self-reliance I'd learned in my hospital crib during those first two weeks of my life gave me a hidden strength. Somewhere inside me, I intuited that being alone was a place of personal freedom and creative thinking—a place of all-oneness rather than aloneness. I had a mind of my own and enjoyed my own company. Like Pollyanna, my optimistic outlook helped me find something to be glad about in every situation.

Oddly enough, I wanted to change my name from Diane to Michelle. I never understood why Michelle was my favorite girl's name. I just wanted to have that name. My books were covered with *Michelle* as I perfected the capital M in a distinctive cursive style. It wasn't until years later that I learned from my biological mother that Michelle was what she named me before leaving the hospital. On some level, I not only remembered the nurses calling me Michelle, but had stored it deep within my unconscious mind as my given name.

To think that a single word had such an impact on me in the first two weeks of my life, demonstrates the power of the human mind. Imagine the impact of the repeated words and actions we experience in the early years of our lives, day after day, month after month, year after year.

Through this impressionable time in my life, I immersed myself in my dancing. With a fury of ambition and a playfulness of spirit, I occupied my afternoons and weekends with ballet, tap and jazz classes. Seeing my love of the stage blossom, my dance teacher entered me into a range of eisteddfods and competitions. Never nervous while waiting in the wings, I gave my all on the stage, competing with myself to perform better each time. I loved the self-expression the stage afforded me, and as my mother wasn't a demanding stage mum, it made no difference where I placed in each dance section. I danced for the love and the joy of it, not to win, although that was always a bonus.

With my creative juices flowing, I created routines which I performed for my parents, godparents and anyone else I could keep still long enough to watch. Many times, I lined up the chickens and the pets, commanding their attention while I performed. Even at this early age I possessed a desire to escape anonymity, to be someone of value who made a difference somehow. Like Dorothy, I skipped down the metaphoric yellow brick road to a creative destiny.

For days, weeks, months and years, I practiced, I dreamed, I studied, I sacrificed much for the future visions dancing in my head, awake or asleep. At the age of eleven, my first big opportunity in the entertainment industry arrived. I was asked to dance for the church's concert. Full of confidence, I put together a small Hawaiian hula routine of four girls, dancing to Dad's favorite tune at the time—Harry Belafonte's "Island in the Sun." Complete with handmade raffia hula skirts, modest tops and leis, we practiced my routine over and over. On the day of the performance, I remember us dashing onto the stage, skirts rustling and smiles beaming.

When we took our positions, the music started, and my hips swayed while my arms snaked from side to side. I danced, doing my best to express the emotion of the lyrics and the image of ocean waves lapping on the sand. In my mind, this was the start of my career, not just as a dancer, but as a choreographer and director. By the end of our performance, we took our bows and left the stage, delighted at the applause. My first foray into fulfilling my young dreams had been a success.

After the recital, and bubbling over with joy, Mum and I walked outside into the church grounds. It was then everything changed. Some of the female parishioners, those holier-than-thou types, found my dance routine offensive. Dressed in their prim dresses and pill-box hats, they gossiped loud enough for us to hear.

"Tsk, tsk," one staunch, straight-backed woman said. "Such a sinful display of flesh and rude dancing on the church-hall stage." Her gloved hand barely covered the wasp sting in her voice as she glowered down her nose at me. Nodding in agreement and casting me accusatory glares, the other women turned their backs.

"I don't know how the pastor allowed it," another haughty voice said.

It was as if we'd swung from poles in wanton nakedness, instead of performing a simple cultural dance.

Horrified at their narrow-mindedness, my meek mother wrapped her arm around my shoulders and scurried me away. "Ignore those women. You were wonderful."

She clung to me, willing her love into my heart. But my mother wasn't a confident woman, and I knew she was also hurt by their pettiness and hateful remarks. She didn't know what to say to diffuse the situation and her loving praise of my performance wasn't enough for either of us.

That adults, particularly women, could be so nasty toward an innocent prepubescent girl who dared to express her love of dance and performance, shattered the rose-colored glasses through which I viewed my world. Having naturally been inclined to look on the bright side of life and applauded for my talents up to this age, I was ill-equipped for their rejection.

In retrospect, I believe this attack on my creativity and dancing had a two-fold effect on my psyche. While my blithe spirit bore a battering, my warrior within reared at the unfairness of the situation, demanding justice. A fateful, fearful chord reverberated deep within me—deep enough to awaken the sleeping saboteur in my unconscious.

Ever since I was a little girl, my parents had told me that I was adopted. They explained what adoption meant, how special I was and how much they loved me. Now, due to this overt, public disapproval by these women, I no longer wanted to be special. If being special meant rejection and abandonment, I didn't want any part of it. Neither did I want any part of being adopted. If being adopted meant I'd be rejected whenever I dared to be me and express my *being*, then I was better off disowning who I was.

I just wanted to be the same as everyone else and fit in. The negative forces inside me kitted up, trying to recruit me with their subversive messages. "Special people get rejected," "Be like everyone else, and you'll be liked," "If you're special, you'll be abandoned, no one will love you." My interpretation of myself and of my world changed. I forbade my parents from discussing my specialness or the issue of my adoption ever again. A promise they honored for many years to come.

Looking back on this event at the church, I realize my fear of rejection and feeling like I didn't belong was beginning to strangle the life out of me, regardless of how much love my parents demonstrated. The public, undisguised rejection of the joyous expression of who I was, impacted me profoundly. I even recall recurring nightmares at this age of being chased by a sinister man with hands outstretched trying to grab me.

I suspect the decision I made that day to not speak of my adoption caused a part of me to be buried. The very specialness with which I'd incarnated, that identified my purpose and destiny, became shrouded. I lost touch with some of my radiance, with some of my *being*. My mind flung the truth of being adopted into my unconscious, and within a year, I forgot that my parents ever spoke of my adoption at all. I shut it out completely.

As an eleven-year-old girl, I was unaware that burying my wound wouldn't heal it. It would fester in the dark recesses of my mind, seeping into my life until I finally dared to face my fears. I changed that day, but I didn't understand why. Even my facial expression in the school photos that year differed from the previous years. The sullen expression of an unhappy, chubby girl replaced my usual Pollyanna smile. Unaware of the confusion which claimed me, my parents thought I was becoming a hormonal teenager. They did the best they could, and although we remained a happy family, something had shifted.

It was also at this age that I chose to never become a parent. I don't know how or why, but deep within me I knew there was a different destiny awaiting me other than motherhood in this lifetime. My decision wasn't based on fear, but on the same compelling drive to explore and dare to be more. I felt I couldn't do both, well. I duly informed Mum never to expect to be a grandmother. She nodded in reluctant acceptance of my announcement, knowing there was no point in discussing it. She knew that once I made up my mind, that was it. She never did become a grandmother, and to this day it's not a decision I've regretted.

★

On the night of my last day in primary school, I lay sobbing on my bed, surrounded by my dolls. Overwhelmed by an increasing sense of loss, I touched and hugged each one to my chest.

Mum hurried into my room, anxious and confused. "What's the matter?"

I brushed my favorite doll's brown hair. "I'm going to start high school next year."

"But you've been looking forward to it?"

"I know. But it means I'm growing up."

Although she tried her best to comfort me, I knew my childhood was over, and I grieved openly for the demise of my first dozen years. Happy, tumultuous, vibrant and inspiring, those years had been good. I'd been loved and nurtured, a lucky kid. But on a hair-trigger just beneath the surface, lurked the fear of rejection and abandonment, though I was unaware of its toxic implication.

After my emotion subsided, I stacked my dolls back onto their shelves, knowing I'd never play with them again. I'd still love them and confide my secrets to them, but play time was over.

And so, it begins...

Our birth is the most traumatic of all events in our lives. When we incarnate, we do so through the constriction of the physical birthing process and emerge, not simply as fleshy, pink bundles of joy with little understanding of what is happening to us, but as intelligent, dynamic entities, ready for the grand adventure we've chosen. Just because we can't talk or move effectively, doesn't mean we're incapable of cohesive process. As any parent will attest, their newborn immediately becomes the focus and head of the family, with all attention and activities centered on the baby's demands.

Perhaps it's all just a universal card game? Before incarnating, we sit around in another dimension, laughing and telling jokes in preparation for another go at the game of life. Then when our turn comes, we begin shuffling the destiny cards, choosing who will be our parents, children, siblings, lovers and adversaries this time around. Once we make our bets and deal the cards, we all slip through heavenly wormholes into this world. Not by accident but by intention—ours.

It's a fantastical scenario which I find not only entertaining, but liberating, as it undermines the blame game and finger-pointing at preceding generations. We are each responsible for our own life. Nevertheless, it doesn't absolve parents and caregivers from loving their children and providing them with safe, secure environments in which to grow. But it does challenge the belief that we're victims of circumstance when in fact, no matter how young, we're the masters of our fate.

I believe we incarnate for different adventures and in doing so, we gravitate toward the places and people who'll provide us with the framework for the experiences we've incarnated to explore this time round.

For me, I chose the nature (DNA) of my biological parents. Inheriting their genetic structure afforded me certain characteristics which predisposed me to overall wellbeing. For my nurture (my upbringing), I chose my adoptive parents, who loved and cared for me. In both cases, I was an only child. No one has the same DNA as I do and simultaneously, no one was reared the same way as I was, in the absence of my DNA donors or siblings. It's an interesting selection of variables on which I often ponder.

Having been an adopted, only child, I sometimes felt misplaced in my world. Like an alien visiting from another planet, I reveled in my new surroundings, but something was missing. I was surrounded by people who didn't look, speak or act like me. Although welcomed with open arms, I was an immigrant in my own family. Natural-born-and-raised children identify with their parents' features, characteristics and mannerisms as a matter of course. This identification brings with it a sense of continuity and familiarity, of belonging in a family unit. Although I was loved by my wonderful parents and carers in my world, I yearned for more. And that longing for more has never abated. Most of the time, it's a blessing for it inspires me to *be* more. But there are times, it's a curse because I know that no matter how much more there is to life, there will always be far more than I can ever imagine. As the saying goes, "The more you know, the more you know you don't know."

When each of us arrives in this brand, new world, we're exposed to a vast range of endless stimuli. We're like thirsty sponges soaking up and storing as much information as we can while we try to make sense of it all. We judge these experiences as positive or negative and begin to interpret the meaning of life based on our limited thinking and repeated actions.

Over time, our interpretations, perceptions, thoughts and beliefs become ingrained, forming the unconscious building blocks on which we construct our lives, and shape our destiny. In these first, formative years and without realizing it, we're developing a master plan of who we'll become as adults, who we will *be*.

Aristotle captured the extraordinary influence of those years when he wrote, "Give me a child until he is seven, and I will show you the man."

Never a truer word was written.

Captured in this poignant photograph are my remarkable parents, Max and Beryl Bowman. Taken in 1941, just as Dad was about to depart for the war, he is resplendent in his military uniform, a symbol of courage and duty. This image serves as a powerful reminder of the sacrifices made and the enduring strength of family bonds in times of uncertainty.

In this tender snapshot, my parents, enveloped in a mix of nervous anticipation and beaming pride, cradle their newest adventure—me. Their expressions, a beautiful blend of awe and love, capture the profound moment of welcoming a new life into their world, forever changing their journey.

Here I am at five striking a pose with the flair of a budding ballerina. Dressed in my best frock, I'm the epitome of youthful exuberance and playful dreams. This photo is a whimsical nod to those carefree days, where every spin was a step into a magical world of imagination and dance.

CHAPTER TWO
Cultivating the dream

High school proved to be a mixed bag of emotional experiences. Now freed from their long hibernation, my hormones raged through me just after I turned twelve. The thrill of watching my body change into a curvy female form enthralled me. I loved everything about becoming a woman. For me, the transition was an exciting display of nature in all its glory, and the attention of the opposite sex certainly added to the appeal. Looking older than my age and being mature beyond my years, I blossomed into womanhood with enthusiasm.

At the age of fourteen, I decided to step across the sexual threshold with my boyfriend of twelve months. While Paul McCartney sang "Let it Be" in the background, we consummated our precious relationship at a friend's house during a party. Having deliberated on this momentous occasion for a few months, I consciously chose this particular evening to become the fuller expression of being a woman. I never lost my virginity, for to do so would mean that a valuable part of me went missing without my knowledge. I didn't give my virginity away to a lover just to appease him. That I'd never do. It was my free-will choice. It felt right. It felt natural. Much like the lyrics of Carole King's number one hit of the time, "Natural Woman", the tender, intense yearnings of first love led us to this moment. A moment filled with romance, respect and reverence. Our young love grew into a strong, monogamous relationship, ending amicably by mutual agreement four years later. In many ways, we grew up together, learning about love, sex and relationships.

The early 1970s saw the world undergo exponential change. With a sense of freedom coursing through our veins, we teenage baby boomers viewed the planet's evolution with passionate optimism, seeking out opportunities to make the world a better place. Because of my broad-minded, cheerful nature, I couldn't understand why other people seemed so hell-bent on defending narrow-mindedness and prejudice. Their dogged refusal to change astounded me. Why quibble over minor issues, when there were more important matters to debate and resolve? This intolerance, illustrated in the sexual mores of the time, impacted me personally when I was fifteen years old. My boyfriend and I were caught at the back of D block at school, having a quick kiss during lunchtime.

"Stop that. No kissing at school. Come with me," demanded the on-duty teacher, who took great delight in ferreting us out from behind the building. With a smug smile, he frog-marched us to the principal's office. Although we knew we'd broken a school rule, my boyfriend and I hadn't committed a mortal sin, and as straight-A students, we expected that our punishment would likely be a dressing down and detention. But to my horror, the principal caned my boyfriend repeatedly in front of me. We were forbidden from going near each other in the school grounds for the next twelve months, otherwise we risked expulsion. The severity of the punishment shocked the student body and teachers. Aside from it being disproportionate to the crime, the imposed no-go zone proved difficult because not only did we take the same elective subjects, we were class captains. Our teachers became our jailers. For many of them, the principal's edict went against their better judgment, but they too had to obey.

My once happy school days became tinged with bitterness. Being powerless against inane rules, and the tyranny of the principal stirred my warrior spirit. Although the courage of my convictions sustained me, the absurdity of the situation added to my deep-seated frustration and feelings of rejection. I was torn between being a good girl and conforming or daring to unleash my fiery spirit in defiance of such autocracy. With no real alternative but to comply, my boyfriend and I continued to study and do well academically, yet inwardly, we seethed. Nevertheless, we wouldn't be broken, and demonstrated the strength of our flourishing relationship outside of the school grounds.

Even as I continued high school, I yearned to make my living in the entertainment business; to be an artist, not just a performer on the musical theater stage, but also a director and choreographer. I lived and trained by my own exacting standards, expecting a lot from myself. My grueling dance schedules of daily ballet, jazz and contemporary classes, in addition to choreographing, teaching and performing were constant reminders of the joy derived from hard work and commitment to my dreams.

Although I was never destined to be a ballerina, ballet was critical for the alignment and technique to perform the other dance styles I loved. As a discipline, ballet was both torturous and transformative, and one which I practiced for over fifteen years. Despite the searing pain of bathing my bleeding toes and heels in methylated spirits after each ballet class, I knew the world of dance and theater was where my future lay, and I was determined to get there. Fortunately, my parents shared in my dream and worked hard to fund my classes and burgeoning wardrobe of costumes.

By the age of sixteen and while still at high school, I graduated as a ballet teacher and began teaching at my teacher's dance academy in the afternoons and on Saturdays. I was responsible for classes of younger students, one of whom was my high school mistress's daughter. Since the head mistress had never agreed with the principal's punishment, I approached her with an idea for a fund-raiser for the school. Having proven my leadership and creative talents as her daughter's dance teacher, she agreed to allow me to produce and direct the high school's first musical production, at last redeeming myself in the eyes of the principal.

However, a familiar pattern was establishing itself in my life. When success knocked at the door, beside it stood rejection. In this instance, rejection was cloaked in the guise of my biology teacher, who, displeased with my theatrical pursuits, halved my final science exam scores for my last year in high school. For the previous year, I'd been one of his best students, scoring top marks. Now I didn't even pass the subject.

I beseeched him to reconsider, to not punish me for my creative endeavors. But he remained firm on his assessment, insisting I was wasting my intelligence on such foolhardiness as dancing and entertainment. This had a disastrous effect on my overall marks, and I missed out on the scholastic level I needed to enter university to become a high school teacher. The injustice of this situation stung, adding more fuel to my frustration and igniting my spirit. But in the mid-1970s there was little recourse against a teacher's actions.

With no alternative, I wrapped my Pollyanna attitude around me and chose to enroll at a nearby college to become a primary school teacher. Yet deep within me, I stewed at the gross unfairness of the situation and my inability to do anything about it. I didn't realize it at the time, but rejection and I were becoming a well-rehearsed duo with more performances to come.

Because there weren't any options of studying full time in preparation for an entertainment career and knowing that school teaching would give me more freedom than a normal nine-to-five job to pursue my entertainment career, I began a three-year Diploma of Teaching course at the North Brisbane College of Advanced Education. At last, here was a place of learning where students were treated as adults. There were plenty of like-minded, creative, passionate people in my circle of teachers and colleagues, and I spent long happy hours on campus. Aside from the compulsory educational foundation and teaching components, I chose psychology and sociology as elective subjects and was fascinated by their insights into human behavior.

With my entertainment career in mind, I majored in music, which gave me added opportunities to learn an instrument, develop my singing skills and showcase my performance and creative talents. Working beside the head music lecturer who wrote original scores for the college musicals, I became the campus choreographer and performed in these productions, honing my entertainment skills. Some of my happiest times were spent at music camps, rehearsing with the cast until midnight, unwinding afterwards with mugs of mulled wine, singing around the fireplace and crawling out of bed the next day to do it all again. Tertiary education and I were the best of friends.

Powering through this third seven-year cycle of life (fourteen to twenty-one), I prepared for adulthood while shaping my identity for the entertainment destiny I dared to dream. Dashing from one activity to the other, I managed my life with abundant energy and high levels of initiative. Performing in and choreographing at least a dozen musical productions during these three years, and cultivating my blossoming relationships with partners and friends, I continued to reassure my parents that the pace I kept was sustainable. With his placid nature, Dad accepted my constant comings-and-goings with good grace. However, Mum worried about my safety and asked that I call her if I was to be late getting home at night. It wasn't easy because public phone booths were scarce. Nevertheless, no matter the time, I always called and heard her relief rush down the phone. I never understood why she worried so much, but then again, I hadn't lived her life. I was too busy living mine.

The mid-to-late 1970s was an empowering time of enthusiasm, peace protests and free love; all bubbling forth from the post-civil and equal-rights era. For me, it was a great decade in which to live, and I slotted into it with gusto. Energized by the women's liberation movement, my warrior spirit waved the feminist flag, spurred on in part by the publication of Germaine Greer's *The Female Eunuch*. I could now govern my life and my body, thanks to the greatest invention of the twentieth century—the contraceptive pill. As young women, we liberated ourselves from living the lives of our mothers and paved the way for generations to come.

In further celebration of women, the Inaugural International Women's Day was declared by the United Nations on 8 March 1975 to celebrate women's achievements. The future for women's equality looked promising. Little did we know we'd still be beating the same drum forty-five years later.

With the sexual revolution changing social norms, we partied and danced our hearts out as we placed our hands on our hips, mesmerized by Rocky Horror's highly sexualized transvestite lead, Frank N. Furter.

Of course, there was a downside to all this love and heady optimism—the Vietnam War. Like many others, I cringed whenever news reports showed the human horrors and senseless devastation of this ongoing tragedy. When the war ended, I breathed a sigh of relief, thankful that our good, young men were no longer being sent to a conflict that didn't concern us.

Mirroring the macrocosm, the microcosm of my life spun in a whirlpool of endless activity and deadlines. Time chased me from one place to another, and while I sped into my future, one of life's tougher lessons was about to unfold. Returning from college one afternoon, I was driving my week-old, second-hand, yellow hatchback Corolla through an intersection about two hundred meters from home. In a split second, another vehicle T-boned me on the passenger side and my car flipped three times in the air, before finally landing on its roof. The sensation of utter helplessness, while simultaneously being protected by unseen forces, seemed to last much longer than the few moments it took for my car to land. Shaken but unhurt, I scrambled out, ready to exchange details with the other driver. By not giving way, he was responsible for the accident and therefore the damage to my car.

Instead, I stood speechless and watched an army officer in the other vehicle speed away. I'd just become a hit-and-run statistic. Once at the scene, the police admitted their inability to find the offender as I hadn't seen his car's number plate. Worse than the inconvenience and unfairness of the situation, was that my car wasn't yet insured.

The paperwork lay signed, ready for posting on the dining-room table at home. As a full-time college student, I received only a small study subsidy and had bought the car with a loan. Without insurance, it took me over three years to pay off that debt, with nothing to show for it because my car was deemed a write-off. I was devastated.

Downsizing from a vehicle which exemplified my bright personality to a broken-down old Mini with a cranky gearbox and slipping clutch dampened my spirits considerably. But not one to be beaten, I reframed this accident as a test in my life, challenging me to grow stronger. I pressed on and traipsed off to dance class that night, refusing my parents' advice to take a night off. Made of tough stuff, I completed my class full of bravado, and then sank into a chair, my body trembling with shock.

The disappointment of my 'dream car' being totaled stayed with me for months. However, like a warrior princess, I readied myself for the next challenge. I dare not let anything stop me. I had dreams to fulfil.

It wasn't until a decade later that I realized the inseparable relationship we have with our vehicles. They act as a mirror, reflecting our mental and emotional states at the time. At eighteen years of age and having been a demanding taskmaster on myself, I worked hard to accomplish and succeed, to *do* everything. I set rigorous standards for myself, and if I didn't measure up, I berated myself. Losing my car, which was the perfect reflection of my journey into my bright, successful future, was the demonstration of how the rigid control I imposed on myself didn't work. But at the time, I didn't understand what my accident was telling me. *Let go, let it be, take it a little slower, everything is perfectly timed.* It would be many more years before I'd finally internalize this message.

After the demise of my beloved yellow hatchback, I pressed on, albeit at a much slower pace in a worn-out Mini. Now chugging rather than speeding into my future, I was forced to pay attention to my car's limitations and, unknowingly, my own. Undeterred by my vehicular misfortune, I remained focused on my dream. For me, putting in the hard yards made for success. I knew talent was never enough. Passion, resolve, confidence and self-discipline were essential to fulfilling my ambition in the entertainment business. "Repetition is the mother of all skill" became my motto, and I seized every opportunity I could to learn, improve and demonstrate my ability.

During my quest to carve out a place in the entertainment industry, my parents' unconditional love and support compensated for some of my feelings of inadequacy and self-doubt. But nothing compared to the applause of an audience to alleviate the fear of rejection, of being abandoned for not being good enough. An audience's adoration is an addictive drug.

No sooner had I graduated from college than I was placed as a grade-two teacher in a progressive, local primary school. Thrilled that I hadn't been appointed to a rural district, I continued performing in Brisbane-based theater productions at night, while school teaching in the day. Working as a teacher was a good fit while I prepared for my "big break" in the entertainment industry.

My twenty-first birthday heralded the beginning of the next seven-year cycle of my life, a time of wanting to leave home and build my own nest. I had a short, sweet engagement to a young performer, who also wanted to forge a career in the entertainment industry. Our goals, dreams and values seemed compatible, but he lacked the drive I thought necessary to achieve great things. Although we enjoyed working in several successful shows together, I ended the relationship. He continued in his civilian life, and I followed the dream.

Laying the cornerstone...

The seven-year cycle of fourteen to twenty-one is when we farewell our childhood personality and welcome in our adult one. The thoughts, perceptions, beliefs, values, emotions, words and actions we experienced during the formative years of our life form the building blocks for this adult personality. Without knowing it, we lay down these building blocks to our future, cementing them into place with either layers of love or fear.

Like any structure, there's a cornerstone, the first block on which the other building blocks are laid. I call this cornerstone to our future our *life philosophy*. It's our deepest buried belief. Most of us are unaware of our life philosophy's existence, much less the enormous influence it has on our lives.

If it's an empowering life philosophy, it supports us. Like the solid, immovable base on which a mighty tower is built, it's the foundation on which the rich rewards of life pile high.

If it's a negative life philosophy, it destabilizes us. Our life becomes unbalanced, collapses and turns to rubble, leaving us to wonder why.

Remember the scene from the movie *Forrest Gump* when Forrest is sitting on a park bench and a nurse sits down beside him. In his innocent, childlike way, he offers her a chocolate. Trying to strike up a conversation, he explains that his mother always said, "Life is like a box of chocolates, you never know which one you're going to get."

In that single sentence, he encapsulates his mother's life philosophy. Each candy, each moment or event in life, is a sweet surprise.

For many people, their life philosophy isn't as cheerful or delicious as Forrest's mother's. Some people build their lives on a life philosophy of competition and struggle. Life is like a football game, there's always someone on the other team out to get me. Or life is like a juggling act, there's never enough money to go around. Or on a more positive note, life is like my birthday, every day is filled with lots of presents. Or life is like one big party, happy days and happy people everywhere.

In my case, it wasn't until much later when my life fell apart that I discovered that the life philosophy I'd laid down in my formative years was complicit in my suffering. Like an archaeologist, I spent months digging through the crumbled ruins of my life trying to find it. Eventually, I unearthed a life philosophy filled with mixed messages of triumph and tragedy, success and rejection.

Similar to a good engineer who finds a fault in a building, I replaced it with a better quality cornerstone. One to empower my life, rather than undermine it. Since then, there have been times when a remnant of my original life philosophy unbalances me, but I dig it out and reinforce the new one. Like a mighty tower designed to withstand nature's toughest elements, I'm still standing, stronger than I've ever been.

I'm seventeen and fully immersed in the thrill of my high school's musical production, which I designed and directed. Here, I'm dancing in a routine I choreographed to the popular tune 'The Look of Love.' It was a fun time blended with leadership, creativity, and teenage enthusiasm, all rolled into one.

CHAPTER THREE
Dreams do come true

After ending my engagement, other doors opened. The more I dared to dream bigger dreams, the more momentum I gathered and the more I pressed on. Although I remained a primary school teacher, my weekends and evenings were filled with rehearsals and performances at one of Brisbane's leading independent theaters. Under the tutelage of well-known director Ken Lord, I became choreographer, dancer and actress in his company's musical theater productions and children's pantomimes. Just like a sapling experiences a growth spurt on its journey to the sunlight, I flourished under the guiding brilliance of Ken. A hard taskmaster and kindred spirit, he's still my beloved mentor and one of the most talented, creative geniuses I know.

As often happens in the entertainment industry, I fell in love with my new leading man. Talented, handsome and intelligent, he was a gifted actor, singer, writer and budding director. Working together was sheer delight as our intrinsic timing enhanced the other's performance. Ever the romantic, I believed our partnership, personally and professionally resembled those famous love affairs of the stage and screen. We were fated to be together and our creative pursuits enriched our relationship.

Many hours we spent at the theater, with Ken, his wife, Margaret, and a gypsy woman named Celia. With her unruly gray hair, a face crinkled by time and a mysterious, almost mystical personality, she'd unexpectedly arrive, day or night. No one seemed to know where Celia came from, but she ensconced herself in a corner like a mystic fortune-teller. Because Ken's grandmother came from distant Gypsy lineage, he never sent Celia on her way. Instead, he permitted her to stay and give random astrology readings. Referencing the ephemeris table, a record of planetary positions throughout time, and with only a person's time and date of birth, she gave readings which amazed everyone with their accuracy. She offered to do a reading for me, but I had no idea of my birth time. Even to this day, there's no complete birth certificate confirming my existence, because most of the birth records from the hospital where I was born were lost to long-ago floods. Celia's amazing gift fascinated me, sparking my interest and study in astrology for several years. The notion of the celestial impact on human behavior intrigued me, and when I gave amateur readings to my friends, I was as surprised as they were with the reading's insight.

On one occasion, Celia called me over to the small table where she perched with her tarot cards, books and charts. "I think you've got Scorpio rising," she declared boldly, shuffling the cards to do a reading for me. "In fact, I'm sure of it. Tomorrow the moon rises in Scorpio and so will you."

I thought no more of it until the next day when I woke to find myself splashed across the front page of the leading weekend newspaper. Never had a story of an actress-dancer made front-page news.

At twenty-three years of age, the metaphorical door at which I'd been knocking since I was a little girl opened. Time for me to leap into the entertainment business full time. I resigned from my teaching position and left home to move in with my leading man. Because my parents and I had shared a happy home life, they were sad to see me go, but it was time to build my own nest. With my new fiancé by my side, we moved into a small unit in the trendy suburb of New Farm in Brisbane, and I embarked on my professional life on the 'wicked' stage with great expectation. My childhood dream, when I wished upon a star, had come true.

Ken's productions became so successful that he opened a theater restaurant in which the four of us performed. With another two children's pantomimes and three major musical productions staged at Twelfth Night Theatre, plus performing in the newly formed Court of the Seven Lamps Theater Restaurant, the following year's schedule burst with energy, joy and creativity.

The theater was my safe place, where my fears and doubts rarely surfaced. Even when the theater was dark, when only the workers—onstage lamps—were on, and no one was there but me and my trusty tape recorder on which the show songs were recorded, I'd choreograph well into the night, making sure the routines were perfect. Even the theater's resident ghost paid me occasional visits during these quiet times.

The first time a figure, clad in what appeared to be a white cheesecloth shirt and pants, wafted across G row to settle into the middle seat of the theater, I was onstage marking out choreography. Because Ken often wore similar clothing and popped into the auditorium before he went home at night, I thought it was him creeping in to watch me work. However, when I called hello, the figure vanished. At the time, I thought I imagined it, but after repeated appearances I knew it was real. Folklore had it, she was the old lady whose house had been demolished to build the theatre, and that after her death, she regularly frequented the property. She and I established a relationship of sorts, and when I was alone working in the theater, she often visited.

In fact, I came to depend on her silent approval of my work, often asking aloud if she liked this step or that. How did I know if she approved? She remained in G row, otherwise she disappeared. Often, after a performance when the audience and crew left, Ken, Margaret, my fiancé and I had drinks in the theater restaurant. The first time we heard running footsteps on the open mezzanine level above followed by crashing pots and pans in the kitchen, we rushed around looking for the intruder. But of course, there was none.

"It's that bloody woman," Ken said, referring to the ghost.

Though she persisted, we ignored her and eventually she ceased her late-night ruckus. Since Sheena had been with me when I was young, the ghost at Twelfth Night Theatre never fazed me. She was my first indisputable encounter with an unseen force witnessed by others. It never struck me as strange to have these experiences. Moreover, I thought most people experienced otherworldly visitations. It would be nearly a decade later before I realized that we only manifest that which we believe.

I loved the stage. I loved performing. The exhilaration of being under the lights gave me the opportunity to shrug off the shackles of ordinariness and let my terpsichorean spirit take flight in all her passionate glory. I loved rehearsals. I loved the hard work. Being directed by Ken to reach further and be a better choreographer, dancer, actress, and all-round entertainer burned away my doubts. Learning to manage injured and exhausted muscles, overcoming sleep deprivation or dealing with the heartache of not meeting my own standards—I loved it all. I had found my purpose in life and my spirit was free.

Another front-page story added to the excitement of my life at this time, as did my wedding. Dressed in coffee-colored lace wearing a Spanish-style mantilla, I walked down the candle-lit aisle of the theater restaurant on my dear father's arm to marry my leading man. An intimate theatrical affair with a tight budget, I planned everything to the smallest detail, even reviving my home-economics cake-making skills to create a two-tiered wedding cake. Elegant, romantic and full of drama, my wedding day seemed plucked from a silver screen musical of the 1940s.

On our honeymoon, my equally theatrical husband surprised me with daily, pitch-perfect acapella performances of the songs from every Gilbert and Sullivan libretto. As we cruised along the Hawkesbury River in New South Wales, his rich, baritone voice serenaded me while I sipped chardonnay and swooned. I was twenty-four years old. Together we set a new sail to a shared destiny in the entertainment industry. Within a year, we established, managed and directed the Brisbane Youth Theatre with a plethora of acting, dancing and singing classes. Since neither of us wanted children, our marriage was complete. We were young, in love and had a promising future ahead of us.

But over time the honeymoon hormones wore off and my leading man no longer shone with the golden glow I first encountered. In fact, his radiance turned decidedly green. No matter who I was with, he questioned my motives. Jealousy grew on him like a parasitic vine, curling upwards to strangle his heart and my joy along with it. Having grown up in a loving home where I rarely heard my parents quarrel or felt friction from unspoken words, I was unprepared for his constant badgering. "Who were you out with? Where have you been? I expected you home hours ago!" His insistence to know my whereabouts rankled me and no matter my answer, it was never good enough. Indeed, it was in this marriage I learned to fight, which saddened me greatly. Together in the theater world we were a successful, professional couple, kicking proverbial goals. At home, we struggled in a worsening tailspin, lasting three long years.

The end of the fourth seven-year cycle of my life was a major turning point, personally and professionally. The youth theater was successfully growing, as was my directorial, choreographic and performance career, both onstage and in television. With my dance troupe, Uptown Strut, I regularly performed on the Channel 7 morning show, back when live acts featured on television. My husband and I also appeared as guest actors on Channel 7's afternoon children's educational program. Here I combined my two loves of teaching and performing, working on the award-winning children's show, *Wombat*.

In stark contrast to this success, I witnessed my father—the man I loved most of all—die a slow, painful death from leukaemia. In his last moments at the hospital, when I wrung out the face cloth to cool his emaciated face, his pale blue eyes flickered open. He smiled his familiar crooked grin and whispered my nickname. "Disy."

On the other side of the bed sat Mum, his wife of forty-three years, holding back tears. With her and I each holding one of his hands, he took a last rattling breath and left, comforted by the women he loved and who loved him most. In my twenty-eighth year, I buried my father, the first person who dared me to reach for the stars. It took me seven long years to stop crying whenever I looked up at the night sky.

As the loss of a loving parent often does, his death inspired me to live my life without regret; to dare to dream bigger dreams, to ignore my past limitations, to remain true to myself and press on. Watching him leave his hard-working, simple life without complaint gave me the courage to believe enough in myself again to make my dreams come true. His passing prompted me to divorce my husband. Without my father's selfless death, and my mother's gritty resolve to start a new solo life, I suspect I'd have stayed in my marriage even longer. Instead, my sanity prevailed, and I chose freedom.

After I made this decision, I asked Mum what she thought about my defunct marriage. "I never thought he was right for you," she said.

"Why didn't you say something years ago?"

She shrugged and smiled. "Because I knew you wouldn't listen."

My mother was a woman of few words, but the ones she spoke had a punch. She was right. I wouldn't have listened.

Within a few months of the divorce and daring to dream bigger, I ran headlong into a new career. Through a friend, I discovered that Conrad Jupiter's hotel was commencing construction on the Gold Coast, complete with a Las Vegas–style showroom.

At full throttle, I wrote to the hotel's CEO offering my services as the director and choreographer, but that role had already been given to Las Vegas director and choreographer Jerry Jackson. Unfazed, I threw my dance bag over my shoulder and auditioned for a spot in the show with every other starry-eyed dancer in the country. I was determined to make my future vision a reality. The moment I took to the audition stage under Jerry's direction, not only did I get in, but I scored my dream job in the first and only multimillion-dollar extravaganzas staged in Australia. These lavish productions, their massive budgets and renowned director/choreographer, set the nation alight, and I'd been chosen from nation-wide auditions to be part of this glittering chapter of Australian entertainment history. You couldn't wipe the smile off my face.

I packed up my life in Brisbane and moved one-hour south to the Gold Coast. Unfortunately, my mother chose not to make the move with me. Instead, she stayed behind in the family home where she and Dad had lived for over four decades. While my life sparkled with my destiny becoming manifest, hers smudged with lingering loss. But she never asked me to stay. She'd worked as hard as I had for this dream, and she wanted me to follow it.

Having been chosen as a dancer, dance captain and then assistant director and choreographer to Mr. Jackson was undeniable evidence that dreams do come true. All the passion, hard work and sacrifice I'd put into the first part of my life had paid off. Adding icing to my new, delicious career cake was Jerry's respect and admiration for my creative talents and teaching skills. Making me his trusted and valued assistant, asking my opinion and taking me into his confidences, he elevated me to a position of authority in the productions for which I'll be forever grateful. With unshakable confidence, I knew the life I'd mapped out for myself was in sight. There was no stopping me from getting to the top of my chosen field in entertainment.

The year 1985 ended with a wonderful beginning for me—eight weeks of intense, invigorating rehearsals for *Starz*, a musical fantasy. At last, I'd arrived. I loved the stage and it loved me. I loved the people, the audiences, my family, friends and colleagues in the business. We were all in love. So, what more appropriate date to show off our love affair to the world than Valentine's Day? On 14 February 1986, *Starz* opened. Never had there been a more fulfilling moment than the one in which I was inextricably entwined.

When opening night arrived, the energy was electric. With my heart racing, I stood in the wings, ready for my first entrance. Akin to when I went off to primary school, I was desperate to get the show on the road. At the end of the overture and on a big crescendo, the heavy proscenium curtain slowly lifted to expose a dazzling light curtain comprised of thousands of brilliant white globes. We were on! I adjusted my black-and-white futuristic costume and took a deep breath. Looking skywards, I said a silent prayer. "This one's for you, Dad. Thanks for getting me here. I love you," and I hit the stage at full throttle.

My time had come.

Game on...

As Charles Dickens wrote in *A Tale of Two Cities*, "It was the best of times. It was the worst of times."

Everything I dreamed of since I was a little girl had now come true. Words cannot describe the joy of finally living my destiny. Yet, I wanted more. I expected more. I drove myself ruthlessly to improve, and in doing so, I expected everyone else to commit likewise. As I grew stronger and dared to succeed, another part of me grew stronger and wanted me to fail. The ego—my conditioned thinking of negative thoughts, perceptions, beliefs, values, emotions, words and actions that I'd accumulated and enacted during the previous years of my life.

Like a bad flat mate, the ego gossiped away in my mind, telling me I wasn't good enough, I had to work harder, that I'll never amount to anything, that nobody loves me, and I'll be rejected…and the list of my shortcomings went on and on.

I suspect that being rejected and abandoned for the first two weeks of my life provided the ego with fertile ground in which to take root and grow. It tended to its poisonous garden of negative thoughts, perceptions, beliefs, values and emotions, shoveling it with the manure of self-doubt, insecurity and worthlessness through those formative years and into my adolescence and adult hood. Using the unconscious underpinning of my life philosophy, the ego subtly haunted me with its subversive, fear-based messages.

Simultaneously, my *being* countered the ego's insidious game. It nourished and supported me, encouraging me to blossom and dare to be more. Within me, there dwelt an irresistible urge expressing itself through my dancing, my performing and creativity. This spark to be authentic, to *be* the fullest expression of me wouldn't be denied. It propelled me forward into a career I loved.

Still, the ego reminded me that rejection and abandonment would be the endgame.

While my external veneer brimmed with confident composure,

I internally suffered from not feeling good enough. I was a living, breathing dichotomy of exquisite pleasure and dejected pain. Like most people, I was totally unaware of the game being played within me, all of which I'd set in motion through my own interpretations and covert negative thoughts, perceptions, beliefs, values, emotions, words and actions in the years before.

The key was turning in the lock to my future awakening, and I lived in ignorance of it all.

In a groundbreaking moment back in 1981, here I am, making history as the first dancer ever to grace the front page of The Queensland Courier Mail. This snapshot captures a milestone not just for me, but for the dance and live theatre community, bringing the amateur arts into the spotlight in Queensland.

CHAPTER FOUR
Tipping point

I was a twenty-eight-year-old woman responsible for and performing in the biggest live entertainment productions in the country. At the top of my game, I was dancing up the metaphorical stairway to paradise. I can feel those shoes carrying me there even now. Because of the wonderful opportunities afforded me during my daring adventure to date, I believed in love, truth and justice. Sounds a lot like Superman's slogan, doesn't it? But who could blame me? I'd been the kid glued to the black-and-white television set, singing and dancing along with all the great movie musical stars, wishing that someday it would be me. Having grown up watching the cowboys in the white hats win in the westerns, and the handsome boys kiss the pretty girls as they danced on top of Manhattan buildings with a full moon painted on the backdrop, I had no alternative but to expect that the good guys would get the good girls. Together, they'd vanquish the baddies and walk hand in hand into the distance while the sun sets upon the golden sands. Ah, MGM did it so well.

Added to this Hollywood-inspired view of the world were the parables I'd learned as a child at Sunday school. I was the eternal optimist and believed that good triumphed over evil. Equipped with this empowering belief but simultaneously conflicted by the deeper fears of rejection and abandonment, I tried to do my best in everything I did, hoping that if I did good unto others, they would do good unto me.

I didn't understand the operating system of the energetic laws of the universe. It's not done unto us as we hope or as it should be. It's always done unto us as we *believe*. And if we have conflicting beliefs, no matter how good a person we are, conflict will be our demonstration.

Once the production was up and running, Jerry returned to Las Vegas, leaving me in directorial charge. My role was to ensure every performance looked as spectacular as opening night. No matter how many performers were injured or sick, and despite the petty politicking back stage, the production relied on my ability to keep its professional, international standard. This meant each show without a full cast needed to be restaged before curtain-up.

With up to nine dancers off each performance, my job became less about keeping the magic alive onstage and more about managing disgruntled, underpaid, unhappy dancers resentful of their peers who took time off, whether for legitimate reasons or not. All of this was made worse because some of the performers smoked dope before they arrived and again during intermission in the car park. I never knew this was going on at the time, but it was obvious that several of the cast were there to have a good time rather than for the good of the show.

Initially, my employer, the producer applauded my strong work ethic and dogged professionalism in keeping the show to its original standard no matter the difficulties. He even promised me a long-term relationship, with him producing more shows and me as his resident director and choreographer at the showroom. My future vision was manifesting before my eyes and my career prospects looked assured.

Regular meetings were attended by management which included the producer and the company manager, and the production team consisting of the stage director, the stage manager, myself and occasionally the musical director. At these meetings, the stage director, who was responsible for the crew, and I would voice our concerns over workplace, health and safety issues onstage, the rights of the employees and production improvement strategies.

Mistakenly, I thought that management wanted the best for the show, but over time, I realized they didn't. Call me naïve, but I was baffled by their unconcealed disinterest in anything that didn't result in increased profits on the bottom line. If rectifying a safety issue cost money, they stalled the repair for as long as possible.

One day, the producer called saying the next production meeting would be held in his hotel room rather than in management's offices. Although I thought this was a strange choice of venue, I discounted my inner nudging to make an excuse not to attend. Ignoring my intuition that day changed my life. It was a sliding doors moment. If I had listened and acted on my gut feeling and not gone, where would I be now? I'll never know, but I do know that since then, I've always acted on my gut instinct. Saying yes to my intuition is a lot easier than saying no to the subsequent circumstance.

On arriving at his room and being ushered inside, I was the only attendee, and when I questioned where everyone else was, the producer intimated they weren't coming.

"Just you and me."

When he sidled up in an undisguised lecherous manner, I broke into a cold sweat. I knew then why my intuition had baulked at coming to this meeting. I should have made an excuse. With thinly veiled sexual innuendos, he wasted no time in trying to seduce me into having an affair with him. "You and I would make a great team, both in show business and the bedroom."

Though shocked by his approach, I didn't want to upset the man who employed me in my dream job. So, I skirted the conversation and the room. With my skin prickling as the gleam in his eyes intensified, I made it clear nothing would come of his lewd suggestions. My rejection of his advances was absolute, and I left. But I had the distinct impression that I had made a powerful enemy.

Not long after this episode, when I spoke with him in his office after a matinee performance, he reached over his desk, pulled down my dance singlet and gawped at my bare breasts. I pushed his hand away and informed him his behavior was unacceptable. From then on, I stayed clear of the producer unless I was accompanied by another person.

All my life I never sold myself short. I had become a successful artist without using sex as a stepping-stone, so the producer's smug, sexual advances galled me. Over time, my refusal of his approaches and my frequent, insistent requests for better working conditions, remuneration and consideration for the overworked cast were received with increasing irritation and little action. No longer the sweet reward he'd hoped for, I became the annoying insect, shooed away and ignored.

During these initial months, I was nudged again by my intuition. This time I acted on it. I approached Conrad Jupiter's hotel and gained their approval to establish a performance academy using their name. After the required legal forms were signed, The Jupiter's Academy of Dance in Entertainment opened its doors on the Gold Coast. J.A.D.E. acted as a training ground for talented dancers and acrobats hoping to become performers in the casino show. The academy gave me the opportunity to not only assess their performance abilities, but also their character and commitment. Even if someone was an outstanding dancer or acrobat, if they lacked a professional attitude, they weren't the right fit for the show. J.A.D.E. proved the ideal audition platform while being therapeutic for me. Teaching bright, new talent at the academy most afternoons before the show, fortified me for the forthcoming challenges at that night's performance.

A few months before the first-anniversary performance of *Starz* and much to everyone's surprise, the producer fired the stage director. The unexplained sacking and the producer's distancing of himself from everyone associated with the business, except his company manager, created uncertainty and friction throughout the company. The stage director's abrupt departure left me in charge of the entire production, including the crew. For all the added workload and responsibility, the producer refused me any extra remuneration.

My simmering indignation at his unwillingness to engage in discussions for the betterment of the show, its cast and crew began to scold my righteous heart. Having managed the Brisbane Youth Theatre with my ex-husband, I was mystified as to how any businessman could simply ignore the obvious safety issues and the escalating human-resource difficulties emerging in his company, by not communicating with the delegate employed to manage these risks. A distant warning bell tolled in my head. I sensed things were unravelling. So, I recorded every event and interaction that happened during each performance in my journal.

Hoping for the best, yet planning for the worst, I decided to produce and choreograph my own late-night cabaret acts for nearby hotels. I figured that if things didn't improve in the showroom, I could at least continue these shows and expand my directorial career from there.

Our group consisted of three female and two male dancers, one of who was my boyfriend of twelve months. Six years younger than me, he'd been one of my students at the Brisbane Youth Theatre. On his own merit, he'd auditioned and been chosen to be part of the male dance chorus for *Starz*. Professionally, we worked so well together that several of the cast and crew didn't know we were romantically involved.

We were a fun-loving couple, a lot like Will and Grace from the popular television series. We laughed, hosted parties at our home and had a great group of close friends. Since we began as teacher and student, we naturally settled into this paradigm in our personal relationship, which suited us both. Despite the apparent incongruity, we loved each other and lived happily together in a monogamous relationship, sharing our love for each other and the stage.

While 1987 tramped on in plodding steps, my body sounded a warning cry. A slight discomfort and irritation in my left eye escalated to painful stabbing. With several doctors unsure as to the cause, and my inability to perform at times, I wore an eye patch in the hope that rest and darkness would ease the condition. However, it wasn't just my eye calling out for rest and darkness. Eyes represent the capacity to see clearly, so I was aware enough at that time to realize that what I saw around me in my world wasn't conducive to my health. Still, I allowed the ongoing battles with the producer to distract me from what my body tried to tell me.

By now the cast was outright hostile. More episodes of incorrect weekly pays, management's unconcealed disdain for the performers and the producer's unpredictable behavior created a fracture within the company that widened into a chasm. The cast became members of the Actors' Equity union and our representative took over the reins of complaining to management about workplace, health and safety issues, as well as matters relating to remuneration.

With mounting anxiety, I visited Dr. Gill, my trusted doctor of many years, who on seeing me was concerned enough to prescribe antidepressants for my elevated stress levels. I knew my health was suffering, but his unconcealed concern over my decline and prescription for pharmaceutical drugs shocked me. Looking back on this now, he was like a little voice of God telling me to get out, the best way he could. On his recommendation I did begin the treatment, but when

I experienced the horrendous side effects of lethargy and clouded thinking, I stopped taking them. I was a dancer, a trouper. The show must go on!

In the middle of this unfolding drama, a rare and uplifting opportunity came my way. I was selected as the assistant choreographer for the Mrs. World Pageant staged in the casino showroom on a Monday night when *Starz* wasn't performing. Since it was the first time this event had been presented in Australia, my appointment to this prestigious position quelled some of my anxieties and self-doubt. The pageant was a top-quality US production and proved the perfect respite from my worsening situation with the producer. I worked alongside the pageant's highly regarded choreographer and television director, relishing the opportunity and challenge to produce a production watched live by millions of people worldwide. We pulled it together without a hitch, despite the bad manners and back-stabbing antics of some of the contestants. Recharged and respected, I thrived in this team of like-minded professionals. With the promise of further work with him if I ever went to America, the choreographer bid me farewell, and I returned to dealing with parochial politics.

By July, the producer refused to pay the *Starz* cast four weeks' holiday pay. He illogically and illegally reasoned that since we weren't performing for a month, we weren't entitled to be paid while on annual leave. Under instruction from the union and the Australian Conciliation and Arbitration Commission, he was forced to pay us our holiday entitlement, but by now, the conflict between management, the cast and crew had escalated to overt episodes of antagonism.

With my world spinning out of control, my body gave up whispering and began shouting. Dizzy spells plagued me throughout the next six months. These worsened in direct response to the increasing animosity among the cast, the producer and me. Ongoing workplace incidents where dancers were injured due to poor backstage lighting, water on the stage caused by malfunctioning smoke machines and friction between performers, escalated onstage with actual physical contact being excused as unintentional accidents.

In one instance, my male partner dropped me from a lift on purpose. Previously, in a fit of rage, he'd put his fist through a dressing room mirror and was granted six weeks paid worker's compensation leave.

I objected to this and requested the producer dismiss him, because his unpredictable behavior and emotional instability were endangering the cast. The producer refused and the male dancer remained in the show, causing further aggravation to the cast due to his protected-species status. I had never witnessed such unprofessional behavior, but as I didn't have the support of the producer, I couldn't manage these actions or performers.

Without any effective leadership from the company, the unacceptable behaviors continued. My allegiance was to the show and Jerry, but because the producer had revoked my authority, my influence waned. Through this worsening time, my body strained to get my attention. During one performance I injured my left knee, damaging the anterior cruciate ligament. In another performance, I badly twisted my left ankle. My right shoulder progressively tightened to unbearable proportions, while my dizziness was finally diagnosed as vertigo. If I hadn't been living in ignorance at the time, I would have read these signs as my refusal to bend or forgive, of feeling undeserving of the pleasures life had to offer, of making life a burden which I had to carry, and of flighty, scattered thinking accompanied by a refusal to see what was really happening.

In retrospect, my body, with its ailments and injuries, was giving me an unequivocal message during this turbulent time of my life—give in and get out. Up to this point in my life, I had been super healthy. Not one to have colds, flu, tummy problems, period pains or any illness, I lived a strong, healthful life. Sure, I'd suffered a few injuries, which most would say were a result of the physical strain my body was under as a dancer. But looking back and knowing what I know now, it was obvious my body tried to tell me what I needed to change to move forward in life with more elegance.

While I struggled to control the situation at the casino, my *being* tried to save me from freefalling into a negative abyss. With my world crumbling around me, my body screamed and reflected the mental breakdown I was sliding full speed toward. A major shift was taking place within me, but because I was ignorant of the energetic laws of the universe, I continued in my suffering. I fiercely clung to my old conditioned thinking, not realizing that the sooner I let go of the old; a richer and more rewarding life would manifest. Added to my deteriorating physical health, my Pulsar hatchback joined the pity party by breaking down repeatedly. My car was turning into a lemon, much like the way my life was souring.

Everything is energy...

I had spent close to thirty years functioning from my conditioned thinking, from a limited, human perspective. Whether it was as a dancer, director, choreographer, teacher, woman, daughter or partner, I had acquired a cache of knowledge, applied and repeated it to get results. My wonderful career at the showroom was testament to my excelling at this process. However, I wasn't consciously aware of the energetic laws of the universe.

One of the world's most brilliant minds, Albert Einstein, encapsulated how this works. "Everything is energy and that's all there is to it. Match the frequency of the reality you want, and you cannot help but get that reality. It can be no other way. This is not philosophy. This is physics."

Everything is energy.

Energy is the fabric of the universe, the essence of life. It's also referred to as God, the Goddess, the Creator, the Universe, Buddha, Knowing, Allah, Creative Mind, Love, the Life Principle, Consciousness and more.

Having grown up in the Christian faith, I was taught a personalized interpretation of this energy. He was a kind old man with a big white beard propped on a throne in heaven. But the notion of a singular embodied God, who is somehow greater than and separate to everything else, seems contradictory to the inclusiveness of everything being energy. Instead, I use the word Consciousness, which is a less religiously charged word to describe this energy.

Regardless of the word we use, in the end, it is all the same energy. We are all the same energy.

Everything is Consciousness, and we are each Consciousness expressing itself through our *being*.

Like a magnificent masterpiece, we're unique. Our beauty (our *being*) sometimes becomes tarnished and dull due to the world around us (the ego), which tries to mask our magnificence. But there are no lasting ill effects, for underneath the ego's lame efforts to taint us, we are still a masterpiece. We just need a little external restoration.

Once we dare to consider that everything is energy, and we too are this energy, this Consciousness, we liberate ourselves from our old conditioned thinking. This frees us to consider the resonance of energy or the universal law of attraction, which is indisputable, inviolable, and we all use it. This was a second break-through for me.

The fundamental clue to the law of attraction is the frequency of our Consciousness. As Einstein said, "Match the frequency of the reality you want, and you cannot help but get that reality. It can be no other way."

The energetic frequency of our thoughts, perceptions, beliefs, values, emotions, words and actions color and create our experiences. When unencumbered by the ego, our Consciousness resonates at its highest level and we live in joyous expectation. This paves the way for miracles, which are unexpected, extraordinary events, to happen in our lives. On the other hand, when the ego's negativity pervades our Consciousness, this lower level of resonance is reflected in a life of struggle, stress and conflict.

Life is simple...Resonate at a high level of Consciousness and receive outstanding results. Resonate at a low level of Consciousness and receive miserable results.

Since everything is energy, and we are that energy, it means that our body also demonstrates our Consciousness at every moment in our lives. Our body works like a mirror, reflecting to us what we need to know. Resonate at a high level of Consciousness and demonstrate outstanding health. Resonate at a low level of Consciousness and our bodies try to get our attention. These messages come as little niggling sensations. I call them whispers—perhaps a cold or stiffness of the joints or an injury. Whispers remind us that we're not resonating at our highest level of Consciousness. If we ignore these whispers, they'll turn into shouts, screaming at us, while discomfort and disease run rampant through our bodies. Exactly as my body did all those years ago.

I now understand what my deteriorating health meant. It was a direct reflection of my low level of Consciousness. The more I focused on what was wrong in my world, the more embattled I became and the lower my energy resonated.

"Everything is energy and that's all there is to it. Match the frequency of the reality you want, and you cannot help but get that reality."

None of what was happening to me was by accident. I attracted in a situation which matched the frequency of my energy at the time. If only I knew then, what I know now.

In this dazzling 1986 publicity shot, I pose alongside the legendary Las Vegas creator, director, and choreographer, Jerry Jackson, for 'Starz'—the most lavish and high budget extravaganza ever staged in Australia. This image captures the glamour and groundbreaking spirit of a production that set new standards in the Australian entertainment scene, marking a defining moment in theatrical history.

CHAPTER FIVE
The gauntlet is thrown

With my mind and body screaming at me, I knew it was time to give up my dream and move on. But I was one day too late. On 11 February 1988, as I set about preparing my résumé to find another job and leave the show, I received a registered letter from the producer. A sense of foreboding crept over me. Written correspondence from a man who refused to speak with me wasn't a good omen. As I stood in my little flat, it took no more than a few seconds for my world to disintegrate like shattered glass.

Loose weight immediately or be dismissed.

Not only was the impact of the insult gut-wrenching, the misspelling of the first word added to my indignation. To receive such an offensive, unjustified letter with no previous discussion on the matter reeked of cowardice and discrimination. Considering I had maintained the same weight since commencing my dance contract in December 1985, I was outraged. Even when I contacted the producer to discuss his letter, he refused to take my calls or meet with me.

The grinding futility of the situation haunted me day and night. Finding alternative employment became critical. I needed money to survive. However, what I needed more was to trust—trust that if I walked away, other doors would open for me. But a "lack" mentality plagued my thoughts by this time: lack of communication, lack of respect, lack of influence. I was living with poverty consciousness and producing a pauper's results.

While the incommunicado zone surrounding the producer tightened, the letter's contents remained unresolved. Unable to present my case and prove that I hadn't gained any weight, I continued in my role with the show, maintaining my professionalism and dignity as best I could. In the meantime, I searched for other work opportunities, praying something would materialize. But opportunity never shows up where desperation hangs out.

Less than four weeks later, I received another letter advising I couldn't perform in one of the numbers in the show because I was too fat and that unless I lost weight, my contract would be reviewed. With no avenue for verbal communication with the producer, I consulted Dr. Gill, who provided a medical report stating my weight had remained constant for the years I had been his patient. He also stated that it would be injurious to my health if I were to lose any weight. Even with this medical report, the producer continued in my persecution. He instructed the stage manager to inform me that management had no intention of paying out my contract. The juices of injustice, rejection and abandonment dripped like a Chinese water torture in my mind. I was being squeezed out.

Preposterous onstage and backstage episodes continued. The Russian lead couple, who had been contracted to star in a spectacular Russian folk dance, possessed enormous egos to match their performances. Previously, the trouble they caused was limited to back stage. But with hostility infiltrating the show, whenever the husband-and-wife pair thought they were being upstaged, they unleashed their fervent displeasure onstage. Using their prop whips, they lashed the dancers or acrobats who encroached into their dance space. Cursing in Russian, they'd hurl themselves onto unsuspecting dancers, pushing and hitting them during the performance. My attempts to discuss this behavior with them proved pointless. By having the audacity to broach their appalling onstage antics, I became the target for the male lead, who slammed into me during the next performance, nearly knocking me off my feet. Of course, management ignored my pleas and allowed the pair to continue in their dramatic assaults.

Because of the tensions, several dancers and acrobats resigned, forcing me to conduct rolling auditions open to the general public to find replacements on short notice. Management advised that because they weren't prepared to pay living-away-from-home allowances, I should only choose replacements who lived locally. They also made it clear that they had no intention of paying allowances to any of us who had relocated to the Gold Coast to take up the original employment contracts.

During these sporadic discussions, never did the subject of my weight, my doctor's report or the producer's request to ban me from a number in the show get discussed. If I complied with the producer's demand and removed myself from the number, the rest of the female dancers would lose their one swing-night off a week due to my permanent deletion. But whenever I tried to open a conversation about the concerns of the female chorus, the producer simply walked away or hung up the phone. He didn't care about how this change impacted the show or the cast. With no other recourse, Actors' Equity union was called in to mediate my situation.

On the day of mediation, the producer canceled the meeting by leaving a letter on my dressing table, advising he was flying overseas. Despite the producer's absence, the union president and I still went to his office to see the company manager. True to form, the producer wasn't overseas. He was in his office, but he refused to see us. Having witnessed firsthand the contempt in which the producer not only held me, his cast but also the union, the president suggested I continue in my role while the union pursued the matter on my behalf. Complying with the producer's written request and on advice from the union, I blocked myself out of the number and forged forward, while the female dancers rightfully complained about their added workload.

I spent endless hours ranting and raving over the unfairness of the situation, trying to work out why this was happening to me. Indignant that I had only ever performed my role for the good of the production, here I was being denied my dignity and ostracized. Since I hadn't breached my contract in any way, the producer couldn't find a chink in my professional armor, so he stooped to making a personal attack on my weight, which for a dancer is sacrosanct. How dare he? My warrior spirit suited up. She wasn't backing down. Pressing on, I posted more résumés to prospective employers, desperately seeking to be free of the situation. The wolves were baying at the door, and I was the main course.

We choose the life we live...

What I wasn't aware of at the time is that *we choose the life we live*, whether we're conscious of it or not.

The concept of attracting conditions and circumstances into our lives has long been chronicled in spiritual, philosophical and scientific literature. Simply explained, the law of attraction means like attracts like. Subsequently, what we predominantly energize in our Consciousness will be evidenced in our lives. Everything we've ever been exposed to and then energized through our thoughts, perceptions, beliefs, values, emotions, words, actions and memories has left an imprint on our unconscious mind. These aren't dead things. They are always active, impacting our Consciousness.

We act like energetic transmitters, sending out signals based on our stored files, attracting to us similar energy in the form of people and experiences. What we think, speak, perceive, believe and embody is returned to us, like for like. The law of attraction never discriminates. It is we who discriminate and fashion our life based on our internal programmed files, enacted through our bodies. In short, we are the master programmers of our lives. Nothing happens to us by chance. Nothing happens to us that we didn't first energize and influence in some way. Whether we know it or not, we use the law of attraction to demonstrate every condition and circumstance in our life. Nothing is random.

We cannot demonstrate in the world of effects (our physical life) beyond what our current world of causes (our Consciousness) embodies. Most of us were raised with a limited sense of our self, which in turn forms our conditioning. It isn't enough to say we attract what we think. We become what we think, and what we become, we attract. Therefore, negatively conditioned and energized people find themselves in trouble easily. Joyously energized people find themselves living abundant, happy lives. We attract to ourselves that which we embody and resonate most. This is how life works and how we govern our destiny.

The level of my Consciousness throughout my life brought me to this situation at the casino. Although I was a good, loving person who acted with strong personal and professional ethics, underneath these positive qualities and behaviors operated a disempowering fear of rejection and abandonment. Although my *being* nourished me, my fears and self-doubt led me to feel persecuted. The producer was my nemesis. He embodied my greatest fear, which was for me to make my dream come true, only to be rejected and abandoned, by him—the person with the most power over my life. It was the same script with which I'd incarnated: that of being born, then rejected and abandoned by my biological mother, the person who had the most power over me. After three decades of carrying this wound around, I still hadn't worked it out.

At every juncture of this worsening time with the producer, I sought resolution. Having been the go-to girl for everyone else in my life, I believed I could fix this too. I tried changing my approach, but the producer refused to interact with me. I demonstrated my willingness by taking myself out of the dance number as requested. I did everything I could to repair my dream job and not lose the future I had worked so hard for. I thought I was dealing with the physical world and conditions outside of myself, when in fact it was about the causes within me, my Consciousness. I set this in motion by my conditioning, and through the power of the law of attraction, it happened.

Of course, the producer was also complicit in this. My refusal to participate in a sexual liaison obviously emasculated him, provoking him to bring me into line any way he could. On some level he was threatened by me. His unwillingness or inability to be honest and communicate meant we couldn't find resolution. The more I tried to find common ground, to stop him from rejecting me, the more threatened he felt and the more he shunned me.

Because I lived with a limited sense of myself as a personality; confusion, frustration and resentment tore through my body like a freight train. I was a good, ethical woman being persecuted by an unreasonable employer. I was right. He was wrong.

Even though I didn't have another job, I could have said, "To hell with it," and walked away. But I didn't.

The vivid memory from my Sunday school days of when Jesus made a stand against injustice flashed on and off like a Broadway marquee in my mind. *I'm going to make a stand too.* And with that one momentous decision, I set the stage for the most critical turning point in my life.

CHAPTER SIX
Do the good guys win?

Less than two weeks after the last letter, my termination letter arrived. That night, an emergency meeting was called by the union. Thirty hostile, worn-out performers sat on the stage venting their frustration, while the audience waited on the other side of the curtain, no doubt wondering what the commotion was. Months of mistreatment reached a tipping point when the cast refused to go on, delaying the show by over an hour. Finally, it was voted by a two-thirds majority to have me reinstated and that unless management did so, there'd be a strike of the next night's performance. The disgraceful way in which I had been treated, and my subsequent termination inspired the cast to make a stand against management on the other unresolved matters that affected each of them.

Despite the cast's decision, and the renewed hope it gave me, the producer arranged a bitter end to my onstage career. Out of nowhere appeared two burly security guards to unceremoniously escort me from the theater. Everyone was dumbfounded. Given no time to clear my dressing table, I bundled up the few belongings I could and was ushered from the showroom in a state of humiliated disbelief. That such injustice could be perpetrated so easily on a person who had done nothing to deserve it was incomprehensible to me and others. The warrior within me flexed, ready for battle. Every insult, every personal attack made me more resolute and resilient. Only behind closed doors did I permit my heart to break. I'll never forget going home alone that night, while the show went on without me. Like water swirling down the drain, I watched thirty years of my life disappear into the blackness of night. I looked to the stars and wished it was all a bad dream.

I spent the next eleven days preparing for my case of unfair and discriminatory dismissal, feeling like Dorothy in Kansas as the tornado wrought its destruction. The union handled my representation by bringing in a senior federal union official from Sydney. Meanwhile, I applied for unemployment benefits, collected Statutory Declarations from supportive cast members, previous colleagues and doctors, tried to find other employment and prepared my case. During this time, the producer acted like the wicked witch of the west and canceled my severance check. The union responded by issuing him a fraud fine. Not only did he decimate my dream and wrench my future from underneath me, but he also stopped my ability to pay my day-to-day living expenses. I eventually received my money, but only after I returned the dishonored check in person to his office to request a replacement. With new check in hand, I left his office accompanied by the toxic twins of rejection and abandonment sniggering beside me.

By the time I arrived at the courts of the Australian Conciliation and Arbitration Commission in Brisbane, I was shell-shocked. How my life could take such an unexpected and demoralizing turn in less than two years confounded me, filling me with profound sorrow. Sporting dark bags under my red-rimmed eyes, my face lax and gaunt, and my body strung out on a constant stream of adrenalin squirting into my stomach, I was an emotional, mental and physical wreck. But ever the dancer, I scrubbed up that morning in a fitted cream blouse, black skirt and high heels, with expertly applied makeup trying to mask the stress in my face. If the producer wanted a fight, he'd picked the wrong girl. After all, in the movies the good guys always won. Right was on my side.

The most important part of my ensemble that day was my journals. For the past two years, I had spent up to thirty minutes after each performance recording everything relating to that show. Keeping a journal provided me with a living history of my daily experiences at the casino and gave me a quiet moment to review and assess what had happened, and to plan the forthcoming day. My journals provided an indisputable audit trail of times, places, events and conversations, both as chronological and factual evidence.

Even now as I write this, those trusted friends, my journals, sit beside me, tickling my memory with their facts. I still commit myself to this regular process and have recorded over thirty years of my life in daily journals, neatly stacked in my library. If given the time it deserves, journaling is an enlightening emotional record of our evolution in this lifetime. Allowing their wisdom to resonate with us, the voices that call from our past infuse us with a deeper understanding to live more fulfilling futures. After all, if our lives are worth living, they are surely worth recording and reading.

As for my day in court, my journals recalled the past and supported me with their indisputable evidence against the producer's planned attack. I walked to the table in the front of the courtroom and sat straight-backed between my local and federal union representatives. At the table across the aisle sat the company manager and the producer's legal representative. The contempt with which the producer held the proceeding was evident by his absence. We all rose when the commissioner entered the room, and I took a deep breath. On the inside, I shook like a leaf clutching to its branch for dear life. On the outside, I was the peaceful warrior who wouldn't bow to the raised sword of the enemy.

Ill-prepared for the case, management's legal representative began his rhetoric and it was obvious he couldn't find a footing on which to claim a case for his client. Fumbling through paperwork, tripping over his insufficient preparation and mumbling questions, management's counsel lacked any evidence to support their case for terminating my employment. I hadn't breached my contract in any way, and he struggled pitifully not to admit it to the court.

On the other hand, my federal union representative offered numerous examples of the unfair and discriminatory way in which I'd been treated. Witnesses were called and statements read. When I took to the stand and referred to my journals, citing dates, meetings and outcomes, the discriminatory treatment was irrefutable. The commissioner adjourned the case for lunch.

I left the courtroom, grateful for the recess until the media swarmed. Having no idea how they knew about the case, I was blindsided by a scrum of pushy journalists and snapping photographers. After being chased down the stairs and weaving in and out of alleyways, I finally escaped and managed to find shelter in a small café. Nobody took responsibility for alerting the press, but their presence added to my feelings of violation and disgrace.

When we returned, the union asked the commissioner to close the court for the afternoon's hearing. He declined. The courtroom ballooned with snoopy, snappy press, and my humiliation of wrongful dismissal turned into a frenzied media feast. Deferring his judgment, the commissioner concluded the hearing later that afternoon, giving the media plenty of time to scurry off to their bosses with the headlines for the next day's news.

The national and local newspapers plastered the story across their front pages the following morning. "Dancer Sacked for Being Too Fat" blazed like a comet across the newsstands. Adding to my shame was that in the fracas the day before, unflattering photos had been taken of me. Jammed next to the headline, these images seemed to prove I was overweight as my anguished face tried to avoid the camera's reach. That I even managed to get dressed and attend the courtroom that second day used the last remaining reserves of my dancer's discipline.

With the courtroom now bursting with print and television media, the commissioner sat elevated behind his austere legal bench and brought down his six-page verdict. Reading from the document, he reiterated the case, the facts as presented and his subsequent conclusions. Throughout his deliberate, even-toned reading, his face remained impassive, and I couldn't gauge whether he would find in my favor. It was the longest ten minutes I could remember. By the end he concluded, "…and so, finding no grounds for the dismissal of Ms. Davidson, she is to be reinstated immediately."

It was over. My body sagged and my breath rushed from me. I buried my face in my hands, trying not to cry from exhaustion and relief. Though I'd been reinstated, I didn't feel like I'd won. It was so surreal. By the time I looked up the company manager was gone.

When I exited the courtroom, I was mobbed by the press pack clamoring for interviews, photographs and the good-news story of how a dancer won against her producer. My case had set a precedent. No performer in Australia had taken their employer to court and won an unfair dismissal and discrimination case before.

I gave a couple of impromptu interviews, stating my hope that communication would improve between management and me on my return. In my heart, I just wanted my job back, to get on with my life, and most importantly, my beloved career.

That afternoon I returned to work full of good will. On the union's recommendation, the company manager called a meeting to inform every one of my reinstatement. But instead of this having a positive effect on the cast, the way she couched the news and the praise she heaped on my interim replacement, did little to enthuse the cast of my return. My enduring hope of "forgive and forget" took a thrashing. I was left sore and metaphorically bleeding before the curtain went up.

Over the next days, my phone rang hot with national current affairs programs and publishing companies offering enormous sums of money for on-screen interviews and the book rights.

Playboy wanted me as their next month's centerfold. "It'll be your chance to prove to our readers that you're not fat."

"No way!"

Channel 9 offered me ten thousand dollars, which was a huge amount of money at the time, to appear on their award-winning program *A Current Affair* and be interviewed by their leading journalist Jana Wendt. Again, I said no. I turned down every offer. I wanted to get back to work, put it all behind me and do what I loved. In my naivety, I thought all could be restored at the showroom, but as the nursery rhyme says, "They couldn't put Humpty together again."

Because I'd promised a few interviews to print journalists on the day of the commissioner's decision, I felt obliged to do them. Again, I ignored my intuition which told me to back out. But no, I had made a promise so I should keep it. It was during these interviews that I became increasingly uneasy when I realized that all the media wanted was to "get the dirt" on what went on backstage.

Jerry called from Las Vegas with his support and offered me work in one of his shows there, but I declined. To leave Mum wasn't an option, although every fiber of my *being* screamed for me to go. That was where my entertainment future lay, not in Australia. But having suffered the terror of abandonment myself, how could I abandon my mother while she was still coming to terms with her widowhood? I don't recall giving Mum the opportunity to express her opinion on Jerry's offer. Perhaps I did. Or perhaps I made the decision to stay because of my love and misplaced responsibility for her. She'd had 'my back' for thirty years and been beside me through this ordeal. Even if she gave her blessing for me to go to America, I couldn't. I needed to finish what I had started.

While management continued humiliating me, the cast ostracized me for fear I might personalize their actions in my interviews. To have most of them renounce me sliced to my very core. I had done nothing but champion their cause by standing up for better working conditions. It was the grandest of all betrayals and completely broke my heart.

By now, the slithering insidiousness of the ego reminded me how unworthy I was. I had deserved to be rejected and abandoned at birth, and I deserved it now. I'd never felt so alone. I'd lost faith in loyalty, justice and humanity, and in doing so, I lost hope. I no longer had the strength to perform. On visiting Dr. Gill, he informed me I was in the throes of a nervous breakdown due to the stress at work and ordered

I take six week's sick leave. On receiving my sick leave certificate, the union called the producer to advise he was responsible for paying my sick leave. He refused.

Within a few days, my confidential sick leave certificate was posted by the company manager on the cast bulletin board backstage for all to see. A shameful act. Management further offered to pay the cast their owed living-away-from-home allowance if they signed a petition to have me terminated again. It was a hollow gesture though, because the hearing for our unpaid living-away-from-home allowance had already been set for a future date at the commission.

Three weeks into my six-week sick leave, a knock at my door heralded another registered letter from management. I opened it expecting to find a check for my sick-leave-pay to date. Instead, I was confronted with another termination letter from the producer. I stood speechless while a gaping hole tore through my soul. Why was this happening to me?

The power of practice and persistence

Having successfully demonstrated my mantra, repetition is the mother of all skill, I knew the power of practice and persistence. By practicing and persisting in my dancing, I had developed the skill to be a professional dancer. I'd applied the same methodology to producing, choreographing and directing my own shows for the previous fifteen years. Through practice and persistence, I'd improved significantly in doing what I loved most. In honoring the calling of my *being* to express itself, I had produced sensational results by scoring my dream job.

What I didn't know was that at the same time, there was another aspect of me that was also practicing and persisting—the ego. My practice of subtle, fearful thinking was also producing results, reflected in the internal and external battles in which I was embroiled.

I hadn't realized the power of thought.

Like everything, thoughts are energy. They are the energetic movement of the level of the Consciousness we currently embody. All thoughts influence our lives because they power up our feelings and emotions.

At this time in my life, my thoughts matched my low level of Consciousness and powered up endless loops of anger, victimhood, powerlessness, grief, righteous indignation, rejection and abandonment. Seemingly trapped, I chased my mental and emotional tail, because I had practiced and persisted in my fear-based, conditioned thinking.

Thoughts are the seeds we plant in the creative soil of our minds until they take root and grow into the beliefs and values which underpin our choices. When we plant disempowering, negative thoughts and embody them in our emotions, beliefs, values and actions, they'll grow into negative circumstances and unhealthy conditions around us. Exactly what happened to me during this time.

Likewise, when we plant empowering, useful seeds—positivity, goodness and success will grow around us. The adage of we reap what we sow, is true. Our life is not random. Our life is what we make it by our Consciousness because all form is first thought, repeated, embodied and enacted.

If we want a better-quality life, we must think better-quality thoughts, ask better-quality questions, make better-quality decisions and take better-quality actions. Instead of asking the victim question of "why is this happening to me," which became my daily mantra, I needed to be asking better-quality questions.

How can I change to get a better outcome?
What am I willing to do to make myself better?
How can I move on?
What is this situation teaching me?

And I needed to be looking within myself to find my answers.

But I was ensnared by the ego. I focused on the external events, asked the wrong questions and blamed other people for the misery multiplying in my life.

At that time, I didn't know Viktor Frankl's well-known quote, "When we are no longer able to change the situation, we are challenged to change ourselves."

But as it turns out, my *being* wouldn't be squashed. My Consciousness groaned and stretched, as if awakening from a long slumber. In moments of fleeting clarity, I sensed that something else was going on. But I had no idea that the purpose with which I'd incarnated was now in motion. Like a shoe that gets too tight when a child's foot grows larger, my life at that time was too tight for my Consciousness. Pressing on past the limitations of the ego, my Consciousness was bursting forth in all its glory, no matter how much I railed and clung to my old, conditioned thinking. Like a baby just before its birth, my time was upon me.

Sacked dancer to seek court ruling

DANCER Diane Davidson is ready to fight for her job in the arbitration court after being suddenly sacked last Thursday from the cast of Galaxies — the entertainment spectacular at the Conrad International Hotel.

Miss Davidson's sacking prompted a walk-out by the 60-strong cast after the Thursday show but a planned one-day strike protesting her dismissal did not happen.

Miss Davidson, 30, was the dance captain of the $25-a-head show and was told of her sacking by certified mail about 3.30pm on Thursday — about two hours before the show's producer Jim McDonald left for a three week overseas trip.

Reason

Miss Davidson was also dance captain (the cast member responsible for ensuring choreography style remains consistent) of the hotel's first gala production Starz.

She has worked as dance captain since Starz started in December, 1985.

"I still don't know why I was sacked. There was no reason given in the letter," said Miss Davidson, who has been dancing for 25 years.

"I think I was unfairly dismissed and it is going to court but as far as I am concerned I would be happy to be re-instated.

"I didn't think there was anything wrong until I got the letter and I thought I got on quite well with the producer."

Actors Equity state secretary Don Summers said the matter would probably go to arbitration late this week.

Sacked Galaxies dancer Diane Davidson

These newspaper clippings, yellowed with time, quietly capture a period of unforeseen heartbreak and humiliation.

Dancer 'too fat' for show, hearing told

THE lead dancer in the Jupiters Casino spectacular *Galaxies* was sacked because her boss thought she was too fat, a Federal Arbitration Commission hearing in Brisbane was told yesterday.

The hearing, before Commissioner Mansini, also was told of low morale among the cast and backstage in-fighting within the Las Vegas-style dance revue.

A male dancer had hit a singer in the mouth and vomited on another dancer on stage, the hearing was told.

Actors Equity has claimed that Ms Diane Davidson, 30, of Mermaid Waters, was dismissed unfairly by Delicado Productions on March 17.

Her contract was cancelled after the company asked her to lose weight around her hips and thighs.

The State secretary of Actors Equity, Mr Don Summers, applied for her reinstatement and compensation for the alleged damage the incident had done to her career.

The Commission was told that Ms Davidson had been employed for the past two years by Delicado, which produced the revue for the Conrad International Hotel on the Gold Coast.

Ms Davidson was dance captain and assistant choreographer in the company's two productions, *Stars* and *Galaxies*.

Mr Bill Parlour, appearing for Delicado, said the managing director, Mr Jim McDonald, had raised concerns that some female dancers in the show were overweight.

Mr McDonald believed the company had to present a "glamorous image" and was embarrassed to hear some of the comments made by the audience, Mr Parlour said.

In a letter to Ms Davidson on February 11, Mr McDonald wrote: "Dear Diane, Please lose weight immediately as you are an embarrassment to the rest of the cast."

In a further letter, Mr McDonald had told her that the weight problem was "particularly noticeable in the Argentinian number, where the cut of your dress is not complimentary."

He suggested Ms Davidson go on the Pritikin diet and attend aerobics classes.

The company had always been happy with her work as dance captain and choreographer, Mr McDonald said.

Mr Parlour said that on one occasion, a male dance partner had claimed he could not lift her because he had a bad back.

All female dancers had their weight checked except Ms Davidson, he said.

Dancers were asked by the company to lose weight when the show went into recess.

Ms Davidson, in a letter to Mr McDonald, said she had been the same weight since the show opened in August, 1987, and was amazed that it had taken so long for the company to disapprove.

She suggested the problem could be solved by a minor alteration to her costume in the Argentinian number.

Mr Parlour said Ms Davidson's contract was cancelled on March 17.

Ms Davidson told the hearing that she had always weighed between 64 kg and 66 kg during her employment with Delicado.

"I am at a total loss as to why I was dismissed," she said.

She said that she had never had any problem with costumes being too light for her.

Ms Davidson then outlined a series of incidents involving other cast members who she claimed had breached their contracts but had not been disciplined.

A male dancer had hit the principal singer in the mouth, had rammed his hand through a dressing-room mirror and chased screaming female dancers backstage, she said.

"He also took Valium before performances and vomited on another cast member on stage," she said.

The soloists in the Russian number had changed their stage positions, which disrupted the routine for accompanying acrobats and endangered their lives, she said.

"Another dancer was hit with a whip," she said.

Ms Davidson said these incidents had badly affected cast morale and despite her repeated requests, the company management took no action.

"The problems backstage were escalating but nothing was done and these people are still employed," she said.

Mr Summers said that the overweight claim was not the real reason why Ms Davidson had been dismissed.

"Delicado seem reluctant to say what the other reasons are," Mr Summers said.

Mr Mansini will hand down his decision today.

MS DAVIDSON leaves the hearing yesterday

This was a time of profound struggle, where the cost of integrity was steep and the journey, unexpectedly arduous.

CHAPTER SEVEN
Crash and burn

On 29 April 1988, I met with the union and the commissioner to discuss my second termination while on unpaid sick leave. Fired up with injustice to the worker and the opportunity to win a second time, the union wanted to pursue the producer again in court, but the commissioner wouldn't be led as to the possible outcome. Nevertheless, he did offer advice on how best to proceed if I chose to do so. Undecided, I requested the union give me a few days to think it over.

I clearly remember how humiliated I felt when standing in line to apply for unemployment benefits. Strangers came up to me, recognizing me as the fat dancer who was in the newspaper. I had always longed for fame and fortune, but this wasn't what I'd visualized. This was shame and misfortune. Disgraced, I skulked out of the unemployment agency and made a hasty retreat home. Being a rejected, abandoned and adopted child, I cared about what other people thought about me. I longed to be accepted. I tried hard to be the good girl, the good student, the good employee. I was devastated by these escalating and highly public events.

During this time, I fronted up for numerous interviews. Pursuing one job after another, I applied for positions in special event management or entertainment services without success. Every interviewer recoiled on recognizing me from the newspaper articles, judging I'd be a liability to their organization. Despite winning my case, I was classed as a troublemaker and a whistle-blower. I was even rejected as a housekeeper and cleaner at a nearby motel with the owner telling me I was too glamorous for the job. I just wanted to work. I needed to work to reassure myself that I was worthy of something, anything. Although I still operated Jupiter's Academy of Dance in Entertainment, the numbers were dwindling rapidly. I had become an untouchable.

Suspecting my entertainment career that once filled me with such joy was irrevocably damaged due to the publicity surrounding my case, I reassessed my options and turned to the one other practice I loved and excelled at, reading and study. Although I had no money to further my formal education, I decided to become self-educated, pouring as much time as I could into studying business management and entrepreneurship.

At the same time, my warrior spirit drove me to continue my stand for justice. I seethed at the flagrant discrimination I'd endured just because I had dared to refuse my producer's sexual advances. Unemployed, and with no money to pay my bills, I chose to proceed with the additional case. Since I hadn't breached my contractual conditions, the union advised I was entitled to receive a payout for the remainder of my contract. I decided to take their advice, get what I was owed and then move on with a new career in another direction.

Weeks passed with the continuing absence of future work and my confidence slid from me like an oversized coat. I spent my days scouring the newspaper for job vacancies, attending interviews, teaching the few remaining classes at J.A.D.E., submitting my fortnightly unemployment benefit form and holding on to the last tenuous thread of hope that a miracle might happen.

In spite of my situation, I was fortunate to have some love in my life. A handful of loyal friends, my loving mother and my boyfriend who had resigned from the casino show when I was fired, supported me as best as they could, while they watched the Diane they knew disappear into a darkening hole.

Just prior to the second court case, I was called to a meeting by the hotel's marketing manager. Sitting in her executive office, I hoped there might be an offer of support, but I sensed a cold blade of steel settle on the nape of my neck.

"Although Conrad Jupiter's sympathizes with your position in this dispute with the producer, the hotel can't have their brand associated with this negative publicity."

The imaginary blade lifted and took aim.

"Therefore, we're revoking our agreement permitting you to use Jupiter's name in your performance academy."

Thwack! I half expected to see my head roll across her plush carpet. It was another blow to my career. With no other option, I acquiesced to their request to cease and desist from using Jupiter's name, signed the paperwork and rose unsteadily to my feet. I thanked her for her time, though I wasn't grateful at all, and left her office.

Once outside, I gathered my reserves again and decided to continue the academy. Despite decreasing numbers it gave me some income. In homage to the mythical bird that rose from the ashes, I renamed it the Phoenix Youth Theatre and desperately hoped my future would do the same.

On the first day of the second hearing, I breathed a sigh of relief when the commissioner closed the court to the media. At least there would be some privacy for this second case. After losing the first case and having to reinstate me, the producer attended this hearing. It was the first time I had seen him in months. Instead of hiring an underprepared lawyer, this time he engaged a Queen's Counsel. Obviously, this was the producer's last-ditch attempt to get rid of me. The QC's first point of business was to try to have my journals excluded. However, the commissioner refused and allowed me to reference them whenever needed.

The tone of the hearing soon became evident when the QC interposed Dr. Gill in the stand. Intimating that my doctor and I had a sexual relationship, he implied this was the real reason for my doctor granting me six weeks' sick leave. Shocked by such an accusation, Dr. Gill strongly refuted this line of questioning. After another fifteen minutes of distasteful cross-examination, my doctor was released. On his exit from the stand, he gave me a piteous glance, like I was an animal about to be euthanized. Despite the sinking feeling in my stomach, I set my jaw and held my head high. No one was putting me down. Or at least, I hoped not. I was then called to testify. Once in the stand, I arranged my journals in front of me and summoned up all my grit. For the next hour, I dared to tell my story despite the constant insidious questions and lewd insinuations by the producer's QC.

When the commissioner adjourned the case for five days, my stomach lurched. After the quick decision with the first case, this lengthy delay only worsened my suffering. I was ready to be done with it all, there and then. My reserves were running on empty.

The resumption of my case saw me in the witness stand for more than five consecutive hours being relentlessly questioned by the producer's QC, who earned every dollar of his exorbitant fee that day.

Weaving, badgering, reverting to previous points and trying to rattle my nerves, he pressed on. Their case hinged on proving I was incapable of returning to work after my sick leave, or that I had no desire to return to work and that my evidence was worthless. Throughout this ordeal I referred to my journals, grateful for the detail I had written in them day after day for the past two and a half years.

At the end of the five hours, the QC turned to me and sneered. "You're good."

To which I replied, "No. I just tell the truth."

The commissioner called a conference between the producer and the union to find a resolution. The producer refused to reinstate me on any grounds, nor pay me any compensation. He also advised he wouldn't abide by the decision of the Australian Conciliation and Arbitration Commission and would take the matter to a higher court if the commissioner found in my favor.

Based on the producer's refusal to consider any resolution, the commissioner decided to withhold his verdict for further consideration. One week later, another resolution conference between the producer and the union was undertaken before the commissioner brought down his verdict. Based on the obdurate stance of the producer, the commissioner decided it wouldn't be in my best interest or health to return to work. I was gutted. I hadn't done anything wrong, yet here was the perpetrator getting off scot-free while I was being discarded like an old bone.

At the time, the Australian Conciliation and Arbitration Commission had no authority to order anything more than four weeks' pay in lieu of notice. For me to receive my owed sick-leave entitlement or to have my remaining contract paid out, I had to proceed to federal court for a repeat performance. Although the union was keen to proceed, I was numb. Everything I dared to dream, every hour I dared to practice, every challenge I dared to overcome in the first thirty years of my life now accounted for nothing. My future had been torn from my arms, like a screaming baby, while I stood helpless in the wings. Depleted and undone, I decided not to live this toxic nightmare any longer. I stepped away with the hungry media nipping at my heels.

And so, on the day I lost the life I loved, I went into hiding, unaware of the powerful shift taking place in the midst of my tragedy. Not that I cared. Curled in a sobbing ball of soul-destroying anguish in my small, rented flat, I wallowed in a pity party for one. The color of the bile-green mosaic floor tiles matched the bodily fluids purging themselves from my throat as my body retched itself inside out. My rejection was complete—even my stomach didn't want any part of me.

If anyone had tried to comfort me or explain the higher purpose of my catastrophe, I would have hurled fury through my fingertips at them, like a true superhero, striking them asunder. Except at the time, I felt anything but super. Just as well God didn't speak to me in his best baritone voice or he would've been promptly told where to go. Humiliation, despair and seething injustice shackled me to the bottom of the barrel, which in this case was the cold, unforgiving bathroom floor, where a churning mass of emotions took turns wringing my heart until all my passion for life was squeezed dry.

Hell is the truth learned too late.

Destiny is repeated experience…

Though I didn't know it at the time, my repeated thoughts, perceptions, beliefs, values, emotions, words and actions from the prior three decades had brought me to this juncture. I'd been born to dance, to perform, to bring joy to people through my creative expression and now it had been taken from me, including any chance of a future in the business I loved. Having practiced and persisted in my battles with the producer, I had repeated the same fear-based pattern of rejection and abandonment over again. Unknowingly, I played victim to his perpetrator, until I was broken—physically, emotionally, mentally, spiritually and financially.

During this whole time, I had done what was right, not what was easy. Like the true MGM movie heroes from my childhood, I refused to compromise my morals. Even when it meant I walked alone; I continued on my chosen path with the character, courage and commitment to see it through. In the face of this adversity, I could no more forfeit my integrity than fly to the moon. The right thing and the hardest thing for me were the same.

Proverbs 10:9 says, "Whoever walks in integrity walks securely, but whoever takes crooked paths will be found out."

But I didn't feel secure at all. I was sinking. Nothing could save me from the misery that consumed every cell of my body while my life crumbled around me. With every anguished thought, I fell deeper and deeper into an emotional abyss.

There was nothing left for me to do.

And in doing nothing, a vast universal energy unleashed itself, exploding my Consciousness, urging me to let go, to let it *be*, to let *me* be.

My spirit, my *being*, was free at last, free at last.

ACT TWO
The Awakening of a Woman

CHAPTER EIGHT
Let go and lean in

Akin to a survivor of a heinous crime, I lay battered, broken and beaten in my bed. I'd reached the bottom of the barrel and possessed no more energy to heave myself up the sides of life. Hopeless and heartbroken, my uncontrollable sobbing continued like an endless river gouging a deep chasm through my soul.

Over the next weeks, a dark, fathomless depression consumed me, tumbling me further into despair. Wrapped in my emotional straitjacket, I was immobilized by a profound fear of the future, while rejection and abandonment danced sadistically on my once passionate attitude toward life. Alternating between hiding under my bedcovers and shuffling around the house in my pajamas, I rode the roller-coaster ride of emotional pain in gut-wrenching terror. Invariably, at the end of each day's ride, I found myself backed into a corner. Rocking back and forth, with my knees tucked under my chin, I deliberated how best to escape this mortal coil.

I had visited Shakespeare's Globe Theatre in London years before and having been a lover of his prose throughout my theater career, I found my mind returning to the soliloquy of Will's tragic hero, Hamlet.

"To be, or not to be: That is the question. Whether 'tis nobler in the mind to suffer the slings and arrows of outrageous fortune, or to take arms against a sea of troubles and by opposing end them? To die: to sleep…" And that's all I wanted to do; to die: to sleep.

I had suffered the slings and arrows of outrageous fortune. I had opposed them and now it was time to end it all. Like phantoms from a long-ago past, concerned friends and family drifted in and out, trying to lift my spirits with happy memories and hopeful promises of a better future. But I was spent. Nothing interested me. I'd given up on myself and life. The more I succumbed to the ego's malicious chatter in my mind, the more I permitted my emotions to join the pity party. Since emotions are energy in motion, they followed suit and partnered with the ego, spiraling me downwards in a suicidal death-spin.

By this time, I obediently took my prescribed medications, unconcerned with the lethargy or possible side-effects they may have. What did I have to live for anyway?

After weeks of watching me nose-dive, my boyfriend and mother removed all medications for fear of what I might do. At her wits end, Mum called for help from my trusted dresser at the Casino. During *Starz*, Judy had stepped me in and out of my costumes every performance, eight shows a week. Dependable, level-headed and compassionate, she'd been my confidante and staunchest supporter. She was a good friend and second mother rolled into one.

Answering the call that evening, she strode into my bedroom full of authority.

"I know your heart is broken, but you must get up and get on with your life."

"I can't, Judy. There's nothing left for me."

"Don't be ridiculous. You have everything to live for."

"No. I can't."

"You can. Now, come on. Up you get," she demanded in a no-nonsense voice. She pulled back the bedcovers and waited. Her insistence and total disregard for my misery cleft a thin fissure in my self-pity. She pissed me off, which is what I think she intended to do. Anything to shake me out of my apathy. With a good dose of tough love, she reignited the smoldering embers within me.

Knowing she would stand there until I dragged my sorry bones out of the bed, I made the choice to get up, reluctant though it was. But in doing so, I also made a deeper choice not to give up on myself. Instead, I chose to give up the bone-crushing pain and pity. Though tenuous in nature and lacking bravado, these decisions had one thing in common—daring. I dared to *feel* something different. I dared to *think* something different, and I dared to *be* someone different. And in doing so, I rose from my bed and the death of depression.

Those daring decisions changed my destiny.

By getting up, I dared to believe in a new life. A life I would eventually move through with more elegance, gratitude and power, by making conscious, congruent decisions. Although the universal law of attraction was triggered the moment I made the decision to get up and get on with my life, none of that magnificent new life materialized instantaneously. It would be up to me to energize my decision with focused intention, aligned action, and applied skills while resonating at a higher level of Consciousness.

That night, and for the first time in ages, I took a deep breath, right down into my very soul. I realized I had to learn a new way to *be* in my world. There had to be more than what I was currently experiencing. Inside me, the belief that I had been born for a reason anchored itself once more. As I shifted my focus to this empowering thought, I gained a slightly surer footing and the vile notion of ending my life was cast adrift.

Over the coming weeks, memories of magic and miracles squeezed through the shadows in my mind, melting the edges of my depression. I was a dancer. I was daring, determined, disciplined and driven. Judy was right. I had an entire life yet to live. Plucking up the last remnants of my courage, I laced up my metaphoric dance shoes to learn the new steps to living a better life. My optimistic attitude of finding something to be glad about in every situation began to flicker, ready to burn once more. Peeking her head out from the recent upset, Pollyanna began to reemerge, albeit with extreme caution, but also with a spark of daring.

With a little more confidence, I ventured out into the world to buy a carton of milk or some other small necessity, though to lift my head and look at the shop assistant while she tallied my purchase proved far more difficult. My posture remained slumped and my eyes downcast with the lingering shame of my case continuing to haunt me. I mistakenly believed that everyone knew my face from the newspapers.

The idea of fifteen minutes of fame (or shame) didn't occur to me. I never considered that my tragedy had been usurped by another front-page story of much greater importance. This never occurred to me not because I thought I was so illustrious, but because the ego wouldn't relinquish its hold over me that easily. Self-doubt, shame and not feeling good enough still plagued my thoughts, but I continued with my conviction to find an answer, not only of what had happened to me, but how to make sure it didn't happen again. Since I'd become unemployable, I gave up knocking on doors for a while. More rejection wasn't something I needed during my healing process. I continued with my youth theater, discovering the best therapy was dancing with and teaching my small group of loyal students, all of whom brought a little sunshine back into my life.

With my boyfriend's financial and emotional support, I spent much of my time reading and studying. Not only did I consume books on business and management, I developed a growing interest in self-development literature and autobiographies. Locking myself away in my own personal world of learning, I decided not to cry over anything again that couldn't or wouldn't cry over me. Anonymity became my perfect refuge, for I knew that to find happiness required valuing my own company above all else. Like a jeweler with a diamond, I set about polishing my rough edges, cutting the many facets of my personality with patience and precision, until out of cloudiness, a pinpoint of luminescence glittered.

As the months passed, the money ran out. I recall standing at the check-out and giving back groceries because I didn't have enough money to buy them. Since I'd been raised a working-class girl, most of the time this didn't bother me. If you couldn't afford it, you didn't buy it.

Martin Luther King Jr said, "The ultimate measure of a person is not where they stand in moments of comfort and convenience, but where they stand in times of challenge and controversy."

After what I'd been through, handing back food proved no great challenge or controversy for me.

The day finally came when I dared to lift my head and face the people around me, the checkout person, the shop assistant and the store owner. I dared to look them in the eye with a new world view. Instead of seeing the world as a hostile place filled with ignorant, deceitful, unkind people, I viewed humanity as a mirror, reflecting my goodness back to me. When I dared to smile at them, little did they know that when they smiled back, it re-energized my faith in my future.

During this time, I wrote pages of observations and notes, expecting to find answers to the questions looping in my mind. My thirst for knowledge drove me ever onward. I needed to know why my dream had been stripped from me, not so much out of self-pity, but from a genuine desire to understand, to find the truth.

Was there something I could have done differently?
How had I contributed to this?
What was it I needed to do to make sure this didn't happen again?

I dared to ask quality questions with the expectation of receiving quality answers. I was now ready to face Viktor Frankl's challenge of: "When we are no longer able to change the situation, we are challenged to change ourselves." I was ready to change myself.

Without finding immediate answers to my mounting questions, I mulled them over and over in mind, scribbling down possible answers, only to scratch them out again. Some would say I was praying, petitioning God to give me the answers, to show me the way. Others would say I was placing a problem in my mind and giving my intellect the instruction to solve it. Debating over what I did, or what millions of people across the world do, is meaningless. The significance of the experience lies in the outcome. Based on my own personal history, I knew success was governed by an unrelenting drive to reach for the stars, dream big and take massive action. My recent experience had also taught me to overcome the staggering blows of adversity and to persevere. The answers I sought, although not immediately evident, were there within reach, and I had to press on until I found them.

Since I had no spare money to purchase new books, my only recourse was a nearby secondhand bookstore. Standing at the doorway of the musty shop, I was embarrassed that I had to buy someone else's discarded books. But a familiar nudging, reminiscent of my ghostly theater days in Brisbane, pushed me through the threshold with no less force than if someone had placed their hand in the middle of my back and given me a shove. Once inside, I wandered around perusing hundreds of tattered books crammed on old timber shelves.

Thud! A book fell off the shelf onto the floor at my feet. Before I took the step, it wasn't there but the moment I did, it literally dropped from the shelves. I bent to collect it and for the princely sum of two dollars, I held the story of my show-business idol in my hand. It was Shirley MacLaine's *Out on a Limb*.

When I read the preface—"This is a book about the experience of getting in touch with myself…about the connection between mind, body and spirit"—I knew something far greater than my rational mind was at work here. With only her story as my purchase for the day, I raced home.

Within a matter of hours, I was halfway through reading the book, or more correctly, inhaling its message. "Hence the answers are all within the self. Your destiny and karma depend on what your soul has done about what it has become aware of. And know that every soul will eventually meet itself. No problem can be run away from. Meet yourself now."

When I drifted to sleep that night, I asked to meet myself. I knew there was a reason, a motive as to why the events in my life had ended the way they had. I knew the cause was there somewhere. I just needed help to find it.

Three hours later I launched upright in bed, blinded by luminescent light and touched by grace. I can still vividly recall the experience. An overwhelming feeling of love enveloped me, making me feel utterly safe. A similar feeling to when I'd had my car accident all those years before, but more visceral.

Those minutes, though it could've been hours, were accompanied by a searing clarity that everything in my life was perfectly orchestrated, and nothing had happened by accident. While this experience rushed through me, I registered a powerful knowing that a new path, a new way of *being* was already shown to me in every moment of every day. My only requirement was to dare to listen, look and lean into the omens.

In my sleep, I'd shaken off the restraints of the ego long enough to experience the activity of Consciousness that I embodied. That Consciousness moved me in such an irrefutable, enduring and irrevocable way that any lingering doubts or disbeliefs dissolved. I had now passed through a door of self-knowing through which I could never return. I was no longer ignorant. I'd tapped into universal Consciousness and had been touched by the wings of angels.

I realized that the events I'd lived through during the past two and a half years were nothing more than my Consciousness freeing itself from the cocoon of my conditioned thinking and limitations. That I hadn't just walked away from the nightmare at the casino when others would have, wasn't me trying to prove I was right. I stayed because I had to. The same desire, the same Consciousness which had supported and guided me throughout my life needed me to consciously register its existence. As the situation at the casino worsened, I'd struggled to hang onto my old life, only to have it collapse. Then in my subsequent mental breakdown, my Consciousness, my *being*, finally got its chance to shine through.

At last, my burden of rejection and abandonment lifted. I became enlightened of the weight I'd carried with me since birth. During these past years, I'd had the courage to follow my convictions, letting everything else and everyone be damned. And now here I was open to everything and attached to nothing. The realization of the absolute interconnectedness of all things being Consciousness expressing itself in movement dawned on me, not as a revelation, but as a remembered universal truth. This was heaven.

I turned to find my boyfriend sound asleep. The momentous revelation I'd just experienced hadn't stir him. Shaking him awake, I explained all that had happened. He became the witness to my epiphany, just as I'd been the witness to my soul's stirring me from my sleep, encouraging me to wake up, both physically and spiritually. The energy coursing through my body uplifted me throughout the rest of the night, and I finished reading *Out on a Limb*.

"But now I don't see life as a battlefield. On the contrary, I believe it can be a paradise, and what's more, we should expect it to be. That is reality to me now. Dwelling on the negative simply contributes to its power," Shirley wrote.

On closing the book at first light, I experienced an abiding peace. I had my answers. I'd been living in paradise but focusing on hell. The only thing that needed changing was not the producer, or the petulant cast members, or the situation, or the commissioner's verdict. All that needed changing was me. Since I was the master of me, this epiphany gave me the permission and power to demonstrate paradise in my life; to manifest heaven on earth.

Buoyed by this realization, I committed to get back in step with my life. My desire for understanding and knowledge had now grown past trying to make sense of my previous experiences. It had grown into a daring passion to discover the real meaning of life and my purpose in it.

It was the end of the 1980s and the dawning of the New Age in metaphysics. In some ways it was a renaissance of the peace, love and flower-power movement of the late 1960s, except it was no longer the private domain of the drug-induced hippy culture. The world of crystals, tarot and angel cards, channeling and higher-self readings crept in from the fringes as legitimate businesses in the guise of trendy New Age shops with a vast array of literature, tapes and videos.

Knowing that the answers I sought were now within my grasp, I reached out, looking for the right connection. Bursting with renewed enthusiasm, I returned to the secondhand bookshop and plucked every New Age, spiritual book I could find off the shelves. Pawing over my budding collection, I began journaling information into dozens of notebooks for easy reference. The more I read, the more I realized my experience was in no way unique. Tomes of information had been written by others who suffered all types of personal, relationship and professional disasters due to their misalignment with life, and how it all could be traced backed to a misguided personal sense of self, leading to poor choices.

Quotes like, "Winners are not people who never fail, but people who never quit," and "There is no elevator to success. You have to take the stairs," reminded me that the ultimate measure of my life would be how I made new choices for change. The journey of giving up the misguided personal sense of self, the ego, was likened to trying to put down a piece of tacky flypaper. The more you attempt to put it down, the more firmly it sticks. Considering how tricky it is to rid oneself of adhesive tape, I suspected a boots-and-all approach wouldn't work with such a clinging long-term attachment.

With far less exhibitionism than Shirley MacLaine's *Out on a Limb*, another life-changing book, *Heal Your Body*, fell into my hands and ignited my life-long love and practice of affirmations. Written by Louise L. Hay, a leading teacher on the mental causes for physical illness, her internationally best-selling book became my constant companion. Having been a school teacher, the idea of writing line after line of affirmations felt natural to me and only added to my conviction of testing their power. Suffering a sore wrist and stiff fingers was little price to pay as I slumped over my notepads, hour after hour, scribbling, reading, reciting and ingesting affirmations.

Affirmations are a powerful tool for changing thoughts, shifting focus and elevating energy. I discovered the real key to their efficacy was to suspend all disbelief when working with them and to integrate them fully into my day-to-day activities. With the works of Florence Scovel Shinn and other amazing authors and devotees of the power of affirmations scattered on my table, I spent hours writing out the most appropriate ones for me.

Using my five senses, I became totally absorbed in the future life my affirmations promised. I visualized myself being in it, tasting it, touching it, smelling and hearing it, energizing the experience deep into the cells of my body until I knew I was living that life. Right in the present moment. Even if my current circumstances demonstrated a contrary life, I remained committed to making my future destiny a present reality.

As I dared to believe in this future vision, three long-lost feelings from my childhood returned. Playfulness, spontaneity and joy. Like eating a three-scoop ice-cream cone of my favorite flavors, I relished each of them, individually and collectively. I was like a kid in a candy store as this New Age world unfolded before me, beckoning me to taste all the goodies on offer.

With my conditioned thinking shaken loose, I realized a simple yet profound truth. Life isn't meant to be about hardship, struggle and lack. It's meant to be wonderful, each moment of every day, for everyone. It's meant to be like a box of chocolates. The Pollyanna attitude from my childhood, which I'd allowed to be buried by the busyness and battles of life, had been my guiding light all along. Now, it lit my way again.

Insights...Be decisive, Be playful, Be spontaneous, Be joyous

In my thirtieth year, my Consciousness broke free while my world disintegrated. In my inability to do anything about my situation, I finally gave up (the depression), I got up (accepted help) and gave in (woke up) to my *being*. In simple terms, the black depression that haunted me was merely the ego and my conditioned thinking running amok in my mind. None of it was real, nor had any true power over me. It was not some random event or emotion. It was me wallowing in my own suffering. Me, rewiring my brain with negative thoughts and words. Me, believing in and valuing negative emotions. Me, engaging in negative, disempowering actions. Suffering isn't a badge of honor. It's a waste of energy.

Somewhere deep inside me, I knew that until I dared to embrace myself as more than a puny personality, I'd remain enslaved by ignorance and arrogance, producing ignorant, arrogant results. Though the loss and grief from losing my career were still raw, I realized that life's greatest teachers are often disguised as our greatest rivals.

As Paulo Coelho wrote in *Manuscript Found in Accra*, "Your enemies are not the adversaries who were put there to test your courage. They are the cowards who were put there to test your weaknesses."

The producer had tested my weaknesses, but I'd been brave and stood my ground. Though it appeared he'd won, I knew inherently I hadn't failed. Despite my fears, I had fought valiantly and triumphed because I was no longer ignorant.

My epiphany when reading *Out on a Limb* was the movement of my *being* registering with me on a conscious level. It was undeniable proof that I was not just a body with Consciousness. I was Consciousness with a body. I was the cause, not the effect.

This seismic shift of perspective radically changed my interpretation of my life; past, present and future. There *was* only one thing going on… "Everything is energy and that's all there is to it." And now I knew that I was that energy, that Consciousness. In that moment, I decided to explore the world from *being*, as Consciousness expressing itself and dare to lean into this new frame of reference.

Since all thought is energy and has power in our lives, then all decisions are likewise powerful. They possess catalytic value for turning our dreams into reality, but it's up to us to harness the power within ourselves and take action. There's virtually nothing we cannot do, if we make a committed, congruent decision and embody it through action.

But what is a congruent decision? It's the one we make with our heart, not our head. The intuitive, gut instinct that nudges in one direction or the other. When we dare to make decisions based on what our heart or gut tells us, we challenge the conditioned thinking we've been taught to value, and in doing so, we are more likely to ignore our past limitations and press on.

Every decision we make sets the direction and destination for our life. Each decision sets in motion the cause which produces an effect in our reality. The great thing about decision-making is that we can change our destiny at any time by making new, congruent decisions.

The revelation of this truth had a lasting impact on me because it reinforced that I was the master of my destiny. I realized my thoughts, perceptions, beliefs, values, emotions, words and actions set the course on which I traveled. They formed the road map for my life. If I enriched them, my experience likewise would become enriched.

The moment I chose to make congruent, inspired decisions in alignment with my *being*, playfulness, spontaneity and joy bubbled up from a well of positive feelings within me. Feelings I hadn't experienced for quite some time. Supported by my new frame of reference of being Consciousness with a body, I allowed these feelings to find expression through me, even if to the outside world, I appeared silly. The more I embodied these three qualities the more opportunities appeared in my life.

For when we approach life with a childlike attitude, we look for the wonder in our lives. We seek out the best in ourselves, in others and our world. This is how young children behave. They experience every day and everything as if for the first time. Filled with wonder, not only do they look for magic, they expect magic to happen to them. When they play, children allow life to unfold around them, reveling in the joyousness each day brings, eager for the next experience. Oftentimes the joy that we, as adults, experience while watching children at play, is a remembrance of our own innocence and childlike attitude. It's a recollection of the inherent playfulness we long to express once more. When we approach life with a childlike attitude, we too attract more playfulness, spontaneity and joy to ourselves.

As children, before we're conditioned by our negative programming, being playful was the key methodology by which we experienced our world. Through play we dared to stand and walk. We laughed spontaneously and joyously at our first failed attempts. But eventually, we succeeded. Being playful, spontaneous and joyous were our first daring steps to success.

Now aware of the universal law of attraction and resonance of energy, I consciously chose to make my decisions based on the brighter future I desired, and not on my past conditioned thinking or limitations. I decided to be more playful and spontaneous in my life, viewing each day as my first rather than my last and experiencing life from a natural, rather than contrived point of view. I consciously chose to be more joyous, to spread more joy to others and to participate in activities which brought me joy. I danced, sang, hugged trees, walked on the beach, anything that unlocked even the tiniest glimmer of joy.

The more I let go of the old me and dared resonate my Consciousness to the energy of these four insights, the more I leaned into the fullest expression of *being* and my new life unfolded.

CHAPTER NINE
Listen and look for the omens

With rekindled playfulness, spontaneity and joy, I took my first steps into a whole new world. Like a child I ventured forth, placing one foot in front of the other, testing my strength, flexing my muscles and stretching my awareness. Aside from energizing myself with affirmations, I decided to play with the significances of replicable omens. Fueled by my New Age study, I actively put everyday omens to the test, using intersection traffic lights as messengers to the guidance I sought. On approaching an intersection, I always prefaced my question with the same phrase is it appropriate for me to…For example, *"Is it appropriate for me to go the long way to the shopping center? Is it appropriate for me to turn here?"*

When I began this process, my questions were purposely simple, because I didn't want to be invested in the outcome. Green lights meant yes, while red lights meant no. I never questioned the answer, my sanity or the possibility that the message from the traffic lights could be meant for anyone else. I suspect many would think me crazy, but this exercise demonstrated my willingness to see my world brand new, without the limited, human perspective I'd previously been conditioned to believe.

Because I dared to ignore my past limitations by actively listening and looking for omens, I pressed on, believing the lights orchestrated their signals solely for me, and without exception, I always followed their message. Over time, my questions became more important and my investment in the answers increased. When I tested the efficacy of each message in hindsight, I found that if I followed the omen, the result was invariably favorable. If I chose to ignore it, the result proved disadvantageous. In fact, what I was doing was daring to lean into my *being* and trust into something far greater than my best thinking.

The availability of parking spaces was another demonstrable omen I used on a regular basis. When driving into shopping center car parks, I projected my desire for a space and listened to whether I should turn right or left down an aisle, always willing to follow the inner nudging. On busy trading days, as others drove around cursing at the lack of parking, someone would reverse out in front of me, allowing me to slip into their space. With a silent thank-you, I'd walk across the car park, watching the frustration on the circling drivers' faces.

Listening and looking for omens was a wonderful game. The more I played it, the more playfulness, spontaneity, joy, faith and hope bubbled back into my life. These love-based feelings uplifted my Consciousness. They acted as positive energy transmitters which attracted reciprocal circumstances.

It was then I integrated the unalterable truth that I was responsible for my life. There were no accidents or random events. When I practiced responsibility, it meant I could respond to my world with love, knowing and grace. Refusing to be responsible limited my power, stunted my Consciousness and inevitably offered me only one option: to react to my world based on the ego's fear-based perspective, leaving me frustrated, impatient and stressed. If I wanted to create a new fulfilling future, I had to be willing and able to respond—to be responsible.

Happiness or suffering was my choice. How I felt was up to me. No one came along and poured suffering down my throat. It was all me happening to me. So, I set about choosing to be happy, but it required diligence. Many times, when I chose for happiness, the ego pushed the buttons in my old programming, trying to disrupt my Consciousness with worry, stress and conflict.

Worry is the aimless movement of the mind and is accompanied by a sense of loss or defeat, which of course is totally unfounded. Its sole intention is to disrupt our mental peace. Stress is another disruptor. It sneaks in and convinces us we can't cope with our lives. We're just not capable of handling the pressure. Then conflict appears, making up the unholy trinity as it presents our lives as unending struggle and opposition. If left unabated, worry, stress and conflict cripple us from taking action and the downward spiral slowly gains momentum toward depression.

Like a game of volleyball, I'd spring up with playfulness, spontaneity, joy, faith and hope to bat the ball across the net and the stubborn ego would slam it back with worry, stress and conflict, laced with the toxins of rejection and abandonment. Except now I knew the rules of engagement. I was no longer a novice in this wicked sport of truth or ego. Discerning the power play in my mind became my new modus operandi. My warrior spirit stood sentinel at the doorway to my thoughts, while my *being* reminded me to choose happiness, and listen, look and lean into the omens with more trust.

During these frequent power plays, one of the most conclusive omens nudged me to a New Age shop, way across town. I'd heard about Luminations and had arranged to meet the owner. On the designated day when I walked into the store, a diminutive lady with a shock of short magenta hair looked up from behind her position at the counter, and said, "Oh, I can help you. Here, come here."

The sense of recognition on her face was eerie. When I joined her at the counter, she promptly told me she was the one I was seeking. But she wasn't the owner. The owner had been unexpectedly called away, and she was minding the store. By now in my journey of self-discovery, I knew not to be disappointed about the owner's absence. The biblical quote of "seek and ye shall find" echoed in my mind, and I knew all was right time, right place.

This effervescent lady in her floating dress and tinkling beads was the answer to my yearning for more knowledge. It was she who became instrumental in opening realms far beyond the New Age movement. Through her, the opportunity to explore a deeper, spiritual experience of myself unfolded. In leaning unwaveringly into the omen on this day, I stepped further into my *being*.

Except for a loyal few, most of the people from my entertainment past drifted away without fanfare. Like silent ghosts, they remained trapped in the past. Out of sight and out of mind, their continuing absence created a yawning space for an enthusiastic tribe of like-minded seekers of truth to pitch their lives with mine. With my boyfriend staunchly by my side, we became a merry band, learning to liberate ourselves with love. We knew that life was energy, a resonance of thought, an activity of Consciousness, of the invisible becoming visible. Unless we provided a greater, receptive Consciousness, we wouldn't be able to accept a greater demonstration in our lives.

We aligned ourselves with Consciousness, never stagnating in our thoughts. We dared to challenge and change our conditioned thinking, ignore our past limitations and press on with more love. But no matter how our thoughts enlarged, we knew we were only scratching the surface to the greatness we embodied, to the Consciousness in which all form, space and time existed.

Insights...Be willing, Be responsible, Be perceptive

This heady time in my life reminded me of the optimism of the 1970's. No matter where I turned another omen carried me forward. I often faltered on my journey of *being* the fullest expression of me, of resonating at a higher Consciousness, but I was always granted a reprieve when I dared to be willing.

Willingness is the ability to see everything, everyone and every situation brand new. In practice, willingness means we look for and invest love into everything going on around us. Although it's not always easy when we're faced with uncomfortable challenges, willingness is a critical step in *being*. For when we dare to be willing, we become responsible.

Whether we make decisions consciously or habitually, we are responsible for everything that happens in our life because of what we've energized and embodied through our thoughts, perceptions, beliefs, values, emotions, words and actions. Each of us lives a life of our own choosing. Nothing ever happens to us by chance. And nothing happens to us because we deserve to suffer. The old saying that everything happens for a reason tends to absolve us from being responsible for our lives. There's a reason that everything happens—the reason is us. Being responsible means being able to respond to our lives, not react to them based on our negatively charged conditioned thinking.

Previously at the casino, I had felt trapped in a living nightmare. But now I knew this had been the process of my *being* revealing itself as conscious experience, while my limited sense of self, the ego, pushed back. The misery and suffering I'd endured was the splintering of the ego. When I had eventually been willing to let go and lean into the experience, I met my *being*, the fullest expression of me.

Now, because I dared to be willing, I realized I was ultimately responsible for how my life turned out; the good, the bad and the ugly. In taking ownership of my life, I accepted my influence over the conditions and circumstances I experienced. My life's challenges weren't meant to paralyze me. They were to help me uncover my *being*.

Unfortunately, most of us aren't taught by our parents, families, schools, communities or societies how to be responsible. On the contrary, we're conditioned to believe that whatever is happening in our lives is someone else's doing or someone else's fault. That we are nothing more than victims of circumstance. Hundreds of disempowering, fear-based thoughts, perceptions, beliefs, values, emotions, words and actions are heaped upon us, usually without malice, in our formative years. Because we judge ourselves and others harshly, and focus on chaotic circumstances and conditions, we create chaos in our lives. This conditioned thinking blocks our birthright to master our destiny of success, health and happiness.

When we're being responsible, we no longer blame others for what we don't have, for what has happened to us or for what we missed out on. We respond rather than react to each situation. Through empowered thoughts, perceptions, beliefs, values, emotions, words and actions we change from looking for problems to finding solutions, from making mistakes to grasping opportunities, from seeing ourselves as victims to being the masters of our lives.

We set a better course for the future, not based on fear, but on love. This simple truth is confronting to our small sense of self, the ego. Whenever we consider being responsible, it dips into its conditioned thinking and memories, pulling out such gems as righteous indignation, blame of self, others or circumstances, victimhood, martyrdom, discrimination, self-pity, self-importance and manipulation. The ego's only means of survival is to keep us caught in the illusion that the external world is a hostile place, and we must defend ourselves against it. But if we want to be the fullest expression of our *being*, we must remind ourselves that we are not creatures of circumstances, unless we choose to be.

Being willing proved a valuable insight as I practiced being responsible. If I wanted to demonstrate a larger life, I needed to be willing to align with Consciousness. I needed to be willing to see things brand new and ignore my past limitations. The more willing I was to give up blame and be responsible, the more I mastered my life. Being willing and responsible were incontrovertible prerequisites to living a fabulous future.

Added to this was the knock-on effect from daring myself every day to be perceptive by listening, looking and leaning into the omens. I developed the mental state of believing that nothing's too good to be true. As Dr. Wayne W. Dyer wrote, "You'll see it when you believe it," and my new belief was a daring counterpoint to challenge my conditioned thinking. Believing nothing was too good to be true empowered me to resonate at a higher level of Consciousness, while giving my future the foundation on which to stand.

By being responsible, willing and perceptive, I leaned into my flourishing Consciousness. Knowing that my greatest challenge had been my greatest opportunity, I was ready to activate a new destiny, a daring new adventure.

CHAPTER TEN
Stirrings of the soul

Throughout the early months of 1989, I continued teaching at the Phoenix Youth Theatre, with many of my students being chosen for work in local and overseas productions. After the last of them left, and with mixed emotions, I closed the doors on the theater. In one way, it had been a safe place for me to rediscover my joy, but on the other hand, it was a constant reminder of what I'd lost. From an energetic perspective, I had risen from the ashes and no longer wanted to be anchored to my past. Time for the band aid to be pulled off clean.

I accepted any work I could find. My services as a choreographer and director were engaged by small club acts and a couple of local theater restaurants, though there was little financial reward. I worked as a waitress, which I wasn't good at because my hands shook whenever I carried a tray of glasses. Reverting to my natural talent, I taught private dance classes for clients, but I needed more. Not just more money, but to *be* more.

Looking, listening and leaning into the omens, I followed the stirring of my soul, my *being*, as it guided me to apply my creative talents in a new direction of my life. I longed to return to the entertainment industry, but work on the Gold Coast was nonexistent, and I still didn't want to leave my mother for interstate or overseas work. My sense of responsibility for her outweighed my longing. Frustrated by the limited options for employment, I chose not to be employed. Instead, I dared to step into a future that I'd be wholly responsible for and filed to incorporate my own company. Because of my past experience, I knew that working for an employer who remained ignorant of the resonance of energy was not in my best interest. Been there, done that. If I wanted a fabulous future, I would have to be responsible for it and make it happen.

By now, twelve months had passed since my court case. The producer had once again been contracted to produce another show at Conrad Jupiter's, albeit on a lesser scale and quality than the first two productions that Jerry and I had done. Mr. Jackson had 'left the building' and so had the magic which opened the showroom in 1986.

Around this time, the producer's company manager, a beleaguered young woman of twenty-eight who had worked for him for several years, dropped dead of a brain aneurism. A sad end to an aspiring life, but indicative of the pressure she obviously felt. Her destiny of death could have been mine, if I hadn't dared to speak my truth and challenge the producer's inappropriate and discriminatory behavior. As tough as it had been, I'd come out on the other side. She died to get to the other side.

We dancers and acrobats, who had relocated from our home base to the Gold Coast in order to perform in the first two productions at the showroom, finally received our living-away-from-home allowances. Actors' Equity had taken the producer to court once more and had won this case under recently introduced new legislation. The producer was ordered to pay the hundreds of thousands of dollars he owed us in entitlements. Laws had changed—he had to pay.

Since live cabaret acts were still popular on the club circuit, I followed the stirrings of my soul and with my money, produced, choreographed and directed a slick cabaret production. Comprised of my boyfriend and me, and another talented couple, the four of us sang and danced our way through months of endless, energizing rehearsals. Being back on the stage overcame most of the emotional demons which still haunted me. I held firm to our budget, siphoning my money into costumes, rehearsal space, recording studios and promotional videos. We then hit the marketing trail, promoting our act, *Star 4*, to agents and clubs alike.

Enthused by the prospect of greater opportunities to demonstrate my talents and abilities, I developed plans with interested investors, for a theater restaurant based on a framework of facilitation, rather than an outdated authoritative business model. But I didn't want to slip back into my conditioned thinking of work, work, work, and become so engrossed in the doing that I'd lose sight of *being*. Respite came in the form of meditation.

As a choreographer and dancer, I knew the best dance routines combined both movement and stillness. I had learned this juxtaposition from watching Fred Astaire. The light and shade, the movement and stillness of his routines created a balance to his dancing. He was often quoted as saying dancing was a sweat job. He was right. At this time in my life, I was sweating in rehearsals and working hard on my theater restaurant project while I followed the stirrings of my soul. My life needed balance and it was the stillness of meditation which offset all this activity. Unlike when I was younger, I now knew the importance of taking time out for myself.

Cultivating a daily practice of meditation, I retreated into the tranquility at the center of my *being*, a space I fell in love with on first meeting. Going within became my sanctuary, a place to meet me, free from the distractions of the world.

Mother Theresa said, "We need silence to be able to touch our souls." She was right. Silence, not experience, is the cornerstone of wisdom.

The more I meditated, the more I came to appreciate the power, peace and poise of silence. For me, meditation was an eternal, lilting routine of the ebb and flow of the invisible activity of Consciousness expressing itself. A dance of energy.

In the beginning I listened to guided meditations, visualizing myself in the different time and space as instructed by the voice on the tape. The intensity of these visualizations transferred into my dreams and my conscious experience, where I encountered numerous adventures both in and out of the body, such as astral traveling which is where I projected my Consciousness out of my body. It's a practice long held in ancient Egyptian, Indian, Chinese and Japanese cultures and is sometimes referred to as soul travel—the soul's ability to leave the body at will or while sleeping, and visit the various planes of heaven.

It became more than a random occurrence for me. Flying or floating to vivid and fascinating other realms on the astral plane added another dimension to my internal search. These experiences reaffirmed that I was not just mortal. I was more than my body. I was Consciousness, being conscious of the eternality and individuality of all things. There are many people who've experienced OBE (out-of-body experiences) and NDE (near-death experiences) and they report the same type of revelation.

Having practiced various methods of meditation, I found the easiest way into the silence required four states of being: being centered, being curious, being receptive and being in communion. Being centered involved stillness and focus, with all my attention on nothing but the center of my *being*. Being centered meant absolute willingness and infinite patience. No matter how long being centered took, I had to be willing and patient enough to dwell in this space before continuing. Without being centered, my mind would simply reboot, and thoughts would tumble forth unabated. Once centered, my mind became like the surface of a deep, languid lake on a still day, gently moving without effort or resistance.

Once centered, I became curious, like a child sitting on the edge of the lake gazing out across the water into the distance not looking for anything, but just seeing if anything of interest is there. Being curious challenged my conditioned thinking and certainty about things and opened me to being receptive. I dared to ignore the ego long enough to receive whatever experience came to me in meditation without trying to analyze or understand it. There's a quote which reads, "Prayer is talking to God while meditation is listening to God," and in listening and being receptive, I became discerning. The more I meditated the more I discerned my Consciousness moving.

Previously, my visual modality was the most acute of my physical senses. I'd often visualized shows or dance routines being performed by miniature performers before my very eyes, as my creativity produced instant magic on a nearby table or countertop. This gift of sight had been a powerful tool in my choreographic career. Now as I meditated, it was my auditory sense that became the most acute, with messages being spoken to me by the still, small voice within.

People often ask what the still, small voice within sounds like. It's not so much what it sounds like, it's what it feels like. Because it often sounds like our own voice, many people ignore it, believing it's just them imagining the conversation. But again, we must dare to press on with the regular practice of meditation, attuning ourselves to the experience and ignoring the limitation of our conditioned thinking. The more we meditate, the more discerning we become. Once we're centered, curious and receptive, our normal day-to-day experience lifts like a mist, allowing our *being*, our still, small voice within, to be heard, leading us into the experience of communion, knowing that everything is Consciousness eternally expressing itself. Like anything, meditation takes regular committed practice to being centered, being curious, being receptive and being in communion which can seemingly take years. But hey! I had nothing else better to *be*, except me.

Despite a commonly held belief to the contrary, meditation isn't an altered state of mind. It is the ego which is the altered state of mind.

Our conditioned thinking is the distorted perception of Consciousness, and when we live from this ego-based state of mind, we can be nothing but reactive to ourselves, others and the world. Meditation is our natural state of mind, of *being* conscious. It's the direct experience of Consciousness in expression, which is sometimes referred to as bliss consciousness, for it is truly heavenly.

When I first experienced the small, still voice within, the ego tried to tell me I was crazy. I was wasting my time with all this rubbish. But I pressed on. Why? Because I'd been brave and broken-hearted before due to my old conditioned thinking. Now, I dared to experience a new way of *being* in my world. One that sustained and supported me instead of demoralizing and disempowering me. I reasoned that if the still, small voice within was only me talking to myself with messages of love and encouragement, who the hell cares? It was me making me feel good, not blaming and shaming me. But I knew it was far more than that, not because I thought it was, but because I felt it was. *Being* is experiential.

To be conscious of *being* Consciousness became my spiritual goal. Knowing the power was within me, I explored the art of deeper and deeper meditation. I also bought decks of different tarot cards, with one of my favorites being The Medicine Cards by Jamie Sams and David Carsons. They became a regular tool at the end of each meditation when I'd shuffle the pack, ask to be shown what I needed to be most aware of and pull a card. The powerful, sometimes cryptic message revealed itself as an animal totem in a Native American Indian parable. At times some messages didn't make sense, but in retrospect I understood a card's deeper meaning and the direction in which it had guided me.

Even today I use an array of different tarot cards as tools to verify the messages I receive in meditation. Recording the card's messages in my journal, I review them on subsequent meditations and glean more meaning and clarity of past messages.

It was toward the end of this second year of my conscious quest, which I affectionately named Life Philosophy 101, when I spontaneously encountered another peak experience in the new house we'd just rented. Thrilled to have left behind the green-tiled bathroom of my wretched past and in the new, white-tiled bathroom indicative of a brighter future with its large hot water supply, I meditated under the shower's comforting spray, sitting cross-legged in the shower stall.

Even as a child, I loved to take long baths. Submerging my head, I'd be enchanted by the echo of the water as it flowed from the spout into the tub. Images of mermaids, whales and dolphins had filled my young mind while I imagined myself swimming with them under the ocean waves.

On this night while I meditated under the shower, the rush of the water drowned out every sound and sensation faster than I'd experienced before. In an instant, I was centered, curious and receptive. With no desire to ask a question, I simply allowed the moment to embrace me, with no expectation of outcome. Then as if a tap of universal wisdom had been turned on, a stream of Consciousness began explaining the meaning of time and space. The detail and depth of the non-stop dissertation flowed through me as a rich, reverberating sound, and I understood every word, phrase and concept. Despite the torrent of information, I wasn't overwhelmed and wanted to remember as much as I could. But my human mind swirled and struggled with the speed, intensity and limitlessness of the experience. This episode lasted well into the hot water turning cold, but I was oblivious to the change of temperature or any external stimuli.

Linear time doesn't exist and is merely a construct of our limited thinking. There's no past, present or future. All experiences exist simultaneously, not as a linear timeline. Like the colored faces on the Rubik's cube, swiveling around from one so-called dimension to another, wherever we place our focus is where time seems to exist. The idea of past, present and future lives is incorrect. For everything is everything, at every time, everywhere. Every event, every lifetime we may or may not experience is happening right now. My experiences in this lifetime or in World War II as a British fighter pilot or in Egypt are not past lives. All is happening now, as are all future lifetimes. If I was being Consciousness unaffected by the ego, I'd be able to consciously choose which lifetime to physically experience and live it now.

A bit like when we dream, and we experience a dream reality which is different to the life we focus on when we're awake. Similarly, while we're not *being* conscious, we live in a dream, thinking that the life we live in our daily lives is real. This presumes we're alone—separate somehow to our lives, to time, to space and acting alone in and against the world at large. Yet if the only thing going on is the activity of Consciousness, then there is no separation, no time and no space in which things apparently take place. All there is, is all there is, expressing itself through individualized movement.

"Everything is energy and that's all there is to it."

Through meditation I accessed reality. Not the limited sense of reality in which we commonly live, but the fourth-dimensional reality beyond time, space and form. And it was in this space, where cowering in the corner of my unconscious mind, I discovered my adoption. For as long as I could remember, I'd always suspected I was adopted. But I'd shut it out completely, I had no conscious recollection that I'd forbidden my parents from speaking about my adoption all those years ago.

Now, at thirty-three and in deep meditation, I saw the image of a sad young woman, my biological mother, leaving a hospital. I knew I was the baby wrapped in the blanket she cried over. She had given birth to me and left me behind.

The next time I saw Mum I told her of my vision, believing my adoption had been kept a secret from me. But she told me the true story. Breathing a great sigh of relief, she explained how they'd adopted me, the little history she knew of my biological mother and how, on that fateful day over two decades before, I'd instructed her and Dad not to speak of my adoption again. When I asked her why she'd kept quiet all this time, she revealed a sad and terrible story.

At the age of twenty-one, my mother's best friend committed suicide when she discovered she was adopted. It had a devastating, long-term effect on my mother. Her deep-seated fear of my doing something irrational resulting in a deadly tragedy, terrorized her into years of silence. When, at the age of eleven, I instructed my parents not to mention it again, they didn't, and my mother would have taken her promise to the grave had I not broached the subject. Now relieved of her burden, we talked about my adoption details openly as adults.

"Do you want to contact your biological mother?" she asked, a new fear surfacing in her voice.

"It's okay. I won't have to. She'll contact me. But she'll track me down through you." I'd already seen this happening in one of my meditations. Old adoption records had just been opened in Queensland, and I knew the sad young woman from my meditation had carried her guilt and shame long enough. She would try to find me and soon. "When she does contact you, just take her name, address and phone number. I'll take it from there. But you don't have to worry. You'll always be my mother." With the truth finally spoken, we embraced and cemented an even stronger bond of love between us.

No longer a secret, my adoption and the wound I'd carried because of my negative thoughts, perceptions, beliefs, values and emotions surrounding it, could be addressed and healed. I was now ready to meet my biological mother.

Insights...Be centered, Be curious, Be receptive, Be in communion

If we're never alone, we can never know ourselves and, without self-knowing, fear prevails. Going within afforded me the space to contemplate my Consciousness and the immortality of *being*. Forever we have been. Forever we will be. We are eternal. It is not something to achieve but to embody. We must stop acting like we're mortals and dare to accept we're Consciousness with a body...Energy embodied.

In being centered, curious, receptive and in communion, I experienced peaceful solitude and touched the eternality of my soul.

Of course, an hour spent meditating didn't save me from the chaos and confusion of the other twenty-three hours in the day, but it did support me in uncluttering and stilling my mind enough to hear the still, small voice within.

It was a grand adventure which I dared to explore day after day. And for those who believe adventures are risky business, try boredom. It will kill you faster than any adventure.

CHAPTER ELEVEN
Releasing my emotional past

By daring to press on with my spiritual awakening, I catapulted myself into 1990 and 1991 with heightened expectation and exploration. But as any explorer will attest, the challenge in their adventure is to stay the course, despite the stumbling blocks. In my case, the challenge was to relinquish the repressed energy from my past. Unless I released my emotional past, it would continue to poke its ugly head up into the inspiring reality manifesting around me. Analogous to a wardrobe filled with old clothes, I was piling new empowering thoughts into my mind and feelings into heart without emptying out the old negative baggage. Releasing my emotional past became a necessary step along my journey.

Like a nervous kid on a seesaw, I fluctuated up and down, up and down, between feelings of elation to dispiriting emotional slumps. Negative emotions of frustration, confusion and self-doubt escalated upward when it became apparent that although our cabaret show was a slick, professional production, the work wasn't forthcoming. No matter how hard we tried, we couldn't seem to get the gigs we needed. I blamed myself for these setbacks. The ego had me tease apart every situation, insinuating I'd got it wrong; I'd wasted my time, I'd wasted my money. I'd failed. The top of the pops on the ego's playlist was the familiar favorite of "Nobody wants me."

The patterns and habits from the limiting, negative programming I'd installed throughout my life sprang up like an evil jack-in-the-box threatening to scare my new life out of me. But I reminded myself that each new beginning offers choice. I could choose for the adventure of a future yet to unfold, or I could choose for the continuous war with the past that would never be won. Knowing that my past wasn't going to equal my future, I clung tightly to the adventure of a future yet to unfold and dared to keep the faith, while denying the ego's chatter.

During these two years, I made a resolute decision that no matter when, where or how, I would release my emotional past. Often, I'd stop and sit on the curb of a busy street and sob. Passing pedestrians picked up speed, obviously uncomfortable with my blatant display of grief, but I didn't care. There was nothing to be ashamed of, regardless of what the ego tried to tell me. I knew that releasing my emotional past was a powerful healing process.

All negative emotions are based in fear. Grief, anger, disappointment, blame, judgment, frustration, guilt, panic, anxiety and stress are the ego's reaction to the world. These negative emotions are energy suppressed at the time of expression. This suppression happens throughout our life, but it begins in our formative years. When we're manipulated by our parents or carers to do something we don't want to do, we feel wronged, but we're not allowed to express this energy. We are told to obey, or we'll be punished. So, we suppress the energy and it festers into fear.

We also suppress negative emotions because of our education system, with its rules and prescribed conformity. Individuality or enlightened thinking is not something education systems encourage or support. If we are different to the norm, we're controlled into compliance. Likewise, society and religion are organized for the purpose of containment and eliminating the extremes. Trapped within these parameters, we may feel ourselves oppressed and suppressed. Added to this, is the collective unconscious where competition is revered and a win-lose mentality seeps into our psyche.

This emotional energy, suppressed at the time of its expression, clings to us waiting to be expressed. If we don't free this energy, it leads to a disposition of hostility. It feeds the ego and becomes a vicious circle of negative self-talk, self-denial and self-destruction.

We can either dive headfirst into the dumpster of our suppressed emotional past and ferret around in our garbage, picking over old wounds and peeling back the layers of grime, until we might eventually clean it out. Or there is another, faster method which I discovered during the process of releasing my emotional past. With love. Love and forgiveness transmute all suppressed energy. They free us to have dominion in our lives, rather than trying to dominate our lives and everyone in it. If ever there was a miracle cure, love is it.

Hours spent in meditation sending love to everyone and every situation in my life that caused me distress in the past became my focus.

Forgiving myself for my righteous emotions, for punishing myself and others, for my self-pity and self-importance, for my manipulations, avoidances and wanting guarantees, liberated me. I transmuted the energy of fear with love, and out of the painful past came composure. And in this sense of peaceful connectedness, I chose to rest my body from decades of contraception and fell pregnant immediately.

Having known from a young age that I didn't want children, I wasn't prepared for this unexpected turn of events, neither was my boyfriend, who also didn't want children. Determined not to overthink the situation and undeterred by the apparent frenzy of energy, I listened, looked and leaned into the omens, and decided to terminate.

It wasn't a decision I took lightly. I meditated on it for some time before finding that peaceful space to hear the still, small voice within. When I rang the clinic to make my appointment, the receptionist asked me if I had a preferred doctor to perform the procedure.

"I've no idea," I said. "Who are the doctors practicing there?"

"Well, we have Dr. Gill…"

I was aghast. "Dr. Paul Gill?"

"Yes."

"Book me in with him, please."

That my wonderful GP who had been my stalwart supporter for the past five years, in and out of court, was now practicing in this capacity in a specialized clinic was an undeniable omen that I'd made the right choice. I was in good hands. On seeing him before the procedure, tears of gratitude sprang to my eyes for all he'd done for me. Here he was again, and as he prepared me, I was at peace.

Once home, I meditated again on my decision. Inherently, I knew it was right time, right place, but the ego tried its best to judge me for taking a sacred life. But what was done, was done. Within me, I knew that the energy of that little one, that *being* who chose me would find me again, somehow, somewhere. All I needed to do was trust.

This termination gave me a deeper insight into the dense energy of judgement and blame. It destroys our happiness by shackling us to our past, perpetuating shame in ourselves and blaming others. Where judgement and blame dwell, there can be no peace, which is exactly what the ego wants. It sends in its vanguard of worry, stress and conflict as its first assault on our peace of mind. Then follows the attack with judgement and blame. But there is a way out. As Nelson Mandela wrote, "Forgiveness liberates the soul."

Forgiveness releases us from judgement and blame. With forgiveness and love, we no longer blame or demean ourselves or others. We no longer grasp for excuses for our actions. When we love and forgive, we no longer play the victim or the martyr, or feel guilty or do whatever we please with no regard for others. Releasing judgement and blame seems a herculean step to *being* the fullest expression of ourselves. Yet the action of giving, receiving and being love is at the heart of every miracle, every inspiration and every beatific experience.

The act of giving love is the fastest, most direct route to the heart of humanity. Whether or not the other person receives our love mustn't influence our willingness to love. We must forgive others not because they deserve it, but because the world deserves peace. Despite the outcome, the love we give makes energetic deposits in a universal bank and changes the world. Love is never wasted.

The more love I shared with myself and others, the more I realized that love doesn't mean turning the other cheek so we can be betrayed or bullied a second time. It doesn't mean we stand by and allow unacceptable behaviors to continue. We mustn't turn away and do nothing in the face of peril.

As Simon Wiesenthal so eloquently wrote, "For evil to flourish, it only requires good men to do nothing."

Yet in our resolute refusal to allow violent or criminal deeds to persist, we must also know the unacceptable action alone doesn't identify the true essence of the perpetrator. We must dare to register the truth of Consciousness, of our interconnectedness to everyone. Love enriches the evolution of human Consciousness, and with forgiveness and love, all is possible.

Throughout these years I dreamed the bigger dream of owning and operating a theater restaurant. More than just a successful commercial venture, it identified my vision for magic both on and off stage, by incorporating sound business practice with higher spiritual principles. Meeting different people with different skill sets to my own, opened doors for me into the business world. *If you build it, they will come.* But as time went by, I was haunted by feeling not good enough for falling short of my goals. The ego reminded me that here I was, committed to expanding my Consciousness, following my heart and *being*, yet nothing seemed to be happening. Obviously, it was my fault.

This muddy thinking proved to be the perfect stomping ground for another elusive emotion to rise like a ghoul. A vague melancholy visited me and took up a front-row seat in the theater of my mind. Keening softly, it introduced its friends of guilt and shame, and together they sermonized me on my lack of deservedness.

Perhaps the most subtle and demoralizing negative emotion of all is feeling not good enough. Without the recognizable fervor of anger, frustration, grief or indignation, it creeps in and leaves us with a sense of stagnation, despair and dread. Even equipped with my epiphanies, affirmations, meditations and congruent, conscious decisions, feeling not good enough lingered in the background, ready for its next performance.

Feeling not good enough is one of the most significant yet obscure causes underlying the human condition. Like the root of all evil, it's buried within each of us, spreading its tendrils deeper, sucking the goodness out of us. Whenever this negative emotion paid me a visit, I sang The Beatles song, "All you need is love" and dared to love myself. It didn't always work, but as a pattern interrupt, it created an energetic shift and gave me enough space to recalibrate my energy.

I also turned to Louise L. Hay who advocated self-love as the most effective cure for whatever ails us. The opening sentence of her well-known, exquisite affirmation on love and loving oneself begins, "Deep at the center of my being, there is an infinite well of love…"

I made copies of the affirmation and plastered them over my bathroom mirror and on the toilet door to constantly remind me that I was love. That indeed I was good enough. To multiply the impact, I even stood naked in front of my bathroom mirror and recited it until I could look upon myself with love. The ego hated that exercise.

"You can't be serious surely?" teased the sinister voice in my head. "Look at you. You're too fat. Your thighs are too big. Look at your stomach. How could you possibly love that?"

The ego's criticisms seemed endless. But I pressed on, repeating the affirmation of self-love. Over time, my denial of its snide remarks worked. Looking into my eyes like I was the greatest love in my life, I came to internalize the last lines of Louise's affirmation… "I am a beloved child of the universe and the universe lovingly takes care of me now and forever more."

By 1992, four years had passed since I embarked on Life Philosophy 101, my conscious quest for truth. In this short time, I'd moved into a new house, dared to be more than before and regained my *joie de vivre*. It was time for me to really let go and surrender my idea of what my life should look like. Since there was no opportunity for me to return to a professional career in the entertainment industry, I decided to offer my dance-teaching services to a nearby medical center. The center's gym facility was only used for a few hours a week, so I commenced an after-school dance program for children.

Within no time the classes grew, as did interest from the mothers who talked with me about their personal issues. Following my inner guidance, I approached the medical center's owner, with a proposal to expand the vision of the facility. Under his enthusiastic mentorship, we established the first health, fitness and relaxation center in the region, possibly the country. He proved to be a generous, forward-thinking man. Quick-witted and driven, he and I possessed similar traits, making us a great team. We joked and laughed often. He financially supported my plans to repurpose the venue, to include not just a schedule of fitness and dance classes, but also meditation and personal development workshops. We promoted it as a one-stop shop for those seeking a mind-body-spirit lifestyle.

By now I was a trained practitioner of Reiki, which is the practice of the laying on of hands for energy to flow through to assist the client in stress reduction and healing. An extension of the natural human response to injury of when we hold our hand to the area of pain, Reiki connects the practitioner and the client through the transference and balancing of energy.

I also studied with Leonard Orr, the founder of rebirthing, which is a system of breathing in a circular manner with no pauses between the inhales and exhales, to heal suppressed emotions. Leonard was considered one of the pioneers of the New Age movement with his concept of overcoming all traumas experienced from birth to senility through the power of rebirthing—the power of the breath. For me, being rebirthed unlocked some of my deeper fears and emotions and was nothing short of cathartic.

I remember one experience while under the guidance of an experienced rebirthing practitioner and friend named Myrilla. I breathed in the normal circular pattern, filling my lungs with deep breaths and allowing my mind to focus on letting go. As the breath flowed through me like hot air from a giant bellows, I drifted to a different realm of time and space. On settling into this place, I promptly stopped breathing, which wasn't normal in rebirthing. While others watched on, Myrilla guided me through the process.

One, two, three minutes passed, and I still wasn't breathing.

Four, five, six minutes passed and still no breath, but my body showed no signs of struggle or distress. My boyfriend became anxious, but I wasn't aware of any of it. I no longer existed as the person known as Diane. I was Consciousness unencumbered by human form. My body waited for me, like a parked car waiting for its owner to return, while I traversed time and space, into different lifetimes and places. I was being conscious of being Consciousness.

Seven, eight, nine minutes passed and still I lay motionless, with no awareness of the scene unfolding around my physical body. Though unconcerned for my physical safety, Myrilla intuited that if I left my body for too much longer, I may choose to leave permanently. So, she leaned over and encouraged me to return.

Ten, and then on the eleventh minute, I inhaled back into my body. In no way was I gasping for air or experiencing any discomfort. Instead, euphoria enveloped me. When I opened my eyes, I was greeted by the others' relieved expressions and the enigmatic smile of Myrilla. She knew where I'd been. I had transcended the human condition to experience Consciousness without a body. I was conscious *being*... eleven earthly minutes of bliss.

I graduated from my four-year self-imposed study course and internship in Life Philosophy 101 with a new career at the health, fitness and relaxation center as center director and stress and life-skills therapist. With complete autonomy, I managed the business, teaching a variety of fitness and dance classes, and personal development workshops, consulting with some of the doctors and their patients, and working with private clients in rebirthing, counseling and Reiki. My love of people combined with my inherent teaching ability found a new stage for expression in this stimulating new career. I'd followed the stirrings of my soul and ended up, not where I thought, but somewhere which was innately right.

Insights...Be love, Be forgiving, Be present

There abides within us an irresistible urge to love and live more fully. This is the stirring of our soul, of our *being*, of our Consciousness. Our purpose is to recognize, acknowledge, accept and act in response to this urging.

For Life is love expressed in the present moment.

Life is what we make it from within, not from without.

Life is measured in consciousness, not years.

All Consciousness is available to us despite our current level of Consciousness. We must challenge our conditioned thinking that says our good comes from outside of us or can be bestowed upon us by another. This thinking weakens the evolution of our current level of Consciousness. It destroys our self-worth, self-value and capacity to love, and extinguishes our radiance.

Being the fullest expression of Consciousness remained my purpose. Never standing still in my life-affirming thoughts, providing a clear, mental likeness of that which I desired, meditating and listening to the still small voice within, being responsible and acting with love; these were the twinkling step lights illuminating my new dance of life.

Like Fred Astaire said, "Do it big. Do it right and do it with style."

In one of my favorite movies, *An American in Paris*, I remember when Georges Guétary struts out onto the stage apron, looking debonair with his cane. He turns towards the proscenium curtain, which opens in grand style and when he steps onto the lower step of a magnificent staircase, it illuminates under his black patent leather shoe. With inimitable style and in his French accent he sings, 'I'll build a stairway to paradise with a new step ev'ry day. I'm gonna get there at any price, stand aside I'm on my way.'

That's how I now lived my life. I was dancing up the stairway to paradise, and for me, that phrase was no longer figurative.

I was deep into the metaphysical study of the power of the mind and how it harnesses the universal law of attraction with every thought, belief, value, emotion, feeling and decision we embody and enact. When we consciously harness its power to expand our Consciousness beyond our current conditioned thinking and limitations, the law demonstrates this as expansive and miraculous manifestation.

Through the practice of expanding my mind and level of Consciousness, I exposed the ego for the fraud that it was. Its survival depended on keeping me ignorant of my power, my capacity to love and of my *being*. By disregarding its negative chatter and by daring to explore a new frame of reference, I harnessed the power which created unexpected epiphanies, experiences and events.

Although the ego tried to persuade me to be disappointed that my theater restaurant hadn't manifested, I became aware that *I* was the reason it didn't happen. Having flung my unshakable commitment to being free of working with those still suffering arrogance and ignorance, and the conscious business principles with which I wanted to operate the venture, out into Consciousness—there weren't investors coming from the level of Consciousness to answer the call at that time or in that place. I finally realized that I'd demonstrated perfectly…if the venture couldn't be done as I dreamed it, it wouldn't be done at all. As I spoke, so was it done.

Yet in its place, another venture did manifest which I could operate under the universal principles—the health, fitness and relaxation center. It was at that venue that I had the freedom and autonomy to stretch beyond my previous experience.

Giving, receiving and being love, twenty-four hours a day is how we release our emotional past. It's how we master our destiny. When we come from love, we find ourselves spontaneously demonstrating happier, more harmonious lives because we no longer invest our power in anything outside of ourselves. We hold firm to the universal truth that we're not dealing with conditions (the apparent outer, physical world around us), but we're dealing with causes (the inner, mental, spiritual world of Consciousness) and in doing so, we live with love and reclaim our power.

All of this happens in the present moment. Not in the past and not in the future. For it is only in the present that we experience life. Life happens now. But there's more. I realized that to be present in my life was more than being in a moment of time. It was about *being* present; being present with the conscious undistorted experience of *being*. To be present was the proof of my existence as Consciousness in movement as the fullest expression of myself eternally interconnected with, and indivisible from, everything.

As 1992 flowed toward its joyful conclusion, it correlated perfectly with the ending of the fifth seven-year cycle in my life. I was thirty-five years old. Over the past five years much had changed. On a deep molecular level, I had tapped into and accessed energetic laws and universal knowing. Like a student of the soul eager to be admitted to the Akashic records, I'd meditated and studied conscientiously, as if wanting to pass some celestial exam.

With a voracious appetite, I'd spent these years daring to dream bigger dreams, challenging my conditioned thinking, ignoring my past limitations and pressing on. At times I stumbled, but my devotion and determination never wavered. I was manifesting a new destiny for myself as conscious *being*, and I would not be denied.

CHAPTER TWELVE
Fire of desire

Complementing the celebration of my life's new direction, my boyfriend and I decided to marry. We'd been together for seven years, sharing our love and desire for spiritual growth. Initially, we'd gravitated together in a teacher-student paradigm, the dynamics of which continued during our relationship. Others probably viewed our relationship as unorthodox. However, we were happy and genuinely loved each other. On some level, we'd chosen one another, and as oddly matched as it may have seemed to others, we felt a deep bond.

At our Gatsby-inspired, white-themed garden wedding surrounded by sixty family and friends, we recited our vows, optimistic of a loving marriage and bright future. A group of musicians playing lutes and mandolins added to the magical charm of the occasion, as did our friend's twin cocker spaniels that dutifully performed the role of my bridesmaids.

After a romantic day filled with promises, love songs and laughter, the wedding night didn't unfold as I'd hoped. Instead of us spending the night together, he chose to remain with a couple of male guests until the wee hours of the morning. It was an uncomfortable, confronting omen that I hadn't expected, but one I didn't ignore.

Edward FitzGerald wrote, "The moving finger writes; and, having writ, moves on: nor all your piety, nor wit shall lure it back to cancel half a line, nor all your tears wash out a word of it."

By the end of this year, my premonition of my biological mother contacting me manifested. She'd tracked down Mum, who took her details and passed them on to me. Over the next week, I meditated and waited until I received a clear message of the right time before calling her, which I did few days later.

"Hello," a woman's voice answered.

"Gloria?"

"Yes?"

"It's me, Diane."

She gasped and a long moment stretched between us. "Diane. I'm so pleased you called me. I spoke to your mum…." She chatted on in an upbeat manner. Her voice had a similar edge as mine. Not quite brusque, but strong with a hard tone. She sounded like I imagined she would, forthright and cheerful.

After a brief conversation, we arranged to meet for lunch over the coming weeks. I wasn't nervous about our meeting, nor was I excited. I had already seen how this meeting would manifest.

Nature turned on one of its super Spring days for the occasion, bright, fresh and crisp. When I walked into the harbor-side restaurant, I paused, looking for someone I didn't know, but who'd given me the precious gift of life. When a woman stood and called my name, I walked slowly toward her, gazing at her face. Like a damp mirror, clouded by mist in a steamy bathroom, the reflection held a faint resemblance. When she reached out to hug me, and I returned the contact, her face opened with a wide smile and the mirror wiped clean. There. For the first time in my life I looked like someone else.

After the initial welcome, we sat across the small table in silence for some time just holding hands. Our eyes scanned each other's face, searching for familiar features. Although no memories connected the dots in our minds, it was the double helix of DNA that linked us. The similarity couldn't be denied. But if I hadn't known who she was, I probably would have passed her by in the street. After all, I hadn't been searching for her. It was Gloria who needed to find me.

She fixed me with a steady gaze. "You have your father's nose. I haven't seen that nose in a long time." Her expression softened as the memory of her first love flooded back and resurrected the young, vibrant teenager she'd been long ago. "I loved him so much. He was Greek and such a handsome man, but he was married with three kids. I was a nineteen-year-old nurse working in Townsville. He never knew I got pregnant. When I found out, my mother sent me to Brisbane to have you. By the time I returned home, he'd left town with his wife and children. I never heard from him again." The sadness in her voice sounded raw with regret. She still suffered from a broken heart. "I never wanted to give you up. My mother made me. For all these years since, each day I've looked for your face on every girl I passed on the street. Wondering if you were okay. Who adopted you? Were they good to you?" Her eyes filled with tears as the years of shame, guilt and uncertainty finally found release. Tiny, hiccupping sobs escaped her, while I soothed her grief.

"It's all right. Everything worked out perfectly." Patting her hand and brightening the conversation, I led her through my life, sharing the highs and lows she'd missed. I told her about my wonderful, loving parents, about everything being divinely orchestrated and that we had all been players in a game of Consciousness that we'd chosen. Using the words of Khalil Gibran, I did my best to reassure her, all was right place, right time.

"Your children are not your children. They are the sons and daughters of Life's longing for itself. They come through you but not from you and though they are with you, yet they belong not to you."

"This is how I've felt all my life," I said to her. "I had great parents, but I was different to them. But then, I've been different to most people. I never really saw myself as belonging to any one family or any one group. I've always seen myself as a kind of child of the universe, like from the poem, "Desiderata." You and my biological father gave me great genes, and Mum and Dad gave me a great upbringing. I'm the lucky one. I'm an only child both in nature and nurture. I get to see things from both points of view."

She gave a hesitant smile, as though wishing she felt the same. "I'm pleased you see it that way." Then she cast her mind back once more. "When I returned home, I married another Greek man and we had five children. The only person who ever knew about you was my mother, who's been dead for some years. No one else has ever known."

Her misty eyes beseeched me to liberate her from this secret, to free her from her silence. This poor woman had given birth to me over thirty-five years ago and had kept this secret from everyone else she loved in her life. As someone who believed the truth will set you free, I couldn't imagine how anyone could keep silent for even one day, let alone half a lifetime.

"You don't have to keep me a secret anymore. You can tell anyone you want. You can tell the rest of your family if you want. You did the right thing giving me up. Really you did." We hugged for the longest time until the energy transmuted, and the present moment polished off the past.

She dabbed her eyes with a tissue. "I named you Michelle before I left the hospital. I told the nurses to call you Michelle until someone adopted you."

"Really? I always wanted my name to be Michelle when I was growing up. I used to write it on my school books."

I hadn't thought about this for years, but now the memory of my writing Michelle flooded back. While I pondered this, an image of a vast ocean of ever-flowing currents and tides flashed into my mind. Consciousness was like that ocean. It too teemed with endless activity and movement. There was motion everywhere. Nothing stood still. Since we're the expression of this Consciousness, our mind is the receptacle for this activity. In my case, my mind had received, stored, interpreted and acted upon the name given to me at my birth. In divulging her story, my biological mother confirmed the universal truth—all movement, activity and therefore actuality come from Consciousness, through us, about us.

Over lunch we talked about her life, her grown-up children and their families. She refrained from identifying my biological father since he never knew of my existence. Because I had no interest in finding him, I didn't push her as to his identity. He'd given me what I needed—great genes. However, a thought rushed into my mind. She'd been a young nurse who fell in love with a married man. Perhaps he'd been a doctor or a surgeon at the hospital at which she worked. These pieces gelled, for as strange as it seemed, if I hadn't been in the entertainment business my next passion was brain surgery. I know this sounds incredible, but I've always been fascinated by large-scale medical procedures. The idea of performing in an operating theater was as exhilarating to me as performing on the stage. Could the reason for my keen interest in life-saving neurological surgery be loaded in my genetic structure? I'll never know for sure, but it's a tantalizing idea.

By the end of our time over lunch, I reaffirmed my blessing for her to not keep me a secret any longer.

"When would you like to meet everyone?" she asked, keen to embrace me into her family. "I know your sisters and brother will want to meet you."

With her high cheekbones and wide smile, I recognized my own face in her brighter expression. It gave me pause to consider how genetic families take for granted the similarity in the faces they see around them every day, and how this must reinforce an unconscious bonding in the group.

Until now, I hadn't seen a resemblance in any face that looked back at me for thirty-five years. Perhaps the absence of that unconscious belonging also contributed to the negative emotions of rejection that had conspired against me throughout the early part of my life. Unless you're adopted, it's difficult to imagine the strangeness of seeing someone you look like for the first time when you've already lived a third of your life. Staring at my biological mother, I intuited there was something about genetic encoding that goes deeper than the science. I found the situation extraordinary, like I was being given a glimpse into the tapestry of life's divine composition.

"No need to make a time for us all to meet," I said. "It'll become apparent. Let's keep in touch." We said our farewells with the fondness of friends, not the devotion of mother and daughter. She returned to her life, and I to mine.

For a lot of people, finding their biological parent or parents and knowing where they came from is a life-long quest. For me, finding my genetic donors had never been a driving motivator because I knew I hadn't come from someone or somewhere. I was more than flesh and blood, skin and bone, genetics, adoption papers or names. My biological mother and father were the genetic vehicles through which I'd incarnated for this adventure. Although I saw some of my features and mannerisms reflected in my biological mother, the encounter only reinforced my convictions. We're all more than we appear to be. We're all Consciousness in movement and individualized in expression. Meeting my biological mother proved it. Nothing ever happens by accident.

I was a fury of energy, burning with desire. Not only was I committed to *being* and helping others through my work at the health, fitness and relaxation center, I attended seminars and workshops conducted by international business and personal development leaders. When inspiring speakers such as Jim Rohn, Anthony Robbins, Louise L. Hay and a dozen others visited, I was there, listening and taking copious notes in my journals. It was during this time I learned the power of written goal setting.

Throughout my life I had always set goals of some sort, but not always on paper. I'd mentally planned where I wanted to be and how to get there. Now, I realized this wasn't enough. Just as writing affirmations had enormous drawing power, I discovered the power of written goals. Inspired to design for myself the good life, I purchased a journal and began to chronicle my goals.

Since I was responsible for my destiny, I knew that if it's meant to be, it was up to me. I'd already reached my goals in the entertainment career, without even being conscious of the resonance of energy. Now, knowing my integral part in weaving life's magic, I was determined to test and trust it consciously. So, I developed my own Conscious Goal-setting System. Unlike dreams, which are nebulous and carry no risks, goals are a "back-to-basics" discipline. They're the nitty-gritty of life, and must be specific, measurable, attainable and realistic, and given a timeline in which to manifest. Under the bigger dreams I dared to dream, I listed five categories of goals—personal, economic, leisure, contribution and relationship.

My personal goals were divided into the physical, emotional, mental and spiritual aspects of life. They identified who I wanted to *be* in my life. I thought about the qualities of my *being* and began with those. For example, I prefaced each goal with the leading phrase "to be," just like Will Shakespeare had done centuries before. For example, to be creative, to be gentle, to be strong, to be persistent, to be loving and so the list went on.

The next element was setting my career, business and financial goals. I knew writing down "having lots of money" was just a broad, sweeping wish with no substance on which to manifest. A wishbone can never replace a backbone, so clearly defined goals were critical. I knew that good economic goals had to identify the harvest I intended to reap from the seeds I'd been sowing over these recent years. I spent considerable time meticulously planning my economic goals, making sure they were specific, measurable, attainable and realistic.

My leisure goals came next and included all the joy, adventure and playfulness of life I desired most. Traveling around the world, owning a fabulous house and lots of other wonderful things were included on this list.

My contribution goals identified how I planned to make the world a better place. I knew that when I gave more, I became more.

Lastly were my relationship goals where I listed what I desired most from a loving, significant relationship.

Beside each goal, I wrote the time by which I expected it to manifest. Some were as short as one month, while others were ten years or longer. I reviewed all my goals and chose the top three in each category which made twelve top goals for the coming year. My system also incorporated the quality-management principles of *plan, do, check* and *act*. Planning our goals is never enough. We must consistently enact the strategy to draw our goals toward us, check our results and proceed to take more action. I called this quality managing my life. I kept my goals and strategy close at hand throughout the year and reviewed them regularly to see how I was tracking on the map to my chosen destiny. The time it had taken to fashion my compelling future and journal my twelve goals demonstrated my love for myself and my life. It also proved I dared to *be* the master of my destiny.

There's no point in writing goals if we don't review and refine them. Locking our journal away for another year will not manifest the results we want. Every time we review, we have another opportunity to refine our destiny, to make changes or to remain on the course we originally set. The time spent setting our goals and formulating an action strategy is but a blink of an eye in a lifetime. Yet the drawing power inherent in this exercise resonates out into the matrix of possibilities, attracting our most desired destiny to us. Even now, over thirty years on, I continue in this process. One of my favorite things to do on New Year's Day is to review my goal-setting journals. Within their pages is the proof of the law of attraction working in my life. Even the home I live in today I can track back to my goal-setting journal of over twenty years ago, where I described this home in detail.

My system may sound like work, but writing down the mental image of the goal and focussing on and feeling it, impressed the desire upon my Consciousness and triggered the enormous drawing power of the law of attraction. When combined with meditation and the deep desire to expand my Consciousness—free will and spirit blended in perfect harmony. Applying my intelligence, my mind and my Consciousness, I enacted what Henry David Thoreau so eloquently wrote, "If one advances confidently in the direction of his dreams, and endeavors to live the life he has imagined, he will meet with success unexpected in common hours."

Insights…Be focused, Be committed, Be purposeful

The difference between those who reap life's riches and those who don't is who they're *being* and how they use their time. If we don't set goals, our lives deteriorate into the joyless existence of making a living. We breed bitterness in our minds, bodies and lives. When we set goals, we demonstrate that we value ourselves. We consciously commit to being the fullest expression of ourselves.

Setting goals signifies that our lives are worth the time it takes to sit for a few hours each year and formulate our plan for living the good life. If we want to live rich, rewarding external lives, we must firstly live rich, rewarding internal ones. Consciously choosing goals is integral to this.

It saddens me that so many people never spend time in contemplative solitude, charting the course for their lives. Instead, they prefer to watch other people's lives on television, on social media or read about them in the gossip pages.

Henry Wadsworth Longfellow wrote, "The heights of great men reached and kept were not attained by sudden flight; but they, while their companions slept, were toiling upward in the night."

While all around you, others waste their precious lives in the pursuit of trying to be more like some celebrity, rather than aligning with the unfoldment of their *being*—fashion for yourself a compelling future vision, knowing that before something happens in the external world it must first happen in your internal world. Your life doesn't change by accident. It changes by intention…yours. Opportunities to fulfil your destiny abound when you hold the vision of your intention with laser-focus and unwavering commitment.

We each live with the economic results of our mind. This is a simple, demonstrable truth. Poor thoughts and limited Consciousness produce poor results and a poor bank balance. My life had been absolute proof of this. At my lowest point when the ego had me reacting in fear, I had no money, no income and no hope of employment. Yet when I dared to change my approach, challenge my conditioned thinking, ignore my past limitations, press on and experience conscious *being*—abundance began to appear in direct proportion to my Consciousness, and my goals began to manifest.

Confucius once said, "If you shoot for the stars and hit the moon, it's okay. But you've got to shoot for something. A lot of people don't even shoot."

Not every goal manifested within the expected timeline. But when I review my journal today, I'm reminded how powerful the universal laws are and how delighted I am for continuing with my goal setting over these decades. In my daring commitment to live my life on purpose, with purpose, I remain focused on *being*…as a verb, not a noun.

Jim Rohn likened life and business to the seasons. "You cannot change the seasons, but you can change yourself."

His message succinctly treated the passing of time not as something to be feared, but as a fact of life that if managed well, is richly rewarded. Learning to handle the winters and not wishing for less problems, he extolled using this time in one's life to become wiser and stronger, to acquire new skills.

Then in spring we must take advantage of the opportunities that present themselves, not wasting time or declining them. The season of spring in life or business is a time to get busy and get it done.

Summertime is for nourishing and protecting our values, our goals, our dreams. In pulling out the weeds of negative thinking and fertilizing our crop, we must remain vigilant against the pests and plagues.

Finally, we reap the harvest in autumn, taking full responsibility for what happens to us. I knew I had handled the winter and I'd buzzed like a diligent bee through the spring. Now, as I came to the end of my summertime, the first sign of a good harvest beckoned.

CHAPTER THIRTEEN
Passion is power

By now, I was on fire with an unstoppable passion for life, energizing myself to stretch further, dream bigger and ignore the past limitations that still tried to restrict my Consciousness. Though uncomfortable as this sometimes seemed, I knew that I was living a life of my choosing, manifested through the power and activity of my Consciousness. Unless I was able to provide a larger Consciousness, I couldn't generate a larger demonstration in my life.

This is why few people excel in their lives. Small-mindedness and limited Consciousness produce small, limited results. We must dare to be mentally alert, spiritually centered, physically healthy and emotionally loving. If we act this way in life, life will act this way through us and return to us likewise. I believe begging, pleading and beseeching God isn't the answer to a person's uncomfortable existence. Entreaty only reinforces the concept of ultimate power being outside of oneself and perpetuates the belief that one doesn't possess the resources necessary to overcome the lack one experiences. By handing our power away to an external force, we unwittingly play into the ego's game of separateness and everything remains the same.

1993 flew past in a whirlwind of energy while I advanced confidently in the direction of my dreams. Aside from splitting my time between managing the health, fitness and relaxation center, attending business seminars and spiritual retreats, cultivating my daily meditative practice and being an active member in my local rotary club, I returned to the stage—this time as a speaker. During the first half of the 1990s, businesses and corporations were keen to train and entertain their staff. They wanted speakers who could inspire their employees to think big and reach for the brass ring. With the pseudonym of the Edu-Tainer, I graced many stages sharing my message of "Dream it, Be it, Now."

In my hour-long presentations, and weaving humor, song, dance and life-skill methodology into an interactive program, I had conference rooms of business-suited delegates up on their feet, "turning themselves on" as James Brown sang "I Feel Good" from the audio system. Featuring key points of personal power, passion, persuasion and purpose, I drove the audience on the super highway to fulfilling their dreams by becoming the person they longed to be.

Although I graciously received accolades from the agencies and audience, nothing compared to the sheer joy of being back on the stage, sharing something of value and entertaining others. Having the speaker's rostrum to myself, I could now adapt my performance to the audience. During these presentations, it was as if I was two versions of myself. Me the performer, speaking, educating and entertaining, and at the same time, I was outside of myself as Consciousness, as *being*, guiding the performer to change course or use different examples. It was exhilarating and enlightening.

This exuberant year morphed into the next with the addition of new interested investors for my theatre restaurant venture. My attachment to this project remained strong and every time someone jingled the possibility bell, I salivated like Pavlov's dog.

Attachment to outcome is a tricky trail to tread. The challenges to hold on are difficult, but this is precisely what you don't want to do—hold on to your attachment, to cling to your investment in outcome. The passion with which I lived my life brought ever-growing opportunities, but saddled onto this energy was the ego, cloaked in the emotional attachment to this project. Like a sinister rider, it would gallop into the darkness of my mind, getting my hopes up and then crush them under hoof. It was in this guise of my big dream coming true and then not, that I learned faith.

Faith is a transformative energy beyond measure and has the power to change everything. It's knowing without doubt or fear that everything will work out for the best, even if it doesn't manifest exactly as planned. Faith is the space between what we cannot see and what we believe, across which we leap. That my theater restaurant which I had poured so much of myself into and still felt compelled to energize remained at arm's length, tested my faith and offered me yet another experience of *being*. The pressure I placed on myself and this project's manifestation brought up old stress patterns I thought I had released.

Repeatedly in my meditations, I asked if there was anything for me to know, or was I on track, or had I got my omens wrong. Every answer came back the same—passion, purpose, power and patience. Live with passion, stay on purpose, you are the power and practice patience. These words pranced in my meditations like four glorious horsemen of revelation, leading me into the center of my *being*.

Enriched by the silence and its wisdom, I would rest, free of the anxiety, to refocus my attention on all is right place, all is right time and that infinite patience brings immediate results. In meditation, with my mind no longer obstructed by fear, my faith stood as the indestructible cornerstone of manifesting an abundant and radiant life. By meditating on the messages of passion, purpose, power and patience, I moved into acceptance. I leaned into my faith as a definite mental attitude, just as I first leaned into the omens.

From a religious perspective, the test of faith conjures up some malevolent external power forcing us against our will, to prove we're ready for the next challenge. I didn't see it that way. I knew my test of faith was a shedding of another layer of my negative programming, a digging down into the deepest, most secret parts of my conditioning. *Let it go, let it be.* The same message I had heard over the years whenever I exerted control over my life still rang in my ears. I was like an onion, being peeled back to the very core by my ever-expanding level of Consciousness. For me to be more, to do more, to have more, I needed more faith. Not just your Sunday-kind of faith, but faith as a conscious choice on a moment-to-moment basis. Like a cane field is burned so the sugar can be harvested, my mind became refined and my soul sweetened. From experience, I knew that faith brings success, while fear brings failure.

Looking back, I gained so much from this time. The most obvious was that with a strong enough faith, much can be revealed. Much was revealed to me in the meaning of perseverance, endurance, steadfastness, detachment, character, sacrifice, love, compassion, trust, humility, and of course, patience—to let go and *be*.

On the blue moon in the middle of 1994, my husband and I moved into our dream home, an architecturally designed, pole house tucked into 43,000 square feet of native Australian bushland, where I'm sure nature spirits danced from branch to branch. With shining lemon walls, stylish white furniture and rainbow-colored throw cushions, our house sparkled with the energy of love, joy and peace. Incense wafted continually throughout the rooms while tranquil music joined the symphony of native birds. Each morning I practiced my dancing on the cantilevered balcony amid the tall eucalypt trees and meditated in nature's serenity. Finally, I nested in a home of my design.

Another year replaced the last and the property in which the health, fitness and relaxation center operated was sold. Since the center was going to be converted into a cosmetic surgery by the new owners, I wanted to give it a fitting goodbye. Several clients joined me and with paint brushes in hand, we splashed our favorite quotes and insights from our years together on the walls. Like kids given free rein to make as much mess as we wanted, we said our farewells bathed in paint, laughter and gratitude. Although disappointed to watch the closure of a space where people had improved their health and well-being on so many levels, I continued teaching personal development workshops, meditation classes and counseled private clients in another venue on a part-time basis.

Not long after, I was offered work as a consultant and trainer for various government departments, conducting lectures to assist the unemployed to return to the workforce. My memory of how no one wanted to employ me six years earlier filled me with compassion for those sitting in the classroom. Exhausted from a life of struggle, they sat dejected and depressed. They were a tough audience, but I knew if I could touch just one person, then I'd fulfilled my purpose for that session.

Understandably, many struggled with the notion of taking responsibility for their circumstances. Blame and injustice still oozed from their pores. Nevertheless, I saw recognition in some faces when, as if waking up from a bad dream, their expressions brightened. From their *being*, from their Consciousness, a stirring registered. By teaching them the life skills I'd acquired, I offered them a key to unlock a better future. What they did with this key was up to them, but I'm sure those who felt the quickening of their *being* that day have flourished.

It was early in this year that an opportunity of a personal kind presented itself. To meet one of my half-sisters and half-brother. When the three of us and my biological mother, Gloria, gathered at her unit, the similarity in facial features, mannerisms, physical structure and vocal tone intrigued us all. We sat there laughing, comparing our knees, feet and hands. My half-siblings gaped at how much I reminded them of their maternal grandmother. The way I spoke, gestured and moved triggered fond memories and surprised smiles.

The eldest daughter, Helena, retold how she'd always hounded Gloria as to where her older sister was. Although she'd never known of my existence, on an energetic level Helena knew from an early age that she had an older sister. Gloria had dismissed her childhood questioning, but it did little to dampen her daughter's insistence. Could my lifetime interest, intuitive connection and love of all things spiritual be genetically encoded? Helena certainly resonated to lots of the same things I did. Like Alice down the rabbit hole, I thought the encounter curiouser and curiouser.

"Here," Helena said on returning from her bedroom. "You should have this." In her palm rested a tiny antique ring. "It was our grandmother's ring. She gave it to me before she died. She wanted it to go to the eldest daughter. You should have it."

"Oh, no. I can't take it."

"She would've wanted you to have it," she said, offering the family heirloom to me.

"Go on," Gloria encouraged.

I accepted the gift of love and slipped it on my finger. A thin band of gold with a tiny diamond, its material value was negligible. But the love with which it was offered was priceless. To not accept this precious gift at the time would have been disrespectful, but to keep it was inappropriate. I wasn't the eldest daughter of this family. Helena was. A few months later, I gave it back to her, which I suspect pleased her enormously. Her grandmother, Gloria, Helena and I shared part of the same bloodline which traced back to good English stock of hard-working, strong women. Though we hadn't grown up in this lifetime together, in that poignant moment of our first meeting, I sensed the hand from a fated past reach through me and touch my heart.

Throughout these years, I never stopped dancing or choreographing, if only for my own pleasure. Just as meditation connected me to my *being* through stillness, dancing connected me through movement. The passion and desire to be creatively expressive never waned in me. Since continual creation was the essence of Consciousness in expression, then finding ways of creative self-expression expanded my Consciousness. Whenever I was being creative, I raised my energy and experienced *being*. In turn, I spontaneously became more empowered and passionate in my life. The cyclical nature of creativity is a powerhouse of energy.

It was from within this space of creativity that I first dabbled with writing. While ideas for children's books flooded my mind, I tapped away on my word processor, enjoying the stories as they manifested through my fingertips. Although I never submitted these stories for publication, writing them provided a platform for my love of storytelling, which I'd had since I was a child. Like dancing, writing was another way of channeling my creativity and expanding my Consciousness.

My thirty-ninth-year affirmation to 'allow the more to be revealed in my life, according to the divine plan under grace', underscored my goals and actions for this year. And since everything is energy and proportional to my expanding Consciousness, I attracted more people and opportunities into my life. The first harvest, which I had devoted my time to was ripening, ready for reaping.

Insights…Be passionate, Be powerful, Be patient, Be fearless

Those who succeed at anything in life are no more talented or gifted than those who don't. Part of the reason for their success is faith. Successful people are fearless in their faith in themselves and that they will succeed. They dare to dream bigger, they challenge the conditioned status quo, they fearlessly ignore their past limitations, and they press on with formidable faith. They inherently know that their faith must be stronger than their fears and understand that fearlessness is not the absence of fear but going beyond fear. The worst enemy we can confront is fear, for fear attracts fear, whereas faith expels fear. The fearless, unfettered mind, the mind filled with faith, attracts only good.

Faith isn't wishing or hoping. It is knowing that nothing is too good to be true. Nothing is too wonderful to happen. Nothing is too good to last. With faith all things are possible. Our faith grows when we embrace the valuable lessons of perseverance, endurance, steadfastness, detachment, character, sacrifice, love, compassion, trust, humility and patience.

Faith is best tested on life's smaller challenges, so it's up to the task in times of greater difficulties. For me, the value of faith during these years prepared me for a future I passionately desired. The firing in life's kiln certainly added more strength, flexibility and power to my faith muscles. Since my affirmations and goals for this year centered around allowing more into my life, attracting situations requiring more faith fitted the vision. I discovered that if I wanted a fast track to my *being*, faith was my get-out-of-jail-free card.

I likened faith to wearing a pair of glasses when viewing a stunning spring day. Mother Nature is in her glory with brilliant blue yawning skies, the greenest, freshest grass, a gentle stream trickling clean and pure down the hillside, and fields of perfumed flowers through which exuberant wildlife scamper. Unfortunately, most of us view this perfect spectacle through dirty, finger-smudged glasses. The image we see is distorted and less vibrant, and so we feel uneasy and restless. However, what we see doesn't reflect the true beauty and perfection of the landscape. It's merely our smudged perception of it. Over time, we come to believe in this distorted representation of the landscape, of our world.

Three options exist for us to see clearly. The first is to leave our glasses in place and rub at the lenses in the hope this will clean them enough for us to enjoy the view. This is referred to as insanity—doing the same things but expecting to see different results.

The second option is to remove the glasses and clean them thoroughly before resetting them onto our face—this is the process of correction, compliance and conditioning, of doing something different but still from the same conditioned thinking as before.

The third option is a leap of faith, where we simply grow tired of the view we're experiencing and throw the glasses away altogether. Sick and tired of being sick and tired, we leap from who we are to who we want to be, without any safety net, except faith in ourselves. That leap of faith provides sparkling clarity because it fast-tracks us to our *being* where we discover we didn't need the glasses in the first place. Faith is a precursor to revelations which cannot be imagined by critical thinking.

Just as we can't see the beauty of the landscape if the glasses remain dirty, we can't demonstrate both fear and faith in our lives at once, as one contradicts the other. The stronger of the two produces the results. During the years since my *Out on a Limb* epiphany, I'd been committed to being out on a limb, reaching for the ripest fruit at the end of the branch and keeping the faith. I knew things didn't happen by chance but by change. I'd attracted into my life test-of-faith opportunities, in preparation for the big changes ready to be revealed. The congruence was inescapable, although not always clearly seen. My metaphoric glasses didn't need cleaning, they needed discarding. And every time I took a leap of faith, they dislodged a little more.

Rather than on hands of prayer, my life was steepled on four principles: passion, purpose, power and patience. With an eternal, unrelenting desire to savor the juice of life and make a difference, being passionate was an intrinsic quality with which I'd incarnated. To temper this passion with the peace from meditation, allowed me to express my passion both calmly and enthusiastically.

The second principle of the purpose of life is two-fold. I believe there's a basic purpose we collectively share. That is to evolve, to give, to receive and to be love in alignment with the unfolding of our *being*. Like a plant can't object to growing, the evolution of our Consciousness is our shared purpose. It's what drives us at a deep level whether we acknowledge it or not. To this mutual purpose, we each have a unique, individual purpose, inherently bound to the stirring of our soul and expressed at an early age. Like everything else, I realized my unique purpose was something I chose. I've often wondered if our individual purpose is genetically encoded before we incarnate, so that no matter how hard we try to find or choose another purpose, we can't. It stirs within us from before our birth and we demonstrate this individual purpose as we grow. For those blessed with amazing voices, perhaps it's their purpose to use their gift to express Consciousness through song and in doing so, bring joy to others. I know of one young performer who had such a gift, but she chose a life of drugs and ended it in despair. I wonder if she'd chosen to keep singing, even for no other reason than self-love, would she have lived.

I feel individual purpose is something utterly personal indwelling each of us. Like a mustard seed, it grows and blossoms over our lifetime. Our sole/soul purpose is to dare to connect with it, placing all our faith into it, and to choose for it consciously.

By practicing patience, I was rewarded when my unique purpose became apparent in words automatically given to me during a kundalini meditation. Kundalini power or spiritual energy exists within each of us and can be activated by intense meditation or breathing practices. Like a sunflower with my face turned to the heavens, I heard the still, small voice within proclaim my unique purpose. A private experience, it's one I've clung to and embody every day to the best of my ability.

The power I refer to doesn't mean power or domination over others, or even intentional influence over others. Power is that which I am, not something given to me from outside of myself, nor something I take away from another so I can accumulate more. Power isn't a game or a commodity. It's our birthright. Power is at the heart of who we are, what we express, where we incarnate and how we live. In living and loving with passion, purpose and patience I unlocked power; not mine, but the power of *being*.

When I embarked on this rich, inner quest, and dared to dream bigger, I also had to dare to be fearless. To keep my eyes on my future vision and go beyond fear. Although there were times when every fiber of my body quaked at the trust I placed in my *being*, I kept the faith and leaped. I had to live the life I came here to live. There wasn't another option for me. I was dancing up the stairway to paradise and there was no going back.

CHAPTER FOURTEEN
Creating a brighter future

As 1996 dawned, I found myself once more hunched over my goal-setting journal, mapping out my future. I remained in awe of the law of attraction and how my energetic resonance acted as a magnet attracting in my personal reality. Since the unraveling of my old life in 1988, I had dared to be more. I had trusted in the awakening of *being* and kept the faith that my big dreams would come true. Sure, there were times when things didn't work out the way I wanted. But hindsight is a remarkable gift because it often brings greater insight. There were times when I looked back and breathed a sigh of relief. If the something I wanted had manifested, it would have ended up taking me on a detour or giving me grief. Obviously not lessons I needed to learn. I'd had my share of those.

Because I passionately engaged in expanding my Consciousness, I attracted an externality reflective of my resonance. The law of attraction worked flawlessly. Now cognizant of its execution, I manifested that which I repeatedly focused on, embodied and energized. As such, my life generated rewarding results.

Still consulting as a trainer at the Department of Employment and Training of Education, teaching personal development, meditation and life-skills courses, and counseling clients, I continued with my onstage performances with glittering speaking gigs for corporate events. In all instances, my message highlighted creating a brighter future. With the world spinning toward the conclusion of the twentieth century only four years away, the energy on the planet accelerated.

I knew no matter how much or how little a person had in their life, everyone hungered for more. This longing was their Consciousness urging them to expand because their purpose demanded expression. Many people didn't realize this was the reason behind their desire, but the push they experienced was incontrovertible. Added to this internal nudging was the media hysteria of terrible events about to befall technology on the stroke of midnight 1999 when the Y2K bug would virtually shut down computers across the planet. The doomsayers were gearing up for the crossing over into the second millennium with references to judgment day, destruction, war and the party being over, just as Prince wrote in his dance hit "1999." The hype surrounding these final years of the second millennium fueled the mass unconsciousness with a mixture of worry, trepidation and frenzied excitement. For those of us who knew differently, we retreated within and chose for the peace and silence in meditation in order to maintain our equilibrium.

We followed Walt Whitman's advice when he wrote, "Keep your face always toward the sunshine and shadows will fall behind you."

Committed to creating a brighter future despite the collective chatter, circumstances and conditions, I kept my face toward the sun.

When I meditated, I engaged my five physical senses and vividly imagined my future—how it would look, taste, smell, feel and sound. I became my future. I energized it by acting every day as if it was already so. Focusing on who I was becoming, how I would act, dress, speak and be in my world, I developed an intense sense of expectancy of my dreams manifesting and of my future fulfilling itself.

I remember the urban myth of Madonna, who as an aspiring, undiscovered starlet used to pretend she had an entourage following behind her wherever she went. What she was doing was visualizing her future as a major music star with all the trappings that came with it, including an entourage of people to do her bidding. For those of us who dare to fling our dreams, visions and destiny out into universal Consciousness with the positive assurance to know and claim it as our own, we will find it is done.

Concurrently with this, I constructed a vision board on which I pinned images reflecting my goals and mapping out my brighter future. Pictures of houses, places in the world I wanted to visit, types of holidays, health, exercise and fitness images—everything that identified my brighter future. My vision board sat pride of place in my home office, where the promise of my future danced in front of my eyes every moment. Behind it lived a huntsman spider the size of my fist. Since spiders symbolize creativity, I accepted its presence as a positive omen and called her Maud. Whenever she ventured out from her hiding place, I checked my thoughts in case she was giving me a message. She lived there for years and like my invisible childhood friend, Sheena, and the ghost at Twelfth Night Theatre, she reminded me that things aren't always as they seem.

Through my workshops and counseling sessions, I encouraged my clients to employ a systematic, personal approach to creating a brighter future. Using the metaphor of a precious jewel, I explained we each possess five basic facets to expressing the fullness of our *being*: physical, mental, emotional, financial and spiritual. For us to *be* the person who attracts a brighter future, we need to polish each of our facets. Only then can the gem of who we truly are luminesce, attracting more brilliance into our lives. When all our facets are polished, we glitter in our flawless integrity, showing our true value to the world.

The most obvious place to start this polishing process is the physical facet. Since we are embodied Consciousness, we have a responsibility to honor and value our bodies—to care for, love and provide our embodiment with the nutrients, exercise, hydration and restorative sleep needed to function most effectively. If we respect our car enough to fill it with the correct fuel, check the air in the tires and service the engine regularly, surely our bodies are worthy of the same attention. With movable joints, our bodies are made for action, not to slouch inactively in front of electronic screens or on couches, hour after hour. Use it or lose it is never more relevant than when applied to the physical body.

As a dancer, I knew the importance of physical exercise and enjoyed the feeling of a strong, flexible body. Although no longer performing, I continued in my dance and exercise regime of five classes a week, keeping my body as close to dance condition as I could. Weight training and aerobic-based activities helped, but nothing ever matched dancing in front of an audience, when the added boost of adrenalin powered up my body. Nevertheless, my body demonstrated its natural state of health, vitality and strength. The more I meditated and listened to my body's messages, the more I knew what best polished my physical facet. When I ate based on my intuitive signals and not my cravings, the better my body responded. It's a remarkably efficient operating system, and I knew I had to honor it by listening and complying with its instructions.

Then there was the power of the breath. Being a dancer, I had learned to manage my breathing in order to perform at peak condition throughout my career. I took this connection one step further in my meditations. Filling my lungs deeply and controlling the rhythm of the breath increased the oxygen permeation in my blood vessels, which in turn reduced inflammation throughout my body. The power of conscious breathing has long been extolled in yoga and meditation practices as a super pathway to support our sympathetic and parasympathetic systems, ensuring healthy physiological responses.

Bret Lyon wrote it most simply in *The Power of Breathing*, "The way you breathe is the way you live."

I believe living healthy, healthful lives is our birthright. It's not random and it certainly has nothing to do with luck. Excusing ourselves from being healthy by blaming our genes, circumstances or conditions is an erroneous, disempowering belief.

Deepak Chopra, M.D., and Rudolph E. Tanzi, Ph.D., co-authors of *Super Genes: Unlock the Astonishing Power of Your DNA for Optimum Health and Well-Being* demonstrate how we shape our gene activity and how genes act as a tool for personal transformation. "Everything you do, every choice you make, whether it is a good habit or a bad habit, is changing your genetic activity." According to the authors, optimizing our gene expression will not only positively affect our life, but also the course of human evolution. "Genes hold the past, the present, and the future of life on this planet."

When we polish the physical facet by honoring our bodies, we align our bodies with our *being*, and we begin to sparkle.

The second step in the polishing process as we ready ourselves for a brighter future is our mental facet. From my own experience, I knew the critical importance of being ever vigilant with my mental health. If we feed our minds trash, we create a future wasteland. And even more importantly, if we feed the minds of our children trash, we create generations of toxic waste. Standing guard at the gateway to our thoughts, perceptions and beliefs, we must allow only those that identify love and abundance entry into the fertile soil of our minds. If we want a brighter future, we must live a brighter today and permit only positive, empowering mind food to feed our mental health.

Mental inactivity, limitation and lack lead to poor mental health, which in turn produces poor results. Unfortunately, there are those who choose mental laziness. They become complacent in their reasoning, slothful of thought, and they scorn wisdom. Instead of expanding their intelligence, they settle for what they have, rather than what they're capable of. Each of us has the choice not to be influenced by the negative messages presented by the media, social platforms, education, political, religious and societal systems, yet many people allow this negativity to shape their lives. In doing so, they become anxious, depressed and even bitter toward those who have more, do more, or are *being* more than them.

A sinister sense of resentment and entitlement pervades their Consciousness as they settle for less, expecting others to make up for the shortfall in their lives. But when we change our mental focus, healing begins. We must choose to mentally stretch, grow and gather more to ourselves. No matter how bright or large the future we imagine for ourselves right at this moment, we must imagine it larger. We must polish our mental facet by expanding our current level of Consciousness so the luster of our *being* can shine through. Life is limitless and it's up to each of us to imagine the boundless possibilities on offer.

The third facet is our emotional nature. Our emotions are energy in motion, e-motion. Positive emotions, which I refer to as feelings are love-based. Feelings such as happiness, faith, passion, trust, kindness, tenderness, empathy, sympathy, honesty, and compassion all have their origins in love—love for oneself and love for others. Negative emotions are fear-based. Anger, resentment, victimhood, deceit, martyrdom, frustration, apathy, bitterness, guilt, shame, and jealousy are emotions based out of fear—the fear of loss, of not being good enough, of being less than or greater than. To polish the emotional facet of our *being*, we must release our negative emotional patterns and choose to embody more love-based feelings.

All disease comes from a state of fear, from fear-based emotions left to fester. Healing is essentially a release of fear. The more love-based feelings we experience in our lives, the more love we give, receive and *be*; the more we are healed. More correctly, the more of who we truly are as *being* is revealed.

The fourth facet is the financial facet of *being*. Volumes have been written on how to make money, get rich quick or win big. However, the basic advice is still the best. When it comes to money, use common sense; spend less than you earn, invest a little each week so your money multiplies, guard your money from loss, make your home a profitable investment, increase your ability to earn, give to those less fortunate, work by the principle of giving a fair day's work for a fair day's pay, ensure a future income and be grateful for what you have.

During these years of polishing my financial facet, I found a small book entitled *The Richest Man of Babylon* by George Clason. Told in simple parables, the powerful message of how to make money still applies today, principles by which I live and recommend. Clason wrote, "Better a little caution than great regret."

As I polished the financial facet of my *being*, I began to more fully integrate that it wasn't more money I needed. It was a changed experience of my Consciousness with regards to money, to substance and supply. Through these years, I made enough to live a 'middle-class' life, but I knew this wasn't enough. There was more. There's always more.

Instead of seeing my financial security outside of myself, I dared to shift my focus to me as the source of my supply, of my abundance. My financial freedom manifested in direct proportion to my Consciousness. The more my Consciousness expanded, the more abundance multiplied in my life. I learned that no matter how much I pursued money; it would always outrun me. Wealth isn't something to get, it's something to be attracted. When I paid attention to my crop within, to my *being*, with the intention of growing my Consciousness—a plentiful harvest without would grow, ready for reaping. This was a massive shift in Consciousness.

The final facet to revealing our luminescent *being* is the spiritual facet, which we polish through introspection, reflection and meditation. My daily meditation ritual afforded me the time and space to explore *being*. In going within, I reconnected with myself on an energetic, universal level.

Castaneda wrote, "In the universe there is an unmeasurable, indescribable force which shamans call intent and absolutely everything that exists in the entire cosmos is attached to intent by a connecting link."

We are that link. The more we pay attention to our inherent spiritual nature, polishing ourselves and expanding our Consciousness, the brighter our future will be.

Every time I expounded the five-facet polishing process to my students, clients and audiences, I reinforced the message back to myself in each presentation. I was my own living affirmation, reminding myself over and over of there being only one thing going on, of only one activity taking place, that of Consciousness in expression. It's always present, always functioning and is all there is to me. Like a De Beers jeweler, I polished my facets, determined to reveal the luster of my *being*.

By March 1996, I reaped my first significant harvest. Contracted as the Orientation and Ethos Trainer for Robina Town Centre, a sprawling new shopping precinct comprising over 150 retailers and restaurants, I developed a corporate personal development strategy and presented it to retailers, who in some cases, were only concerned with increasing their revenue, complaining about management and possessed little interest in seeing the world with any degree of emotional intelligence. In fact, some of these interactions reminded me of my days dealing with the cast, crew and management at the casino. Nevertheless, I remained unaffected by the bickering, stress and tensions. By now, my view of the world and humanity were vastly different to before. I presented myself as a facilitator, a state-inducer, and linked my message of kicking life goals to the greater vision of corporate and public harmony. I was dubbed "the goal kicker" by the press, which I found infinitely more agreeable than my previous tag of a "fat dancer." I thoroughly enjoyed working in the corporate arena and interacting with a range of contemporary associates. It gave me the opportunity of sharing what I'd learned and applying it in a results-driven environment.

On the personal front, my mother and biological mother finally met. I instigated the meeting so they could dispel any emotions they carried about my birth and adoption. Both women, although a little hesitant, were gracious and curious to know the other woman in my life. Gloria questioned Mum on my childhood—what was I like growing up? How did I like school? Did I get any childhood illnesses? She delighted in hearing the stories Mum told her. On the other hand, my mother's curiosity about who I took after was finally satisfied. In Gloria, she witnessed the same strong-mindedness, forthright personality, vocal tonality and collection of mannerisms which I possessed. The three of us had a delightful few hours filled with laughter, compassion and acceptance.

After Gloria left, I hugged Mum tightly. "I'm so pleased you're my mother. We're so good together."

She lifted her gentle face, her ethereal blue eyes moistening with tears. "Me too."

Like we'd done so many times before, we retreated to the kitchen to wash the dishes and chat about the day. My mother had always been the one I could turn to and count on. She had my back. No matter if she agreed with me or not, she never faltered in the love and commitment we shared. As far as I was concerned, she was the best mother, my only mother and we had chosen each other long before my incarnation. Did she believe this too? Since she usually agreed with me, I've no idea what she genuinely thought. Mum was a reserved woman, not often taken to revealing her deeper thoughts, but on a soul level I think she knew this to be true.

The highlight of this year came when I finally convinced her to leave Brisbane, and the home she and Dad shared for over four decades and move to the Gold Coast to be closer to me. She'd spent the last ten years living there alone, and at the age of seventy-five she finally allowed this change into her life. She was a healthy, young-minded, independent woman and with her two cats as a deal-breaker, she refused to move if they couldn't come with her. I promised I would find somewhere within her meagre budget where she could be happy with her furry babies. The criteria was tough; a well-appointed unit, somewhere close to me, able to have pets, in a managed independent-living retirement facility with minimal entry cost.

During my search it became apparent how limited the options were. No matter where I inquired, nothing worked. With no other recourse, I gave up and gave in. I threw out into Consciousness what I needed and believed it would be done unto me. I lived with faith, trust and a detachment from outcome, believing all was right time, right place. While Mum teetered between wanting and not wanting to move, she waited with unconcerned patience. Then one day, when I was driving past a retirement village not far from my home, I decided to inquire in person. My first phone inquiry a few weeks earlier had proven fruitless, but on this day, I listened to my inner nudging, turned the wheel and headed for the estate's office.

On being ushered in to see the manager, I met a well-dressed, blonde-haired woman with a sweeping smile. She introduced herself and informed me she was the new manager. With the bells and whistles clanging in my head, I told her Mum's story and our predicament with funds. She whipped out a calculator and did the math, then offered me a deal I couldn't refuse. By increasing their commission on the unit buy-back when Mum left, she reduced the entry price to a more affordable sum. Since I had no interest in Mum's share of the unit on her death, we shook hands on a tentative deal for the one and only unit available.

The following weekend I drove Mum to the unit which she promptly loved. In no time, she was happily ensconced with her two cats in her bright, new home and making new friends. I hadn't seen her so settled in years. She built a new life for herself and with it she found a new lease on life. Like me, she'd embarked on a brighter future.

Insights...Be peaceful, Be healthy, Be disciplined, Be driven, Be determined

Being peaceful, which renders calm, collected knowing and poise, was a central tenet to creating a brighter future and keeping my life on track. Knowing the truth of how the law of attraction worked, I became more conscious of choosing my own destiny, sustaining my health and energizing my *being*. Life was a gift, but it was up to me to accept it. Committed to impressing the future I desired on my Consciousness while valuing my peace simultaneously, I aligned with the unfoldment of *being* and accepted my future with open arms.

Being physically, mentally, emotionally, financially and spiritually healthy is about installing good habits in our lives. When we see life as a gift and not a sentence, being healthy is a natural state of *being*. We deserve to be healthy so we can enjoy the gift of life more. We feel a oneness with our body, our mind, our emotional nature, our abundance and our *being*. Too many people think they must make massive, immediate changes with their health in order to create a brighter future. This can often work against them because every time they fail the ego convinces them of their unworthiness. *Hey, you're going to die anyway, so why not drink, eat, smoke and drug yourself to death?*

Like polishing a precious stone, it's the smaller, incremental changes that lead to the highest luster. Once we learn to love and value ourselves, being healthy becomes second nature. Confronting as this seems especially for those with chronic illness, the more we reconnect with our *being* and authorize our body to release whatever isn't necessary for its perfect functioning, the more we empower our bodies to respond accordingly.

The three d's—being disciplined, driven and determined—come as a powerful trinity to creating a brighter future for they relate to "practice makes perfect." But beware. They're not about practice from the limited, human perspective of trying to force the future to happen, but rather from the new frame of reference of going within and relinquishing the ego in favor of *being*.

There were times when I faltered and lost faith in myself. Times when I lost my way. But this was when being disciplined, driven and determined acted as a terrific fallback position. These three qualities held me in good stead. They supported me like an army of strong, well-trained troops, while I advanced boldly into my new future, fearful and weak. Being disciplined, driven and determined rekindled my faith, and I became the conduit through which my brighter future manifested.

In that space of renewed faith and being peaceful in my meditations, I heard, "There is nothing for you to do, but everything for you to *be*."

CHAPTER FIFTEEN
Reaping the rewards

With Mum settled into her new life nearby, my husband and I settled into feathering our nest. We spent many pleasurable hours shopping for knickknacks, decorating, working in the gardens and finding a comfortable groove in our bright, new home. Both artistic by nature, we expressed ourselves creatively through writing and painting. While he enjoyed oil painting, I wrote a series of seven, short children's fantasy stories. I found the experience of being guided in my writing, inspiring. It was yet another way in which I could honor my *being* as it nudged me to *be* more.

We lived in a companionable, peaceable fashion. Ours was not an epic love affair of sweeping passions and possibilities. Rather a comfortable cohabitation between two loving people who, having supported each other and endured hardships, were committed to enjoying a brighter future together. With our Persian cat, Topaz, as our object of affection, we were content. Yet the still, small voice within me kept asking why I was settling with being content. If I was gathering a brighter future to myself professionally, then why wasn't I gathering a brighter future to myself personally? Did I not see what was happening? Did I not realize I wasn't *being* all I had come here to be?

My husband and I had numerous conversations about our relationship and the lack of intimate contact. Too much time was spent with me acting as his counselor and not his wife. We continued in our marriage albeit with some discord over his secretive nature, unwillingness to communicate and reluctance to release his emotional past. Yet, underlying it all, I felt an overwhelming sense of responsibility for him. But my still, small voice within wouldn't be silenced. As the stalemate between us continued, I came across an old Chinese proverb which I thought most apt, "The gem cannot be polished without friction, nor man perfected without trials." Deep within me, I knew another test of faith was on its way.

A professional highlight of 1996 was being emcee for Charlton Heston when he launched his autobiography, *In the Arena*, in Australia. When I was a little girl, I used to sit on the floor, nestled between Dad's legs while he lounged in his favorite armchair smoking a cigarette, watching Charlton Heston's award-winning films and performances on our black-and-white television set. The Hollywood star had been one of my father's favorite actors and those days held special memories for me. So, when I was offered the chance to emcee for the great actor, I jumped at it.

In the ballroom of a leading Sydney hotel and in front of an elite group of three hundred guests, I took to the stage to introduce him. Epitomizing the true Hollywood legend, he was a real man's man, who oozed charisma, power and a commanding presence from which people couldn't avert their gaze. In introducing him, I also welcomed his wife, Lydia, who I knew would've been the wind beneath his wings throughout their long marriage.

He stepped onto the stage in long nonchalant strides while the audience clapped and cheered. Even at seventy-three years of age, with his chiseled jaw, broad shoulders and striking good looks, he embodied the quintessential alpha male. When I stood aside to allow him access to the lectern, he leaned close to me. "Well done, and that's my professional opinion."

To be so close to him sent shivers up my spine, let alone to receive his compliment. When I returned to my place beside Lydia, the room hushed and like everyone else, I fell under the great actor's spell.

Articulate, lyrical and dynamic, he spoke about aspects of his life and career with great humility and fondness. Although this evening he was a little tired, he still finished his presentation by performing the soliloquy from Shakespeare's *The Tempest*. Rising to his full acting height and grandeur, he transformed into the character. "Now my charms are all overthrown, And what strength I have's mine own, Which is most faint: now, 'tis true, I must be here confined by you, Or sent to Naples."

His delivery so captivated the audience, they gave him a standing ovation. He returned to our table, and being the consummate gentleman, held out my chair for me and then for Lydia. I was keen to know if he'd share any gems of wisdom, and since he was a devoted family man, I asked him what life advice he gave his young grandson.

He instantly replied, "Do your best and keep your promises." This prompted a discussion between us on life philosophies and we chatted like chums through dinner.

Photographs with Mr. Heston were strictly banned unless previously arranged with his personal assistant and taken by his approved photographer. Since I was the emcee, I was permitted to be photographed with him and able to purchase the photograph directly from his photographer. This one photo, with me wearing a beaming stage smile, my flaming hair piled high on my head a la Lucille Ball standing beside a lop-sided grinning Mr. Heston, fills me with delight whenever I walk past it in my office. Looking back on this event now, Charlton Heston resembled an angel come to earth to give me a pat on the back, encouraging me to keep going. But then he did play larger-than-life characters such as Ben Hur, El Cid, Michelangelo and Moses—nothing like having the "big guys" on your side.

The remainder of this year continued to flourish professionally with my short-term contract as the Orientation and Ethos Trainer extended into the role of Marketing and Promotions Coordinator at Robina Town Centre. After a couple more months of proving my ability to meet challenges, manage resources, people and projects, and design and implement innovative, creative campaigns, I offered them the retention of my services in the role of Tourism and Special Events Manager. They accepted, and I reaped a substantial financial harvest.

All the work, faith and dedication to expanding my Consciousness and *being* had paid off. I was learning a new business in the tourism sector and doing what I loved in special event management, while simultaneously maintaining my independence to perform keynote speaking presentations and work with a select group of private clients who I still counseled. What I had thrown out into Consciousness and claimed as my own all those years before was now upon me. My brighter future had manifested.

Generating a lot of media hype at the time was Robina Town Centre's star retailer, the first Disney store in Australia. As the Special Events Manager, I had the pleasure of working alongside the Disney Corporation's production team flown out from America to stage a spectacular parade for the store's opening. Being Disney, nothing less than perfection would do.

Walt Disney had said, "When we consider a project, we really study it—not just the surface idea, but everything about it. And when we go into that new project, we believe in it all the way. We have confidence in our ability to do it right. And we work hard to do the best possible job."

And this is what I did with the Disney team for the grand opening of their first national store. Every detail was considered, planned and executed and in the end, it was a hugely successful parade, not only for the Town Centre and Disney, but for the hundreds of people who lined the streets eagerly awaiting the store to open its doors.

For the third time in my career, the opportunity to work in America presented itself. The first was when Jerry Jackson offered me a position with him in his Las Vegas shows. The second was from the Mrs. World Pageant's choreographer and the third was from the Disney event manager, who offered to have me on his Disney events team in the States. I declined.

In reflection, I wonder if I had missed this repeated opportunity because my focus was elsewhere. Had I been waiting for my ship to come in and missed the boat? Although flattered by these three offers, I'd chosen not to pursue them. Instead I remained in Australia, close to my aging mother, who had no one else but me. On the other hand, if I had gone overseas, which I am sure Mum would have supported, then what?

One thing I've learned is that if one door shuts, another door opens. Too much time and energy can be spent on regret, which is just another way the ego tries to bind us to the past, while keeping us from gathering a brighter future and reaping rewards. Living with regret is not, and never has been, on my agenda.

Abraham Lincoln wrote, "I don't really have any regrets, because if I choose not to do something there is usually a very good reason. Once I've made the decision, I don't view it as a missed opportunity, just a different path."

With Mum as my very good reason, I chose to stay in Australia on a different path.

By the end of 1996, I planned and managed a massive New Year's Eve event, the likes never seen on the Gold Coast in any shopping precinct. With an early fireworks display scheduled at nine o'clock for families and another larger fireworks at midnight, plus an array of entertainers, bands, food stalls and children's entertainment, Robina Town Centre rocked into the new year. Blessed with a decent budget and a supportive executive management team, I created a visionary outdoor event which attracted over four thousand people to the shopping town, which had only been opened for a few months. After the bump-out of the final contractors and performers, I called it a wrap at about two o'clock the next morning and released my team of hard-working crew. I drove home pumped and pleased with myself, my favorite music blaring in the car.

Propped up on the balcony of our home overlooking 43,000 square feet of bushland, I sipped a glass of chilled French champagne and ate caviar in celebration of my success. No longer unable to make ends meet, I had graduated into my destiny and it felt damn good. Free from the self-inflicted pain of the past, I was living proof of what David Thoreau wrote, "What lies before us and what lies behind us are small matters compared to what lies within us. And when we bring what is within us out into the world, miracles happen."

That night I toasted the past and future year and gave thanks for all I'd learned and experienced. Most of all, I realized I had only scratched the surface of conscious *being* and the best was yet to come.

Insights…Be persistent, Be strong, Be thankful

"Nothing in the world can take the place of persistence. Talent will not; nothing is more common than unsuccessful men with talent. Genius will not; unrewarded genius is almost a proverb. Education will not; the world is full of educated derelicts."

In my experience, Calvin Coolidge's quote is true. Being persistent, relentless and never giving up on my vision fueled me to *be* more; to be more passionate, powerful, purposeful and patient. My persistence in *being* had created a brighter future, and I reaped the rewards.

In today's vernacular, these traits are referred to as grit. Angela Duckworth talks about gritty people as those who believe "everything will be all right in the end, and if it's not all right, then it's not the end." For me, it was more than a selection of character traits. It was about enriching my inner world of thoughts, perceptions, beliefs, values and emotions, and embodying them through my words and actions, which led me to experience a life of richness. Persistence pays off.

Interestingly, Charlton Heston, an actor renown for playing strong characters, appeared in my life at this time. I had always admired the strength of his characters' convictions, no matter the struggle. They epitomized what Paulo Coelho wrote, "Difficulty is the name of an ancient tool that was created purely to help us define who we are."

In mustering the strength of my convictions, my will and my *being*, I'd been able to face difficulty and redefine myself. In being strong, I'd anchored the truth of Consciousness so profoundly into my frame of reference that I refused to be cast adrift by advancing storms of the ego. I had changed and my world had changed too. I was reaping the rewards of *being*.

Throughout this time, I lived with an attitude of gratitude and the list of what I was thankful for grew daily. I no longer saw things as good or bad. Everything was simply Consciousness in expression. That I was an integral part of the movement of this Consciousness sustained me, heightening my gratitude. Pollyanna was back.

Being thankful helps us view life as a glass half full, rather than half empty. It fixes our focus on being optimistic rather than pessimistic. The more we practice being thankful, the more our worldview changes and subsequently our own personal reality changes. Gratitude is a force which gives birth to fulfillment and success. When we live with gratitude we grow and glorify Consciousness. This heightened resonance and radiance act as a vibrational magnet which attracts to us more to be thankful for. To reap life's rich rewards, we must embody an attitude of gratitude.

To this day, I lie in bed each night and list what I'm thankful for. While my conscious mind practices this gratitude exercise, my *being* carries me into deep, restorative sleep from which I awake grateful once more with my morning affirmation. *Today is my day. I give thanks for my perfect day.*

In 1996, I had the extraordinary honour of being the emcee for Charlton Heston's Australian book launch of his autobiography, 'In the Arena.' Standing alongside a Hollywood legend as he introduced his life's story to the Australian audience became one of my career highlights.

CHAPTER SIXTEEN
Attention and intention

Like a stonemason laying bricks on a foundation stone, I built on the previous year's triumphs in steady succession. Empowered by my new role and the connection with my expanding Consciousness, I forged into this year with more attention and intention. Spurred on to further myself professionally, I became a registered consultant with the Queensland Industry Development Scheme in human-resource planning and cultural change and graduated the management-skills-development program from the Australian Institute of Management.

Affiliated with several business and charity organizations, I gave of my energy and time, interacting with my professional peers and supporting others less fortunate. My role as the Tourism and Special Event Manager opened the door to more learning, business networks and work travel, igniting a life-long love of exotic locations and different cultures. As one who enjoyed being productive and being of value, I actively sought out more opportunities and accepted them.

Continuing in my speaking engagements, I performed a range of presentations including "Energize Your Business," "Don't Jump off the Cliff," "Living Dynamics," "Mind Aerobics" and one of my favorites, designed specifically to empower women entitled "Women of the 21st Century."

On the stage in front of all-female audiences, I fiercely encouraged women to claim their feminine energy and appreciate our timeless characteristics of beauty, gentleness, tenderness, grace, power, resilience, compassion, mystery and joyousness. Speaking about self-empowerment, my presentations never focused on male-bashing, gender inequality or men being the enemy. To me, those messages were counter-intuitive and spiritually destructive. Instead, my message centered on the feminine energy within everyone. That as women, we have the power to lead, not from the male-dominated perspective, but as communicative, intuitive, nurturing, creative and insightful leaders, directing a new way into a brighter future. Exampling the feminine associations throughout history of Mother Earth, the wise old crone, the medicine woman and the mystical enchantress, I presented women as way-showers, demonstrating how feminine energy was essential to return balance to the world.

Leading my audiences through the four steps to self-empowerment—recognition, acknowledgement, acceptance and action—I charted a course for them to consider and follow. The press jumped on the feminine energy bandwagon with a story on my message entitled, "Waiting for the new Millie-ennium." A catchy play on words by journalist Rachel Syers, who finished the one-page article by writing, "By following the steps Diane has outlined, you may find yourself armed to the teeth with enough feminine energy to make one hell of an impact in the new millennium. Look out world!"

Before I knew it, New Year's Eve 1997 heralded the end of another year. Based on the success of my previous year's event, the crowds thronging through Robina Town Centre mushroomed to fifteen thousand people, ringing the retailers' cash registers. What a sensational finish to an equally sensational year. A bittersweet moment though. The owners of the massive shopping town found themselves in a tight financial situation and suspended all external contracts. Despite my contribution to the center's success, my contract wasn't renewed when the calendar ticked over. Although a little disappointed, I was unperturbed. I'd spent two rewarding years on a thrilling rollercoaster ride of creativity, growth, contribution and success. Capping it off with a New Year's Eve event attended and enjoyed by thousands of people, sweetened my departure. At forty years of age, my life now diametrically opposed the one of shame, heartache and poverty I'd lived only a decade before.

Armed with strong business and tourism experience, I launched into the marketplace, willing and able. Abiding in my intention of finding another fulfilling role which reflected my *being*, I gathered my resources and prepared for an even brighter future. Serendipitously, I bumped into the previous owner of the health, fitness and relaxation center from a few years before. Though he and I hadn't kept in contact, the law of attraction had brought us together once more.

As fate would have it, he'd decided to go into the tourism industry after selling the center. He had recently purchased a lavishly appointed seventy-foot yacht and was preparing to embark on a strategic sales-and-marketing campaign for his new luxury product. Based on my recent industry experience and our previously successful working relationship, we struck a mutually beneficial deal.

Launching a high-end product into the tourism marketplace required a little black book of contacts locally, nationally and internationally; contacts who possessed the cashed-up clients to charter such a superbly equipped yacht and crew. I had the national and international tourism contacts, but the challenge was to capture the imagination and patronage of the local "A" list. I set to work designing a campaign with an irresistible offer.

Over the next fortnight, four sunset cruises set off on the tranquil Gold Coast Broadwater, crammed with the city's elite and powerful, who jumped at the invitation. Like a popular television show at the time, *Lifestyles of the Rich and Famous*, I rubbed shoulders with seemingly ordinary people, living extraordinary lives, some of whom became life-long friends. By raising my resonance, I expanded my Consciousness and attracted in a new set of friends and fulfilling relationships. My vibration within had changed, and so too had my tribe without.

During this time, I developed an even more inspiring relationship. For years I meditated on being centered, being curious, being receptive and being in communion with the still, small voice within. My sense of *being* one with universal Consciousness, with everyone and everything had expanded. Embodying my mantra of *infinite patience brings immediate results*, I perched on my meditation stool, asked a question, expected an answer and waited, poised in the peace.

On one occasion something changed. Like a soft breeze blowing in from the shore, a presence floated around me and settled. This encounter was accompanied by a profound feeling of home. A majestic benevolence and familiarity enfolded me, as if a friend I hadn't seen for a long time had just appeared and sat down beside me. With a grateful, spontaneous smile, my face instinctively lifted upwards, while warmth coursed through my body.

Then the conversation began—the conversation with the goddess. Despite my initial interpretation of this energy's specific gender assignment, it was made clear to me that the goddess represented the feminine energy indwelling everyone. It wasn't an external, supreme entity separate to my *being*, but an integral aspect of Consciousness. Considering my intense passion for and interest in the feminine energy, my work in the empowerment of women, my name, Diane meaning moon goddess and my choice to incarnate as a woman, it made perfect sense to me that the goddess within would make her presence known.

Throughout the years, I'd taken a notebook with me whenever I meditated, in case I needed to jot down an insight or feeling. Although I hadn't experienced automatic writing, I had experienced the joy of being in the moment of inspiration when words flowed unrestricted from a stream of creative Consciousness when writing my children's stories. On this night, I experienced something different. Aware without, yet attuned within, I took up my pen and notebook and began to write my first conversation with the goddess. The flow, pace and accuracy with which the conversation proceeded signified that what I registered was more than my thinking or reasoning. The answer to the question I'd asked at the beginning of my meditation revealed itself as I transcribed what I heard. At the end of this session, I re-read the text, marveling at the insightfulness of the message.

It was a significant moment in my evolution of *being*. Just as I'd trained as a dancer, I had rehearsed my meditation routine for years, preparing for this experience until I was ready for the big night. This was that night.

Buckminster Fuller wrote, "Everyone is born a genius, but the process of living de-geniuses them."

I had spent the past eleven years daring to place my intention and attention on having a deeper connection with my *being*, with my genius. Responding to my request and heightened level of Consciousness, the goddess answered my call.

With a widening circle of fabulous new friends and a home energetically invigorated in which to entertain, my husband and I socialized regularly and enjoyed our flourishing life. But something was still out of balance. As I created a brighter future and reaped the rewards, he struggled to keep up. Aside from the personal issues that tormented him, which we often discussed, I knew there was something else. In my solar plexus, my intuition jiggled madly, like a cat in a box scratching to escape. Unable to ignore this insistent nudging, I pressed him on what else was going on. After some ducking and weaving, he finally admitted he'd been hiding a secret. When he confessed, I was mortified. On one level I knew why he demonstrated deceitful, self-sabotaging behavior, and on another level, I wanted to throttle him. Even though I felt betrayed by his admission, I proceeded to counsel him while simultaneously stating the importance of honesty, integrity and communication in a marriage. I asked why wasn't he happy at home? Why would he jeopardize our marriage? But my questions hung like a broken kite on a tree branch. He offered no answers.

Guilt, shame and remorse took up residence in his body and the tenuous thread of trust in our marriage stretched to breaking point. Not wanting to make any rash decisions and despite my outrage, I was willing to put this behind us and move forward. Like others who choose to forgive an indiscretion, I recalled the old saying of not throwing the baby out with the bathwater. We'd invested a huge amount of love, time and energy into our marriage. He had stuck by me in my darkest hours, so surely this one indiscretion wasn't worth destroying all we had built. Nevertheless, I did clarify my expectation for the future without reservation. Filled with regret and shame, he made a promise which I accepted. I think we both knew it would be broken, but hope kept us together.

The end of another seven-year life cycle dawned in the middle of this year. At forty-two years of age, I had built enormous momentum due to my energetic resonance and my expanding Consciousness. Professionally, I continued in my role as the Marketing and PR consultant for the luxury yacht, as a conference speaker and corporate trainer, and as an event manager for various high-end corporate events. But I knew there was more for me to *be*, to do and to have.

Astrologically, this seven-year-life-cycle itch is because of the Uranus opposition which happens to everyone around their forty-second year. There's a yearning to break free of the family trance and live from your soul. And there was such a soul push for me at this time to break free, I wondered how it would manifest.

It was my husband who gave me the opportunity. As the distance between us widened, our marriage deteriorated. Lack of intimacy, communication and growth signaled our relationship breaking down under the pressure of being married. Both unhappy and unfulfilled, we struggled with the inevitable. Unless radical change took place, our time had come. He needed to find himself and be who he truly was, rather than pretending to be someone else.

Confronting him one day, I questioned where he had been, and again he admitted to his secret liaisons. It was the proverbial straw that broke the camel's back. The veil of family trance, of obligation, of misplaced karmic responsibility lifted from my eyes, and I gathered myself for a brighter future.

I listened within and made a congruent, empowered decision.

Turning to him, I said, "Betray me once and it's your fault. Betray me twice and its mine. I'm over it. I refuse to play victim to this situation any longer. We're done."

Once more I chose freedom and my soul danced for joy.

Insights…Be intentional, Be generous, Be undefended, Be courageous

We are energetic beings. The evidence of this is demonstrated in the life we live. Because of the law of attraction, we call to ourselves circumstances and conditions of a similar energetic resonance. Therefore, if we want our lives to change, we must change. Our life doesn't change by accident, but by intention—ours.

Once we accept that we're responsible for our destiny, we can *consciously* harness the power of intention. For intention is more than wishing and hoping. It's more than dreams or goals. It's being convinced that it's already so. Intention is a connection to our *being*, to its enormous drawing power to manifest. When we become accustomed to *being*, we are a conduit for this power, and we can gather brighter futures to ourselves. We can channel our intention to make the invisible, visible.

Having spent the past years refining my intention, focusing my attention on *being*, while demonstrating faith and trust, I consciously harnessed the law of attraction. In the early part of my life, when I trained as a dancer, my *being* propelled me forward with the same laser-focused intention. The difference this time was that I was *conscious* of what power I conducted. This was reinforced whenever I blew up my household appliances. Many an electric toaster or frypan shorted when I touched them during an intense energetic moment. I never received a shock, but when I tried to use them, they didn't work. Working one minute, and not the next. You may think that this is what happens to appliances, but not repeatedly, and not to new ones that haven't been used.

Numerous people are high conductors of energy, but don't realize it. If you've recently increased the electro-magnetic Wi-fi frequency in your house or office and have since suffered headaches, investigate safe-guarding yourself. I had to hard-wire my office and remove my Wi-Fi because of my body's high conductivity. "Everything is energy and that's all there is to it."

Through the power of the law of attraction, my intention had manifested. I'd reaped the rewards, which in turn gave me more to give. In being generous, I shared my *being* and was further enlightened by the gift of giving. Instead of allowing doubt, fear and lack to infiltrate my thoughts about finding another contract after my tenure finished at Robina Town Centre, I focused on right time, right place and right people. I dared to trust in a destiny I couldn't yet see.

Of course, it was challenging to be out in the marketplace again, but I believed an opportunity would present itself if I stayed the course and remained undefended against my inherent good. I trusted that the world was a friendly place, that life was on my side and that all would unfold perfectly in alignment with my *being*. The situation reminded me of the old Bible quote about the lilies of the field and how they grow. Like them, I deserved to have my needs met.

Just as a warrior summons up her courage before battle, I summoned up my courage to continue to *be* the fullest expression of Consciousness, despite my professional circumstance and marriage breakdown. I had spent years following the omens, acting on my guidance, going beyond and within to my *being*, and I'd reaped the rewards. My role now was the same as it'd ever been—dare to dream bigger dreams, challenge my conditioned thinking, ignore my past limitations and press on, until those dreams or something better manifested. By being courageous in my convictions and applying a liberal sprinkling of trust, I happened upon my previous employer, who contracted me immediately. I had placed my intention and attention on letting my life *be*, and in doing so, I became more empowered.

I was shifting from the limited, third dimensional perspective of viewing the world as separated space, time and form; to the fourth dimensional frame of reference, which was the conscious experience of *being*.

When considered from this frame of reference, the collapse of my marriage was understandable and predictable. The end of a marriage isn't failure, and divorce isn't shameful. It results from the disparate rate of growth of the two people involved. Without both partners being willing, responsible and intentional in expanding their Consciousness, they can either remain in the marriage and self-destruct, or go their separate ways.

We are each responsible for our own awakening.

We are each responsible for our own suffering by our unwillingness to awaken.

We are *not* responsible for another's awakening.

In the end, I chose to no longer be responsible for my husband's awakening. We knew the only intelligent way to end our marriage was with love and forgiveness. We had spent sixteen years together awakening. To have ended on bad terms would've only proved we learned nothing.

Mark Twain wrote, "Forgiveness is the fragrance that the violet sheds on the heel that has crushed it."

Rather than dwelling on the crushing of the marriage, we moved forward, fragrant as friends, each responsible for our forthcoming results.

Like a dancer longs for the stage, I longed to experience the fullest expression of the movement and harmony of *being*. The stairway to paradise beckoned, and I laced up my dancing shoes, ready for the next performance. I was forty-two years old and had continuously lived in relationships with men since I was fourteen. It was time for me to dance life as a solo performer and be the choreographer, director and event manager of my life, solely and souly.

CHAPTER SEVENTEEN
Magic and miracles

After spending a day crying, revisiting fond memories and allowing the grief to be released, my husband and I toasted to our brighter futures. Parting ways didn't mean erasing each other from our lives. Our relationship simply evolved in a different direction. We remained living in our house as roomies, awaiting the sale of the property. That we still cared for each other sustained us during the transition from couple to independent individuals. Finally freed from our obligations to the other, we began our single lives.

Living independently of a partner for the first time, I launched into a whole new world. Instead of staying home at night, I ventured out with girlfriends, dancing the night away at clubs and shedding the few extra pounds that domestic discontent had packed on my body. More joy, passion, energy, hope and faith bubbled up within me, effervescing with the divine feminine. The goddess was taking up visible residence in my body, and I felt a surge of sexual energy rising through me. I had become desirable again, not just as a woman, but as a human *being*.

Empowered and enchanted, I explored my first-time single life with unrestrained passion. Not at all interested in a relationship, I kicked up my heels with a variety of men as a free, independent and self-reliant woman. Never had I dared to embrace my sexuality with such abandon.

Heterosexual alpha males fascinated me. They were a new breed I hadn't intimately experienced and they proved easy studies. Unashamedly sexually motivated, their conversations and behaviors entertained me as they engaged in their mating ritual. At times, I felt like David Attenborough observing the silverbacks of the highland gorillas. Just like their genetic ancestors, these men glowered, poked and prodded nearby females trying to get their attention. Then with a quick swipe or scowl, the women dismissed their advances, leaving the male to turn his attention to his next quarry. Knowing the pain of rejection, I felt sorry for the male of the species at times. But they were so single-minded in their endeavors I couldn't help but be amused.

Intrigued and perhaps threatened by my forthright attitude, some men backed away from my feminine power, while those with more charm, confidence, intelligence and determination found my game of verbal thrust and parry a thrilling aphrodisiac. These encounters nourished me, giving rise to more laughter and levity in my life, restoring my confidence in being an attractive, desirable woman again.

Never once did I attract an unsavory or problematic situation when on my daring sexual adventures. Because I resonated my divine feminine energy, I attracted only powerful, charismatic men and rewarding liaisons. After all those years of polishing myself physically, mentally, emotionally and spiritually, I expressed my luminescence more at this time than I could remember.

With the much-anticipated arrival of the year 2000, I partied and danced until the wee hours of the morning in Sydney at one of the biggest fireworks spectaculars in the world. I was in the thick of it, squeezing every drop of juice out of that historic moment.

Having chosen to incarnate when I did, my life traversed two millenniums. As a child, I'd grown up when you could go out and play without fear of molestation or abduction, and like the rest of the world, I had sat enthralled watching Neil Armstrong walk on the moon. Instead of mobile phones, computers or personal devices, my young adulthood was spent enjoying face-to-face communication and dancing the night away. I had lived my passion and been paid for fulfilling my dreams while experiencing two marriages with all the love, laughter and learning they entailed. But most importantly, I had engaged in radical personal change, every moment of which I used to expand my Consciousness.

And now as I stood on the cusp of another new age of spiritual growth, I decided to take every opportunity as it presented itself to me. I couldn't waste another moment. My faith and trust in life returning bountiful harvests remained steadfast. The greatest freedom I experienced was not the freedom from my marriage or being in a relationship, but the freedom from my smaller sense of self, the ego. The demons of doubt, despair, disillusionment, distress, delusion and disease couldn't find a footfall in my life. I lived, loved and thrived, expecting every day to deliver miracles to me. My glass of life was no longer half full. It overflowed.

More omens led me to a variety of personal and professional opportunities. With my unswerving intention of following each one, they appeared thick and fast. My exploration into the interconnectedness between spirituality and sexuality opened new vistas, and after further studies, I developed the Great Sex Seminars. A program designed for couples to empower their relationship from a deeper connection within.

Following my intuition, I decided it was time to relocate and move to Sydney, so I asked for an omen as confirmation. On my next visit there, a stranger at a nearby table eavesdropped on my conversation with a girlfriend, and on hearing I was looking for a publicist, leaned over and told me the name and number of his. This extraordinary synchronistic moment was the sign I'd been looking for. I thanked him and set up a meeting with his well-known publicist, who took me on as a client.

I returned home to the Gold Coast ready to make the move, but needed to complete some professional commitments, sell our house and finish a non-fiction book to accompany my seminars. On the research path, I met a range of people and couples who lived fascinating lives outside of the cultural norm. Demonstrating how sheltered my life had been, these experiences acted like quick-release fertilizer on my rapidly expanding Consciousness. I flourished at high speed, like a blossom in time-lapse photography.

In the middle of this effervescing energy, I realized an important truth. Why stand at the door to my destiny and knock? Why not become the door through which my destiny rushes toward me in the present moment? Living with love, laughter, freedom and independence afforded me this insight, which in turn I practiced gratefully. I was back. I joyously lived as a fuller expression of *being*, in harmony with life as the magic and majesty of the goddess shone forth.

Then the unexpected happened. Of course, nothing is unexpected because we attract to us that which we become, but for me it seemed unexpected in the instant of its manifestation. A couple of years prior to this moment, when my marriage was faltering, I had worked with a new intention. During my regular dance classes, I'd placed my intention on having a man in my life who loved, lusted and longed for me—someone who matched me on the physical, mental, emotional and spiritual levels.

I hadn't thought about this intention for some time, certainly not since my marriage ended. Thoroughly in love with my new single life and the freedom it gave me, I didn't want a serious relationship. I was having too much fun flitting from one man to the other, like a hummingbird drinking the nectar from the flowers in the garden. But it happened when I least expected it. I met a man. Not just any man—a successful, opinionated Australian-Greek man, with an intelligent mind, witty repartee and generous spirit. That he was of Greek heritage was yet another sign. My biological mother had fallen in love with a Greek man—a love affair which had produced me. The coincidence danced with divine providence.

With our Type-A personalities, passion for life and personal power, he and I experienced a meeting of minds, the like of which neither of us had ever encountered. The inexplicable nature of our introduction and the similar character traits we shared was an irony not lost on either of us. Pushing back on his advances, I made it clear of my intention to gather brighter futures without a partner. As an alpha male, he found my rejection challenging and pursued me with vigor, but he was married and of no interest to me.

Thwarting his romantic approach, I struck the palm of my hand to his chest. "I'm no one's mistress."

"I don't expect you to be."

"Good. I'm glad we cleared that up."

Though I wasn't convinced he'd respect my boundaries, over the following weeks, our friendship grew, and he bade his time.

Meanwhile, the opportunity to appear as a weekly guest on a syndicated radio program offering advice on love, sex and relationships manifested. It was the perfect opportunity to share my message with a wider audience, but I needed a pseudonym that suited the night-time programming. After toying with the idea for a few days, the answer appeared in a flash of inspiration in one of my meditations—the Goddess of Love. How appropriate. The message of love for self and others was at the heart of my teachings and presentations, while the reference and reverence to the goddess who guided me gave credit where it was due.

The Goddess of Love hit the airwaves, broadcasting to millions of listeners who called in asking for advice or a chat. Covering topics such as relationship patterns, fantasies, the most romantic event in your life, breaking up, sex in public places and more, I sprinkled my advice with a good dose of humor while chatting with the resident radio broadcaster. We set the airwaves alight with our cheeky, irreverent banter and the phones rang hot. With my new brand of the Goddess of Love gaining traction, I contacted my publicist, who set to work on photo shoots and hawking me around Sydney town.

Marlene Dietrich's husky voice sang in my head, warning me that I was falling in love again though I never wanted to. Yet the omens surrounding the man who played Greek god to my goddess of love were undeniable. Yianni ticked the boxes. He possessed the qualities I wanted in a man, qualities I had energized for some time. Try as I might to ignore him, there remained a compelling connection. Something uncannily familiar haunted us whenever we were in each other's company. Not covertly sexual as much as mysteriously supernatural. The bells and whistles were once more clanging in my mind.

I'd only been single for three months, my career seemed poised to take off in Sydney, but the unexpected appearance of this man unsettled my equilibrium. Was falling in love really the next step for me? The heady delirium I experienced indicated it could well be, but distress flares flashed in my mind. Here I was, at the beginning of my next seven-year life cycle with a brand-new life unfolding before me. I needed clarity on the most appropriate direction to take.

Rationalizing the pros and cons of a new relationship while simultaneously meditating on the issue was bringing me undone. I was too invested in the outcome. Yet I intuited that Yianni offered me the opportunity to further integrate all I had become. Perhaps he was a match, and we could explore *being* together. So, I followed the advice I had given to clients for years—dare to let go, listen and let it *be*.

I chose to allow the situation to unfold in its own timing and did my best to relinquish my attachment to the outcome. I ignored the yammer-yammer in my mind with its running commentary of everything that could go wrong, and I chose to give up control, and trust. *Que sera sera*—what will be, will be.

Just as I had done a dozen years before, I tested the efficacy of the omens every step of the way. Over the next couple of months, my personal and professional lives thrived harmoniously in parallel. Working on radio, conducting the Great Sex Seminars, teaching and counseling clients, dancing and writing, I focused on raising my profile with my publicist. I lived every day to the fullest. I was in love with life, with my life and with all I came in contact.

Being a man of action and determined to fulfil his own intentions, Yianni made a serious conscious decision of his own. He chose to end his marriage, proving he was one of the few who dared take the grand adventure into the unknown. He was willing to lose in order to love. Even though he'd made this life-changing decision, I told him I had no intention of moving in with him when his wife left. I wanted things to unfold organically between us. With plans to live alone, I wasn't ready to give up my hard-won freedom to be tied to a man.

Four weeks later my ex-husband and I finally settled the sale of our house. However, at the eleventh hour of settlement, my new accommodation fell through, leaving my belongings stacked in the removalist's van awaiting delivery to a new residence which no longer existed. A strange, unforeseen event. But ever trusting, I knew this situation was nothing more than another omen, and I refused to negatively energize it.

While we stood on the balcony of our home one last time, discussing where I could stay for a few nights until I organized new accommodation, my phone rang. Unaware of my homelessness only an hour or two before, Yianni called to say his wife had moved out that afternoon. "I know you're got everything organized, but if you want to, you could move in here, today."

And the omens just kept coming. Nineteen weeks to the day since we first met, I mirrored his leap of faith, transported myself and my belongings, and set up residence with a man who dramatically transformed his life to be with me. All had unfolded organically, though much faster than I could have imagined. Like a chess piece, I'd been picked up from one life and placed into another one.

The idea of falling in love and being in love with someone else sets our hearts racing. For many, it fills us with eternal hope, while for others, it clutches them with anxiety because they fear they might lose the person they love. That the human brain generates its own pharmacy of love drugs such as dopamine, serotonin, oxytocin and vasopressin, indicates we have little defense against love, which is an evolutionary master stroke.

If we consider love, we eventually recognize a simple truth—when we fall in love with another, we're falling in love with our *being*. The other reflects our own radiance, Consciousness and immortality. Like a mirror, they shine with all good, all light, all godliness, and we respond in kind. Through the reflection of another, we glimpse each other's souls and fall in love with our *being*. Everything and everyone in our world become brand new because we're willing to give love, receive love and be loved.

We spontaneously act with caring, responsibility, respect, humility, intimacy, courage, honesty, vulnerability and commitment with the intention of creating pleasure, security, safety and trust for the other. We're enraptured, and we live in the rapture of everlasting love. In truth, love is the willingness to recognize eternal Consciousness in each and everything.

For those who are addicted to the euphoric feelings of love, they can only sustain a relationship for short periods of time because they crave the high of new love. Unmet expectations and escalating boredom mean they move on in the false hope of finding "the one"—never realizing the one they seek is within themselves, their *being*. They become emotional cowards who turn into emotional cripples, because they lack the courage it takes to be in a relationship. Those who thrive in long-term, fulfilling and successful relationships appreciate the commitment to the giving, receiving and being loved. With love, all else flows…respect, honesty, patience, forgiveness, kindness, intimacy, empathy, growth, support, freedom, understanding and communication.

Both in our forties and each of us having been married twice before, Yianni and I bore the financial scars of our past marriages; scars which would deepen, especially for him in his forthcoming divorce. With wisdom gained by experience, we knew another romantic turn around the park might prove disastrous for each of us. However, we both lived life with a similar passion, power, purpose and aligned values.

My intention from two years earlier had been to find a partner, who like me, desired to *be* more and live life as an unfolding adventure. Someone daring enough to explore the deeper meaning of life and Consciousness. Without hesitation, Yianni accepted the challenge, and we stepped boldly into a new life together. I remained true to my purpose and continued dancing up the stairway to paradise, this time with a new, dynamic partner by my side.

Insights...Be optimistic, Be open, Be bold

During the early months of 2000, I remember numerous occasions when the 1983 pop song "I'm walking on sunshine" by Katrina and the Waves played around me. The song exemplified the beat, rhythm, energy and infectious optimism with which I lived. Whenever I heard its driving tempo and happy lyrics, I sang and danced along like a kid. I loved that song because it represented me. I was walking on sunshine.

Being optimistic had been a part of my childhood nature. Now, at forty-two, I consciously chose to be optimistic, and in doing so, I became more open and emboldened to take bigger leaps of faith.

It's like the chicken and the egg. Which comes first? Being optimistic, or being open, or being bold. There's no right or wrong answer. Inseparable, they formed a circle of trust from which I took bigger leaps of faith. I believed magic and miracles would happen in my life, and as a result, they did.

Magic isn't something that happens from without, but from within us. It's the refinement of our senses which spontaneously occurs when we register every circumstance and condition as guidance and dare to follow its direction even though it may be an unfamiliar and risky path. When we come from this frame of reference, which is the conscious experience of *being* and undistorted by ego, we experience magic and miracles, which are the endless creation of Consciousness as it unfolds.

Living in a realm of reality where extraordinary things manifested, I caught glimpses of this life of enchantment. I was like Alice in a wonderland of limitless love, possibilities and opportunities.

My life was like a gift, right here, right now, and I dared to follow its lead, accepting it with open arms.

This playful publicity shot from 2000 for 'The Goddess of Love,' captures the essence of that milestone year perfectly. Radiating confidence and a touch of sass, this image is a vibrant celebration of the joyous and timeless allure of the Goddess within.

CHAPTER EIGHTEEN
A new role

In those first couple of years together, Yianni and I built a stable, loving relationship and family base. Within no time, I wore the mantle of bonus mum to his five children, who lived in Sydney with their mother, his first wife. They ranged in age from young adults in their twenties to the two youngest boys in their preteens. Suddenly, I had a new role, that of part-time parent when the boys holidayed with us during their school holidays. It was a role I loved, and a time we anticipated with great joy. The boys filled our home with laughter, love and heart-warming moments whenever they visited, and we missed them when they returned home. I particularly appreciated the irony of my never wanting children and then ending up with five through marriage.

Over the coming years, Yianni's daughter, Natalie, spent most of her time living with us, enriching our lives and that of my eighty-year-old mother's—for Mum now had the granddaughter I think she'd always wanted. Very similar in personality, she and Natalie enjoyed each other's company, often going on shopping excursions and coffee dates. My thoughts of relocating to Sydney got shelved, but I continued conducting workshops and keynote presentations interspersed with my appearances as the Goddess of Love on radio. At times, I wondered had I made the right decision by staying. But whenever this doubt raised its nagging voice, I tuned into the other voice. The still, small voice within which had never led me astray, and I asked for an omen. In confirmation that all was right time, right place, my publicist secured me guest appearances on *Beauty and the Beast*; a national daytime panel show aired by the Channel 10 television network. The format required one man, a confrontational provocateur who elicited the opinions of the six women panelists on viewers' questions. I lived on the Gold Coast, but I still got the gig even though it was filmed in Sydney over five hundred miles away. There was my answer. I didn't need to relocate. The work came to me.

From the beginning, it was apparent what a formidable team Yianni and I made. His presence filled previously missing parts in my life, and I did likewise for him. It was obvious that if we worked together in business, the level of success we could manifest would fulfil both our financial intentions. My professional commitments didn't require all my time, and because of my management and training skills, I consulted to his business, the Capital Group, the largest national limousine transportation provider in the country.

Although working together sounded good in theory, there were tough times in the early stages. Both being charismatic, dynamic leaders, neither of us was used to another disagreeing with our opinions. The challenge was particularly difficult for Yianni because I threatened his sense of manhood. Having been reared in a traditional Greek home where the man is the provider and the head of the household, he disliked being challenged. In 2002, while we were watching the highly successful movie *My Big Fat Greek Wedding*, he finally got the message. In a turning point of the film, Toula's mother explains the roles of men and women to her daughter. "The man is the head, but the woman is the neck, and she can turn the head any way she wants."

Aside from the humor, the not-so-subtle message rang loud and clear.

Yianni represented what I had flung out in the Consciousness all those years before—a mental match—and he was at once charming and challenging. Had we met earlier in our lives, I've no doubt this challenge would have proved exasperating and one of us would've walked away. Nevertheless, we rose above the ego which wanted a win-lose relationship. Pledging to the "we" rather than the "you" or "me" in our relationship, we consciously chose to play win-win.

Over those first years of the second millennium, I continued in my part-time role as the corporate facilitator in the Capital Group, developing a new vision for the company and training staff across Australia. Concurrently, I worked as a trainer for Women at Work, an organization specializing in re-skilling and up-skilling professional women. I spent three rewarding years teaching women the self-empowerment and professional tools with which to generate more success and fulfillment in their lives during my "Empowering Women in Business" workshops.

In one of these workshops, a woman named Victoria recognized me from my court cases fifteen years prior. Though she was delighted to meet me, her recognition unnerved me. I had kept my past confidential and was ill-prepared for this unexpected exposure. When she recognized me, the eleven-year-old girl who'd been rejected in public by the nasty women at church all those years ago reappeared, anxious and uncertain. But the fear was short-lived because I knew it wasn't real. It was just the ego trying to snag me into believing its bag of lies. In front of the class, Victoria explained that she'd studied my case along with most of the classes at Queensland University's law faculty back then.

Because my cases had set precedents, Victoria said they had been instrumental in the abolition of the Australian Conciliation and Arbitration Commission and the introduction of the Australian Industrial Relations Commission. The new *Industrial Relations Act 1988* ensured no worker would suffer the type of discriminatory treatment and lack of recourse I had endured. I was staggered by the news. I had no idea. Unexpected tears sprang to my eyes while she explained the extraordinary, positive impact my case had made on her, her fellow students and teachers at the time, as well as its impact on industrial law, especially regarding discrimination against women in the workforce.

My immediate emotional response blindsided me. I had dealt with my pain in private for all those years and thought I was done with it. Yet on this day, it was obvious I still suffered from residual trauma and heartbreak. Victoria's recall of the impact my stand for equality, truth and fairness had had on her life and that of others at the time, cauterized the wound.

Even though my Consciousness had expanded over the past years, I'd tucked away a little stash of emotions left over from that catastrophic event at the casino. They'd laid dormant for fifteen years somewhere in my unconscious. Unbeknownst to Victoria, she had shed light into their hiding place, releasing the last lingering hooks of unworthiness, denunciation and loss. After thanking her for liberating me, I told my story in public for the first time. The women in the class were shocked that such a situation could have happened in Australia only fifteen years before. It was good to finally be free of the secret, free of being that "fat" dancer who took her producer to court. Instead of teaching the women how to empower themselves, I became a living example of self-empowerment, thanks to Victoria.

In offering up my story and the insights I had learned during the casino experience, I fulfilled part of my purpose for the evolution of human consciousness. At last, I wasn't forsaken. Others unknown to me had applauded and stood by me, when many didn't. My stand had made a difference. All that I'd endured had real meaning, not just for me, but for the higher good.

Kindness is often cloaked in small, seemingly inconsequential words and actions. For those of us who receive such kindness, we often feel like we've experienced a miracle. Victoria's kind words and actions were my miracle. They reaffirmed that the stand I took all those years ago had value. Something changed deep within me that day. The radiance I had cast into my unconscious mind decades before shimmered a little brighter, lighting my way.

When I accepted an executive manager's position in the Capital Group, the pace of life accelerated. Yianni and I settled into a "work hard, party hard" lifestyle, expending vast blocks of time and energy into the business and pleasuring ourselves with the rewards. A hectic travel schedule, nation-wide for business and internationally for leisure, filled our calendars. We had found our rhythm and attracted success into our lives.

I knew that every person, place or enterprise resonated to its own level of Consciousness and that energy determined what was drawn to it. Successful people, places and enterprises attract more success. The challenge to succeed lies not in what we do, but in the energy, we embody and expend. As Yianni and I expanded our Consciousness, we energized our lives, personally and professionally. We'd each longed for a partner who matched us and now that we'd found each other, we were unstoppable.

A few days before my forty-sixth birthday, I returned home after being at dinner with a girlfriend and our house reverberated with shouts of "Surprise!" Yianni had gathered about sixty of our friends to celebrate my birthday. During the festivities, my girlfriend instructed me to sit on a chair in front of the guests. Everyone hushed when Yianni, dressed in a black tux, strode into the room singing Elvis Presley's "The Wonder of You."

On the final note, he dropped on bended knee and removed a ring box from his jacket.

My breath hitched. *Oh no.*

When he opened it, his dark eyes twinkled, "Diane, will you marry me?"

Everyone gasped while I struggled to breathe.

The voice of a dear female friend of over twenty years chimed from the crowd. "Be careful, Diane."

I never wanted to get married again and had made my intentions clear to Yianni on numerous occasions. Yet, as usual, he had his own plans. How do you say no to someone who has given you so much? To someone who loves you. To someone you love in return. After a brief pause and on the advice from my still, small voice within, I accepted his proposal and the surprise birthday party turned into an impromptu engagement party. Cunning as a fox, my fiancé's strategy had proven faultless, and he'd captured the hen in the coop.

A wedding followed on Valentine's Day the following year. Although we wanted to marry on the twenty-ninth of February, as it was the date we'd met four years earlier, that date was already booked. So, we chose the fourteenth instead. Yet another omen. It was the same date that *Starz* had opened at the casino eighteen years before. Eighteen years. I'd completely turned my life around and dared to be all I came here to be. Both *Starz* and my marriage to Yianni were life-changing, magical events. They both held the promise of a brighter future and abundant harvests. However, with my marriage, I was more conscious of *being* and better equipped to fulfil my destiny.

Finally living my girlhood dream of a white wedding with bridesmaids and all the trimmings, Natalie and Yianni's two youngest sons joined the bridal party as bridesmaid and groomsmen. When the chant began, I stepped over the threshold and glided down the aisle of the Greek Orthodox Church. Veiled, crowned and clutching an enormous bouquet of white lilies like my mother had done nearly sixty years earlier at her wedding, I was overwhelmed with the energy coursing through my body. By the time I reached my adoring fiancé at the altar, I trembled with such spiritual elation the priest asked if I was nervous.

"No," I said with a radiant smile. "Not at all."

If I told him I was channeling the Holy Spirit he'd think me mad.

Men of the cloth often have a hard time witnessing what they try to convince us to believe. My maid of honor, my best girlfriend of forty years, stared at me, concerned my flowers were going to shake out of my hands. We had grown up together as dancers, and she'd never seen me tremble with nerves over anything.

"Are you all right?" she whispered, eyeing off the St. Vitus dance of the lilies.

"Never better," I whispered back. It took every ounce of my willpower to channel the energy and not throw the flowers into the air and dance around the altar in wild abandon. I wanted to sing to the heavens, to grow angel wings and fly to the balcony. Instead, I surrendered to the euphoria without trying to suppress it or analyze it. During the thirty-minute ceremony, the energy subsided, but the love and joy didn't. I was *being* in it. I was *being*.

After the service and on our way home for photographs, Yianni and I chatted happily in the back of the wedding car. "When did you know you wanted to marry me?" I asked.

His eyes glittered, soft and sincere. "The moment I met you. I had been searching for you all my life, and I knew I couldn't let you slip away."

Pieces of the cryptic conversations I'd heard in my meditations over the past four years fell into place. My wedding day was more than a promise of a fulfilling, successful future. It was the culmination of four years of trusting my guidance, of having faith that this was where I was meant to *be* despite how hard the ego tried to convince me otherwise, and most importantly, of daring to love.

There had been times when I wanted to walk away, to not be a man's therapist or life coach again, to focus on just *being*. But Yianni's love and insistence on our remaining together, my conversations with the goddess and my willingness to listen, trust and keep the faith manifested in a marriage of unfolding Consciousness.

Insights...Be kind, Be intuitive, Be flexible

Thinking kind thoughts, speaking kind words and embodying kind actions begins the process of being kind. The more kindness we demonstrate to ourselves and our lives, the more kindness we have to share with each other. Imagine if everyone waiting in queues at airports, bus stops, taxi ranks etcetera, spent those moments in solitude, focusing on kind, loving thoughts rather than their phones. I'm sure there'd be an increase in spontaneous acts of kindness which would, in turn, change people's lives. Being unconsciously and constantly connected to our electronic devices disconnects us from our *being*, and from humanity. Looking for the opportunity to perform random acts of kindness reconnects us with *being* and expands our Consciousness.

Being intuitive is a quality we each possess, but due to our conditioned thinking we lose touch with our intuitive nature, and in doing so, we miss messages of real importance. Intuition is often referred to as gut instinct, because the sensation of being intuitive resides in the solar plexus' region. Whenever I make a decision, I check in to see what my intuition tells me. If there's a sense of peaceful calm in my solar plexus, then I'm on the right track. If there's an unsettled, swirling energy, then I need to reassess my choice or action. When in doubt, don't.

We develop our intuitive nature in silent solitude and by listening to the still, small voice within. When we switch off everything else, including the chatter of our mind and reside in peace, we let love guide our actions, rather than relying on our best thinking.

But what if we haven't developed our intuitive nature so well? Then we must use our common sense and be flexible enough to change ourselves, our thinking and our approach. A rigid mindset hinders being intuitive.

In my case, I listened to my intuition and dared to be flexible and change once Yianni appeared in my life. During this time, there were several forks in the road. Every step along the way, the only assurance I had of making the right choice was the still, small voice within and the escalating omens pointing me in the direction of this new role. The ego certainly raised its head on occasion, but there was nothing for me to do, but *be*.

On Valentine's Day 2004, in a moment that seemed destined, The Goddess of Love finally married her Greek God. This enchanting image from our wedding day captures the culmination of a journey filled with love and serendipity, as if the universe itself conspired to bring our hearts together in perfect harmony. It was a day when myth met reality, and we embarked on our lifelong odyssey, arm in arm.

CHAPTER NINETEEN
Fulfillment and success

During the first three years of married life, we lived, loved and worked well. Just as I'd visualized and written in my journals years before, my intention to live the good life manifested. The Capital Group grew more successful, and we won numerous accolades, including state and national gold awards for business in 2005, 2006 and 2007, as well as other local business excellence awards in these years.

During all this achievement, there were certain things I wouldn't compromise—my own private time and space. Whether I was meditating, dancing, teaching private dance classes, reading or writing, I carved out time to *be*. I knew the insidiousness with which the busyness of doing and having could swallow my life and had experienced firsthand how the ego dragged out the "too busy" excuse to disconnect me from my *being*.

I knew the value of the advice I had given clients who made excuses not to exercise, or meditate, or read, or grow. "It's far easier not to do something good for yourself, than it is to do it. Far easier to sit on the couch, watch mindless media and allow your thoughts to turn to mush, than to become self-educated and empowered. But the long-term rewards for those who make the effort and stretch past their comfort zone far outweigh the results of laziness. Like sugar, laziness gives quick-fix highs only to drag you into all-day lows. If you dream of success and fulfillment you must motivate yourself. If you can't, you will live a life of mediocrity no matter how clever, talented or creative you are. Living a fulfilled, successful life is about expanding your Consciousness and valuing *being* above all else. We are either waking up or dreaming a dream."

Travel to exotic, wondrous locations like Africa, Egypt, Dubai, Italy and China broadened our minds and connected us with people and cultures vastly different from our own. It also reconfirmed that despite our seeming differences, we're all interconnected at the level of *being*. Yianni and I experienced many life-changing adventures, but for me, those that included the animal kingdom were the highlights. Personal encounters with elephants outside our tent at night while they tiptoed over the tent pegs, feeding giraffes face to face as their slippery blue tongues licked the food pellet from my mouth and immersing myself in the untouched beauty of the natural world in remote places filled my heart with boundless joy.

Not surprisingly, it was during these years that our family gained a new member—the golden child, a clever little shih tzu we named Koko joined our five-year-old Persian cat, Precious. The later addition of another shih tzu, Chanel, and a border collie, Gypsy, took our furry head count to four, adding an endless source of love and entertainment to our lives. Since Yianni's children hadn't grown up with pets, our furry family gave them a wonderful opportunity to connect with animals and realize the important role they play in life. I have no doubt being surrounded by pets at our home contributed to their being kinder, more considerate and responsible adults. The unconditional love given by furry children is a healing balm.

One Easter, I was surrounded by my furry and two human families celebrating at our home. With my mother, my biological mother, my three half-siblings and their two girls, and Yianni's two youngest sons seated at the dining table for Easter Sunday lunch, I gave thanks for our wonderful life. Everyone chatted and feasted while the puppies lay sleeping at my feet. I watched the scene around me and knew this was family…all of them. It had nothing to do with bloodlines, nothing to do with names, nothing to do with birth or growing up together. Family is a feeling of connectedness, family is Consciousness expressed, and family is love. I scanned their happy faces, and for a fleeting moment, felt transported to a time when we'd done this all before. Different place, different forms, but the experience of being together was real. At the other end of the table, Yianni lifted his head and smiled. I was home.

Our first wedding anniversary introduced us to Vanuatu in the South Pacific, where good friends had recently relocated. This pristine tropical island archipelago, which existed in a time warp devoid of easily accessible connectivity, was awarded the global title as the happiest place on earth.

Flying low on our landing path toward Bauerfield International, I gazed out at a place that time had forgotten. "We're going to buy a block of land here."

Trepidation creased Yianni's brow. "Let's just get off the plane first."

"We'll buy a block of land here before we leave." Of that, I was certain.

Our friends had booked us into a quaint boutique resort, located on 239,000 square feet of lush property edged by thousands of square feet of ocean-front, white-sand beach. The next morning when Yianni and I rose, we opened the door of our coral cottage and stepped outside into sparkling daylight. Green grass, white sand and blue ocean spanned our one-hundred-and-eighty-degree view.

"Wouldn't you like to own this place?" we said in unison, enchanted by the resort's untouched natural beauty and unhurried lifestyle. We were hooked.

Within a week, we'd bought 43,000 square feet of beachfront land just down the road from the resort, with the intention of one day retiring to the island.

Not long after this, and because of the country's stable government, strong growth and investment opportunities, we partnered with our friends and invested in an innovative residential building project in the capital, Port Vila. Our life branched in directions we'd not previously considered, and we strapped ourselves in for the ride. We raced into 2007, dividing our time between our Australian and Vanuatu businesses.

It had been half a century since I'd come hurtling into this incarnation, fifty years dancing up the stairway to paradise and expanding my Consciousness. Rather than looking back on where the last fifty years went, I kept my focus resolutely on the future, while living in the present. I knew life wasn't measured in years, but in Consciousness. I certainly wasn't going to allow the negative concept of age or aging to influence me. Some people would say I'd reached a milestone, a time to slow down, not work so hard and allow the inevitable grim reaper through the door. After all, by the time you're fifty you're on the downhill slide.

Absolutely not! Chronologically, I figured I was about halfway through this lifetime, with the best yet to come. Like an experienced jeweler, I had polished my physical, mental, emotional, spiritual and financial facets over all these years. My Consciousness continued urging me to stretch and grow, to be the fuller expression of *being*. For me, turning fifty meant all the repetition had paid off and my life with all its love, health and bountiful rewards was living proof of that. Although my life had manifested in some ways differently to how I envisaged it would, the outer results were indicative of my inner growth.

I celebrated my fiftieth birthday at the little resort in Vanuatu with a dozen of my closest friends where we partied for three days under the tropical sun and in the warm, blue waters of the Pacific Ocean. A glorious highlight of my life, but it didn't surpass the birthday present awaiting me back home.

The Capital Group was a benefactor of the Dalai Lama's visit to Australia, and we were given the opportunity of meeting him. On the Brisbane leg of his tour, Yianni and I waited with about sixty nuns, monks and other benefactors in a private function room at the Brisbane Entertainment Centre. Eventually, his minders arrived. They presented each of us with a white rectangular scarf, a *khata*, which they explained we were to offer to His Holiness as he passed. He would then recite a blessing, place the *khata* around our necks and move on to the next person. They said not to expect an up-close-and-personal encounter as meeting His Holiness was a fluid affair because he was prone to change his mind and do something completely different. When they finished explaining the correct protocol, we lined up like eager schoolchildren.

By the time His Holiness shuffled in, the room buzzed with energy. His face was creased in his signature smile as if he lived in a perpetual state of amusement, which I've no doubt he did. I glanced at those nearby, and like me, they could barely contain their joy. His enlightened Consciousness touched everyone, opening our hearts and minds. The same energy which had blasted my body on my wedding day took up residence once more.

When I bowed my head on his approach, His Holiness took my hand and moved to a row of chairs. Drawing me beside him, he nodded to his entourage. Though obviously surprised by his move, they hurried everyone into position for a group photograph.

Throughout this shuffling, he clung to my hand, chatting and laughing with me. I was dumbstruck. He was *being* with me. His grip was certain, his skin was soft, cool and delicate. We sat straight-backed like children in a school photo, me with the biggest grin. His hand never released mine until after the photographer nodded.

His Holiness rose, turned to the group and bowed. "*Namaste*."

He shuffled from the room, leaving everyone enthralled by the brief encounter. Many came over and asked about my experience.

"What was it like?"

"How did it feel?"

"I wish it'd been me."

"Wow, how lucky are you?"

Yianni stood to one side, an enigmatic smile on his face. He knew it wasn't luck. It was the law of attraction. I couldn't have hoped for a better birthday present. In His Holiness choosing me, he acted as the best omen I could receive. Bring on the next fifty years.

Insights…Be inspired, Be valuable, Be intelligent

It was 2007. I was fifty human years old and had spent two decades on my conscious quest for truth and personal enlightenment. My rich, rewarding life was a continual testament to this. Meeting the Dalai Lama and being in his extraordinary presence reaffirmed that love was the common denominator in everything.

With love comes inspiration, the state of being inspired or "in spirit." Inspiration is the essence of fulfillment, and without fulfillment, success is hollow. My inspiration guided me in expressing the creativity of my *being*, for throughout all these years, I'd continued with my first love of dancing and choreographing. My body had responded and none of the freedom or exhilaration of the dance had waned. The music and the movement still filled me with love and illuminated my *being*. Writing also continued to inspire, and I knew that one day my books would be published when I placed my full intention and attention into my writing career. Inspiration, imagination and intuition weren't something happening to me, but me happening to me.

In whatever form it takes, the creative expression of our *being* is critical to expanding our Consciousness. It's the portion of our Consciousness which we haven't yet embraced which guides us through this intuitive creativity and opens us to be more. Too many people give up connecting with their inspiration as they get older. They mistakenly believe they're too busy with the kids, work, family and commitments to give themselves any time to play the guitar, paint, sing or engage in the creative expression or project. It's this sacrificing of the very thing which identifies our *being*, that limits our Consciousness. When we reconnect with our creative expression, we rediscover joy, playfulness, hope and love, and our Consciousness expands.

Patanjali wrote, "When you are inspired by some great purpose, some extraordinary project, all your thoughts break their bonds, your mind transcends limitations, your consciousness expands in every direction and you find yourself in a new, great and wonderful world. Dormant forces, faculties and talents come alive and you discover yourself to be a greater person by far than you ever dreamed yourself to be."

With love comes being valuable and aspiring to help others, for there is little fulfillment without service.

How can I serve the greater good? Whenever I was unsure as to which direction I should take, I'd ask this question. I knew that if I followed the guidance given in response to this question, I'd align with the unfolding of my *being* and it would be the right direction for me. Until we're willing to accept our own value and *be* of value and of service to others, very little of value will manifest in our lives.

Fulfillment and success cannot be forced into reality. They manifest as the consequence of the loving intention and attention we give to *being*. When we set aside time to go within, to meditate, connect and reflect, we move beyond the habits of ignorance which prevent us from living the good life. It is us who make our lives successful and fulfilling. No one else; most certainly, there's no such thing as dumb luck. Yet many people believe they are unlucky. They feel separate from their lives, believing they're powerless, and that while success and fulfillment bless others, they are left to struggle.

With such limiting beliefs, these people often feel resentful. They accuse, criticize and blame successful people as if they are somehow responsible for their lowly lot. Suffering from a deep-rooted sense of inequality, they fail to understand that we are all equal. We are all Consciousness expressing itself. We're all *being*. There is no more or less. There is only *being*. We must stop defining prosperity and success as something separate from ourselves, as something we have no power over.

Like everything, success is energy. It's a state of mind, a state of *being*. If we are expanding our Consciousness, aligning ourselves to our *being* and supporting it with action, we are living in the space of prosperity consciousness.

Because we're adding value and *being* more, we attract more success into our lives. This success manifests in different forms, as people, opportunities, money, a new job or contract, or a loving relationship. Conversely, if our habits focus on lack and limitation, we dwell in the space of poverty consciousness, and we reap reciprocal results.

Everyone experiences exactly the amount of success and abundance they can justify receiving. Whether we live with prosperity or poverty consciousness, the law of attraction still applies. Whatever philosophy, values, beliefs, perceptions, thoughts, feelings, emotions and decisions we embody and energize, will return to us, like for like. Sending out the desire for more money to pay the bills, when all we think about is how much money we don't have is nothing but wishful thinking.

If we desire more money, we must disregard our conditioning of lack and limitation, expand our Consciousness and *be* the embodiment which draws in the money. Just because we wish for it, doesn't make it happen. Thought can only attract to us that which we continuously enact, embody and energize. If we only work for money, without any enjoyment or fulfillment, then we're trapped in poverty consciousness. We'll never have enough money; we'll never find time to enjoy money and no amount of money will ever be able to compensate for the lack we feel in our lives.

Money isn't the root of all evil. Poverty consciousness is. Worrying over, talking about and acting out how much we don't have or why we can't afford something, only ingrains poverty consciousness in ourselves and our family. When we realize we're not dealing with the form of money or success, but with the energy of abundance and supply, we graduate into a new level of prosperity Consciousness.

Once we know that our *being* is the source of our supply and abundance, we need only align ourselves with it and move forward. Abundance and supply always respond when the desire and dreams that we dare to fling into Consciousness, reflect the fulfillment of our *being*. That is why it's so important to listen, lean into our intuition, look for the omens, follow their lead and then let it *be*. Trust and faith are powerful partners in generating a successful, fulfilling life.

One of the saddest things is this misperception of lack, particularly with money. I had no money at the beginning of my conscious quest. No one would employ me due to my reputation as a troublemaker and whistle-blower. Instead of wallowing in what I didn't have, I dusted myself off, dared to change and went in search of how not to *be* in that situation. I didn't expect anyone to do it for me. I did the personal work in order to attract in the professional work. If I had sacrificed my responsibility, freedom and independence to "crying poor," I would still be living a life of lack.

There is law, order, harmony and an infinite intelligence to the universe—the same intelligence which constitutes our *being*. Try as we might to ignore this infinite intelligence, we can no more change or manipulate it than we can change the rotation of the earth. As such, the power that flows through infinite intelligence flows through us, demonstrating in our reality. Once we align ourselves with this power, accepting our inseparable connection to it, our results will reflect our blossoming prosperity consciousness. Our wealth never far exceeds our Consciousness. Once we dare to embrace ourselves as indivisible from our success and fulfillment, we make it so.

Meeting, marrying and working with Yianni demonstrated this principle manifesting in my life. Out of a matrix of infinite universal possibilities he manifested, representing the mirror image of all I had become. Together we reaped the harvest we sowed. Because we were both functioning within our destinies and the unfoldment of our *being*, love, magic, miracles, mystery, success and fulfillment abounded in our lives. Content but never complacent, we celebrated our success with resolve and gratitude, sharing it with others.

Yet as our Consciousness expanded, a sharp hairpin turn lay in wait down our yellow brick road.

In a moment of profound serenity and connection, captured here on my 50th birthday, I experienced the rare and humbling honour of holding hands with His Holiness the Dalai Lama. This extraordinary gesture symbolized an unmistakable milestone in my journey and was testament to the unexpected, yet deeply meaningful encounters that life can bring.

CHAPTER TWENTY
Setting the trap

We worked by the ant philosophy. Ants never quit. They think winter all summer. They think summer all winter. And ants gather as much as they can. We had no intention of trading this attitude for regrets. Having lived and energized this philosophy over the previous seven years, the beginning of the next life cycle commenced with further success. Years of intention, attention and action now manifested in our winning a major contract on which we had focused our energy for three years.

Elated, we launched Capital Parking. A national domestic airport parking business, it was one of the airline industry's gold-standard contracts with a leading Australian airline. With only an eight-week lead time, we set to work on the necessary planning, systems and recruitment of nearly two hundred staff in readiness for a massive four-state takeover from the previous company. At the stroke of midnight on the designated day, four teams of our people began the process of bumping in the business across the country, ready for the first customers to check-in at 5AM. A mammoth logistical endeavor.

Though the handover progressed smoothly in three of the four states, in the remaining site we were plagued with internal sabotage, theft and resistance to change by some of the previous company's staff we had retained. Since hard work wasn't something we shied away from, Yianni and I remained interstate dealing with this demanding time, working day and night to minimize the risk and impact to the business and customers. Being able to withstand the staggering blows of this ongoing debacle proved demanding, but I knew challenge provided those with the courage to face it with vast opportunities to grow. It reminded me of the quote by Roger Crawford, "Being challenged in life is inevitable, being defeated is optional."

Throughout this period, we met the challenge a day at a time until we triumphed. Finally, a month later, we returned home and proceeded to manage the business with a hand-picked, excellent team of managers and staff, who over the years, added great value to the business and its customers.

It proved that people are integral to success. None of us can do it alone. Whether you're a one-woman show or managing hundreds or thousands of employees, you'll always be in contact with people. Like the weaving of an epic tapestry, it requires many different threads to create the intricacy and beauty of the design. Similarly, it takes many people to weave success. Staff, customers, suppliers, colleagues and stakeholders…people are inseparable from success.

If you can communicate your vision to people and persuade them to stand with you as you enter the dark night of the soul, you'll produce the brightest stars. This new business provided me with the opportunity to lead and empower others to reach for personal and professional excellence, and in return, they became my brightest stars.

As the General Manager of Capital Parking, my role extended into every facet of the business and produced a sixty-to-eighty-hour-week workload, which I threw myself into with unrestrained passion.

Years previously, I had dreamed of owning a theater restaurant; a business which, based on the resonance of energy, would demonstrate success and fulfilment. Although the theater restaurant never manifested, the dream did. It crept up on me in the guise of a national car parking business. One that I never thought I'd be involved in, but one which gave me the opportunity to manage on the principles I embodied and energized. It was one of the most rewarding times of my life.

Certainly, there were challenges through the first couple of years, not least because we still worked in our limousine business and completed the residential project in Vanuatu. There never seemed to be enough time in the day and our travel commitments meant many hours spent in the air. Nevertheless, if it was meant to be, it was up to me.

With significant success behind and before us, we led a busy and blessed life. Yianni's children were grown and branching into their own independent lives, of which we enjoyed being part, while we prospered spiritually, mentally, emotionally, physically and financially.

Unfortunately, my mother was diagnosed with early-stage dementia. Obstinate and fiercely independent, she refused to believe the diagnosis and continued in her joy of living and managed on her own with the addition of a health carer.

My biological mother died while Yianni and I were holidaying overseas. On taking the phone call from my half-sister, I stood looking out at the delphinium-blue skies in Greece. I lit a candle and placed it in the altar sand at the church we were visiting, smiling at the irony. There I was, with the Greek blood of my unknown father coursing through my veins, my Greek husband standing beside me in a Greek Orthodox Church set high on a hill in Mykonos. What better place could I be than right where I was when Gloria left this lifetime?

The year 2010 marked the beginning of one of my greatest growth spurts. As a seeker of truth and enlightened Consciousness, I had stood at the leading edge of my life for over twenty years and dared every step along the way. I'd challenged my conditioned thinking, ignored my past limitations and pressed on knowing that my dreams or something better would manifest…and they did.

My choice was still the same as it had been two decades before—dare or die, though not by suicide as it had been then. But dare to press on *being* or die of an inert Consciousness. Whether by suicide or inertia, I had no intention of dying either way.

Over the coming months, Yianni and I spent more time enjoying the fruits of our toil with friends and family. Just as life eased into a more relaxed holding pattern of elegant living, another opportunity arrived. The boutique resort in Vanuatu at which we'd been holidaying for the past five years fell into receivership. The resort's previous management had neglected this slice of paradise and now the property appeared on our radar.

It seemed a no-brainer—six private cottages nestled on 239,000 square feet of pristine ocean-front land, local staff who lived on site, an iconic well-established business and the opportunity to develop it further into a successful venture we could manage through our planned retirement. When we stayed at the resort for the first time five years earlier, we had both commented on how we'd love to own it and grow the business. Here was that opportunity manifested before our eyes.

We decided to test the efficacy of the omen, so Yianni offered a ridiculously low purchase price. We figured the receivers wouldn't take it, but if they did, then it would be a sign for us to buy the property. While we waited for their response, I questioned the veracity of the decision to take on another project. Was this really the right course of action?

It wasn't that I questioned the obviousness of the omen. But I knew this was Yianni's dream, not mine. I was willing to support him, but I also intuited this project had the potential of being one hell of a life lesson. We discussed the pros and cons at length, and on Yianni's assurance that he was up to the challenge, I agreed to stand by him. After all, it wasn't my role to deny him his dream, his swan song. His free-will choice was as valid as mine. If I had succeeded in talking him out of buying the resort, I'm certain there would've been another challenge of equal or greater proportions lying just around the bend. Within five days an agreement was struck, and we prepared to be the proud owners of our own little piece of heaven on earth.

The resort could best be described as plucked from the pages of Somerset Maugham's *Tales of the South Pacific*—an idyllic location where guests relaxed in their veranda hammocks while being waited on by attentive staff. Where sea breezes caressed the pandanus trees along the grassed edge of the pristine white-sand beach and the tropical sun warmed the shimmering azure waters. A serene, tropical paradise landscape in which to find oneself. We planned to develop it with a gentle, authentic touch and raise the standard of living for the on-site staff.

On the flight back home, a touch of uneasiness settled in my stomach. When I mentioned this to Yianni he recapped the positives. Capital Parking was thriving and producing record months of revenue. The resort's purchase price was terrific value for money and the investment prospects for Vanuatu and its tourism industry were solid. I remained quietly cautious and we began planning this next phase of our lives. Side by side, we would see this project into the future, giving us the perfect space and place in which to unwind in the years to come.

As successful business owners, we knew that the biggest challenge in any business was finding good staff. Recruiting and training a resort manager became our number-one priority as well as managing the myriad operational and business requirements. We contracted an experienced manager who had worked previously at another resort in Vanuatu and began the handover from the prior managers to our new manager. We expected this process to be seamless. However, this wasn't the case, as on their departure from the resort they divested the business of everything, leaving us with nothing but two paper clips—an action which saw them taken to court by angry receivers.

Their action impacted our start-up significantly, leaving us to launch the business from scratch. Not a booking remained, no customer or supplier contacts, no computers, no files, nothing. Added to that, they absconded with our head chef, who broke his contract with us, leaving the resort in an untenable position. Weakened by these events and with only a limited pool of talent available, we forged forward. The next blow came when our new resort manager smashed the rental vehicle we'd supplied him. Witnesses stated he was drunk when he fled the scene. He was never seen again, but we heard he left the island the next day.

Yianni and I gritted our teeth. We knew success was an energy which resulted when we perceived impossible problems as challenges, then as opportunities and finally as success. No one triumphs without overcoming challenges. We had done it before, and we'd do it again.

We endured this baptism by fire in a third-world country which was obviously not the happiest place on earth when you tried to operate a first-world business, and enacted Joseph P. Kennedy's advice, "When the going gets tough, the tough get going."

Having no replacement manager in sight, Yianni and I played country tag, spending three weeks each in Vanuatu managing the resort while the other remained in Australia managing our other businesses. Like ships in the night, we passed each other at airports once every few weeks when we swapped countries. This lasted for over six months while we searched for a decent manager or management couple. Moreover, we'd begun a major house renovation before we bought the resort. These building works were underway and couldn't be delayed. Although taxing, neither of us buckled under the pressure because our attention remained firmly on the growth of the resort, our future and ourselves. There was no turning back. We had to see it through.

Nine months in, we were up to our third resort manager and finally found a reputable chef. While all this transpired, I launched a massive tourism marketing campaign with major travel wholesalers, inbound tour operators and wedding specialists to increase international business. Due to a malicious island grapevine, several of the local expats who'd previously frequented the resort never returned. We later found out the prior managers blamed us for the receivers' court case, ensuring a large portion of the expat community no longer supported us. Still we juggled the resort, our major businesses in Australia, my ailing mother and a spiraling house renovation.

Just before her ninetieth birthday, Mum suffered a massive heart attack. Unfortunately, I was stranded at the resort and unable to get an immediate flight home. Speaking with the surgeon on the phone, I authorized him to operate and insert stents into her heart, and prayed she was strong enough to recover. By the time I arrived at her bedside the next evening, she was recuperating. However, the general anesthetic affected her thinking processes, escalating the dementia. With no other recourse, I placed her in respite care, where she stayed for a month before returning home to her unit.

When I waved goodbye on her first day at the hostel, I wanted nothing more than to have some respite myself. My intuition prompted me to curl up in the bed beside her, like we'd done all those years ago when I was a little girl, and she'd read stories to me at bedtime. The memory was as sweet as her gentle smile. But at the time, I was so wrapped up in being busy instead of *being* love, I denied us both that intimate pleasure of *being* together. Driving off, I scolded myself. Given the chance again, I'd take her in my arms and gift us both with that simple gesture.

The balance had shifted. The world was in a freefall from the global financial crisis and as such, many catastrophic events transpired due to collective conditioned fear and poverty consciousness. When major banking players stumbled in the US, their downward movement reverberated across the world. The energy shift in the macrocosm was palpable, and we experienced its rippling effect in the microcosm of our lives.

In Australia, the airline to which we were contracted underwent a crippling grounding which sliced deeply into our revenue stream. This impacted our ability to financially prop up the resort when required. In Vanuatu, road infrastructure changed, leaving our resort stranded from the new ring road around the island. Our passing trade was lost, and our access road remained neglected by the local council. Moreover, the resort still suffered the after-effects of the initial difficulties from its first eighteen months of operation.

Global and individual Consciousness stretched and groaned as people grappled with fear and growth. The Buddhists refer to it as monkey mind—undisciplined and agitated thoughts, anxieties, worries and fears swinging from branch to branch in our minds. At this time on the planet, the monkey mind had a wicked old time, collectively and individually.

I dared to lean into the circumstances and conditions around us, knowing that what was happening had no real, significant impact on my *being*. The biggest challenge was that Yianni had become consumed by the external world, leaving me to paddle a one-person boat of trust and faith. I clung ferociously to *being* while I railed against his reluctance to acknowledge the truth. Although I knew I wasn't responsible for his enlightenment, the ego convinced me that life would be easier if he wasn't so goddamn stubborn. The trap was set, and with my eyes wide open, I was lured into it.

It was at the end of this year that my body launched its first blow across my physical bow as a warning signal. While relaxing together under our Christmas tree, I sprang to my feet, angry at something he'd said. When I turned, I wrenched my right knee and buckled in excruciating pain. Most would see this as a freak accident, but I knew better. The message was as shatteringly acute as the pain.

The past couple of years could be likened to a philosophy of, life is like a buffet, except we'd piled more on our plates than we could handle. I was angry at myself for allowing this to happen. I was angry that I felt guilty whenever I wanted to opt out, to just *be* and reconnect with my peace. I was angry that I couldn't control Yianni, and I was angry at letting anger, frustration and resentment become squatters in my thoughts again.

Like a mouse in a wheel, I ran around and around, not getting anywhere and it was my fault. I'd left the door to my Consciousness cracked open and the ego had made a targeted assault on it.

Knowing I needed rest, I took a few weeks off. While I hobbled around on crutches, there was no other option but to give in, to let my life *be*. What really needed recovery wasn't just my knee, but my Consciousness. With all the busyness of the past couple of years, I'd forfeited my peace and allowed my Consciousness to stagnate. I'd allowed myself to come off track and had ignored the whispers to slow down and go within, illogically thinking I had too much to do, and I couldn't let Yianni down.

How proud and egotistical was I? Full of self-importance, I figured that I would rest and reconnect when things got better. The ego had captured my attention, and I'd become obsessed with doing. Playing into its misgivings and misperceptions until, seduced by its illusion,

I sacrificed my peace. I'd become so caught up in everything, I'd forgotten the most important thing—my *being*. Pride comes before a fall and my wrenched knee felled me.

With my underpinnings knocked out from under me, my *being* brought me to a grinding halt. A non-negotiable wake-up call. It proved a sharp learning curve, but one for which I was grateful. Had I not chosen to listen, regroup my senses, meditate and find my peace, poise and power from within again, I could've manifested something much more severe than a simple knee injury as the external message. I resumed regular meditations and like welcoming a good friend home, my peace returned without blame or judgment. As my peace grew stronger, so did my Consciousness and my knee. My external recovery was the result of my internal revitalization.

Eventually, I discarded my crutches and began to set pace once more, albeit at a slower, more conscious rate. I committed to not give my power away to the ego, a person or situation no matter how seductive the payoff of anger, blame, control or righteous indignation appeared. My injury had proven a tough lesson. At fifty-five, I received negative opinions from doctors who thought my knee would never make a full recovery and that I was expecting too much from my body.

"You'll never be able to dance again."

"You're too old."

"Just as long as you can get around, be happy with that at your age."

I all but leaped across one doctor's desk, furious at his condescending attitude. I was the master of my destiny and knew that life wasn't measured in years, but in Consciousness. As such, I ignored their limited, medical opinions.

Over the following months, I retreated within, reaffirming my perfect health and expanding my Consciousness. In direct proportion to my return to *being*, my knee's flexibility, power and strength returned. Within a couple of months, I unfurled my gossamer spirit wings and stepped onto the dance floor. Tentative yet faithful, I was confident my knee would support me once more in my beloved dancing. And despite medical opinion to the contrary, it did and has continued to do so.

From a business perspective, the beginning of 2012 proved promising at the resort as our new manager, chef and administration manager settled into a steady rhythm. We had found a team who worked tirelessly on building the business and who valued personal and professional excellence. Producing special events and flying in Australian entertainers to perform in them, I managed my resort responsibilities more remotely than in the previous years. With local expats returning and a growing international customer base, the resort blossomed.

Although Yianni and I still traveled regularly each month and juggled our businesses, house renovations and my mother's worsening health, I carved out space in my life. I made time for me again, without the guilt and angst of having to be in control and fix everything. Personal and universal space yawned open within me like a peaceful chasm filled with inspiration. Out of which resurfaced my other great love, writing.

Over the past few years, I'd shelved my creative writing projects to produce the necessary business proposals, tenders, strategic and marketing documents, and a vast number of training and quality manuals. True, I had manifested success and prosperity with Yianni, but I'd sacrificed much of my personal fulfillment. This was the real cause of my dissatisfaction and frustration. By ignoring the expression of my creative essence, I had strayed from the unfoldment of my *being*, from my destiny.

Instead of self-nourishing, I'd become self-neglecting. My expression of self-love had dried up and so too had the magic and miracles. Knowing the best company to keep was my own, I retreated within where peace, joy and inspiration embraced me. Balanced and back on the keyboard, my energy lifted while my fingers tapped away in an inspired frenzy. Creativity flowed and the ego sulked out the back door, deflated but not defeated.

Over the next twelve months, the energy in Vanuatu changed radically. Not long after the introduction of the global telco, Digicel, the government destabilized. Corrupt politicians and repeated elections triggered a domino effect which began to topple investment. Reading the signs, we decided to sell the resort and reclaim our lives back in Australia. With the energy of the country in a tailspin, our manager and chef resigned at the end of their two-year contract. The island had taken its toll on their psyche, and they returned to their familiar lifestyle back home.

Our professional and personal responsibilities demanded more than ever and the desire to be free of the resort weighed heavily on Yianni's mind. While he battled with the ego, I removed myself as best I could. Trying to live emotionally detached from him while he waged war against himself was difficult. Some days I was up to the task of holding the energy of love for both of us, while other times I ran out of patience and succumbed to the ego's blame game. My daily meditation ritual proved the perfect panacea. It was where I reconnected with my *being* and listened to the whispered words of wisdom I'd long come to trust.

Our completed renovations proved a welcome blessing. Aside from realizing our dream home with plenty of space for visiting friends and family, I included a Zen room in the project—a sacred space where technology was banned, and peace reigned supreme. Using Feng Shui principles, I incorporated the elements of water, fire, earth and air into the Japanese-inspired garden outside. Filled with candles, incense, tarot cards and other tools for meditation, relaxation and introspection, the Zen room exemplified my dream of a spiritual sanctuary. I retreated into its resonance daily and encouraged Yianni to join me. Although not often, whenever he did, he found a brief respite from his rising stress levels.

Predictably, the more I reconnected with my *being*, the more I longed to follow my destiny. During a meditation, the name Bryce Courtenay bubbled to the surface. Following the lead, I bought his latest novel at the time, *Jack of Diamonds*. On finishing the book, I discovered this would be his last novel due to his terminal stomach-cancer diagnosis.

Researching more about the author, I discovered he didn't start his fiction writing career until he was fifty-six. This was the omen—I was fifty-six. I'd been dabbling with my writing for years, and now was the time to give it my committed attention and intention. A new chapter in my life was calling.

Throughout the coming days, weeks and months, I fulfilled my business obligations, but instead of taking time off at night, I remained in my office, absorbed in my new destiny, feeling the energy resonate in my body. Once more I followed the still, small voice from within and signed up for online creative writing courses and workshops for the remainder of this year. I was back on track and my increasing energy levels proved it.

While I experienced the freedom and independence available to everyone when they reconnect with their peace, power, purpose and passion, Yianni's ego battles intensified. His moods darkened as his impatience and frustration grew, lowering an oppressive curtain over our marriage. No matter how I tried to lighten the energy or encourage him, the ego sucked out his life force. I empathized because I remembered how I'd felt all those years ago.

But having been there, I knew that when we feel ourselves shoved in the corner and think we're going crazy, we're actually standing on the leading edge of illumination. Hidden in our darkest hours, burn our brightest revelations. If we dare to go beyond the terror of these dark moments, our conditioned thinking and limited, human perspective finally desert us. And in their place, revelation happens.

Dr. Wayne W. Dyer wrote, "The essence of greatness is the ability to choose personal fulfillment in circumstances when others choose madness."

Insights...Be creative, Be gentle, Be intimate, Be balanced

The ego is illegitimate. Either everything is energy, the activity of Consciousness, the expression of love, or it isn't. The assumption that we are somehow separated from this energy, this Consciousness, this love, is a lie. The ego cannot exist of its own volition. It's the ultimate trickster, because it hasn't any existence to defend. It's merely that part of our Consciousness which we haven't embraced or accepted yet. It's disowned *being*.

Therefore, it's needy and greedy for our attention. We mustn't be fooled by its insistence that what's going on around us in our external world requires all our attention. In its insatiable efforts to get our attention, its actions are corruptive and corrosive. If the ego hooks us into thinking that it's the real us and that our circumstances and conditions are the real world, we're in an active state of denying the truth, which is our indivisibility from Consciousness, from *being*.

Our *being* is constantly calling into play our capacity to recognize this truth.

Our *being* is constantly daring us to be the fullest expression of Consciousness.

Our *being* is constantly affirming to us that love is real, while fear is not.

Despite knowing all this, over these last couple of years I had sacrificed my peace and had allowed the ego to convince me that *doing* was more important than *being*. Even as this happened, there was a part of me that recognized what was going on. I shifted my attention back and forth, between living from ego and living from *being*. My balance was off, which was the deeper meaning of my knee injury. I was off balance with my *being* and my body reflected it. Instead of balancing spirit and will, inspiration and discipline, love and law, beauty and reason, feeling and intellect, knowledge and intuition, the scales had shifted. I'd allowed the ego to take control, and in all the *doing*, I'd neglected my *being*. Yet even through it all, I dared to trust that I was going through some sort of a transition into transformation, which one day, would lead to transcendence. I clung onto *being*, hoping that soon I might truly master my life.

Mastery is to give, receive and be loved right in the face of madness and adversity. Mastery comes when we allow the world of circumstances and conditions to do its little jig while we remain in the peaceful space of *being*. This doesn't mean we walk around in a dopey daze as if stoned. On the contrary, if we respond to our world from our *being*, our true self is revealed.

That which lies beyond our sense of limitation isn't beyond our capacity to understand and comprehend. We must each dare to step beyond our limited, human perspective, in order to experience a new frame of reference, so we can master our lives.

Just like the space between the bars of a cell signify freedom to the prisoner, so does space in our lives. No matter how distracting the external world appears, no matter how many bars of busyness seem to imprison us, we must choose for space so we can be free from our conditioned thinking and limitations. We must dare to be gentle and intimate with ourselves, each other and our world. To stand undefended against our good, daring to see the goodness in others. We must tread softly and be balanced in our life, always giving ourselves time to be creative and go within.

If you've traveled to or lived in highly populated countries, you'll have experienced the discomfort of not having enough personal space. Bodies crammed against bodies on public transport, bustling along the street or queuing for hours can feel energetically overwhelming. Whether it's physical as in overpopulated spaces, or mental as in the negative thoughts swinging through our minds, or emotional as in the topsy-turvy states of fear-based emotions, we lack the spiritual space to *be*. While we jam, cram and slam more stuff into our lives, we sacrifice our space, our peace and our *being*.

Just when Yianni and I had created the space in which to live elegantly, we bought the resort. Following the omens and with the best business practices, we cultivated the resort physically, emotionally, mentally and spiritually to produce a space in which our staff, guests, and we could enjoy. The challenge wasn't in making the resort work. That was the easy part. The challenge was to *be* the space within ourselves in the process. For without space, there can be no peace.

I'm not suggesting that without a physical space we cannot find peace. On the contrary, each of us *is* the space in our lives. It lies within us, and we access it through meditation. Every time we shift our attention from the bars of busyness to the space of solitude within, we align with the unfoldment of our *being*.

I knew the challenges at this time weren't real problems. They were greater opportunities to expand the level of our Consciousness. Shifting from a finite to the infinite viewpoint meant shifting from separateness to unity, from judgment to discernment. While we sat in judgment of ourselves, each other and the apparent events going on around us, there was little space in our lives for love. Love cannot reside where there's no space for peace.

Like the latest must-have technology, judgment has been sold to us as a global solution. In fact, we feel justified to judge. We're insidiously encouraged to rate and judge what other people wear, what they do, what they say, how they look, what gender they are, what color their skin is, what age they are and what religion they worship. Banning the labels of black, white, rich, poor, man, woman, Christian or Moslem does little to remove the judgment which is the root cause, not of the words or labels, but of the separateness of which the ego has falsely convinced us. Acts of bullying, brutality, violence and global conflict are a result of judgment, of people feeling less than or more than another.

Judgment spreads like a suffocating algae bloom over our hearts, leaving no space for love. It chokes the fabric of love, removing kindness, patience, respect, compassion, tenderness and inclusiveness, and replaces them with resentment, contempt, hostility, intolerance, superiority and exile.

When we judge, we separate ourselves from our Consciousness, from our oneness, from our unity. Ultimately, we destroy ourselves and our relationships. If people are integral to success, know that every time we judge ourselves or another, that judgment acts as a silent sniper and will take down our success. We can never master our lives or our destiny while we sit in judgment.

When Yianni and I judged each other's actions, my Consciousness pushed against my limited, human perspective. During our heated debates, there were isolated times when I experienced *being*. I stepped out of the dynamic of the argument and like watching my own avatar, I witnessed the third dimensional me, stating its case. I found my avatar's performance disappointing. In witnessing my judgmental words and actions, I realized how much of a master I wasn't. In judging my husband, and vice versa, we were squeezing all the love, magic and miracles out of our marriage.

I reminded myself of the words written by Deepak Chopra, "Never forget your real identity. You are a luminous cosmic stardust being forged into the crucible of cosmic fire."

This not only applied to me, but also to Yianni. We were the same Consciousness, the same *being* unfolding itself. Regardless of our seeming differences, we were one.

And as my *being* urged me to master my life, the challenge once more was to dance up the stairway to paradise with more light, love and expanding Consciousness.

This snapshot of Yianni and me captures our delight and pride in winning another Business Excellence Award. These awards, from the years 2006 to 2008, mark significant milestones in our journey of building businesses side by side. Each trophy celebrates our partnership, dedication, and the entrepreneurial spirit that drove us to success year after year.

Nestled on the pristine shores of Southeast Efate, our resort, Tamanu on the Beach, was a slice of paradise, evoking the enchanting allure of the South Pacific. With its idyllic location perched right at the ocean's edge, this haven offered guests a serene escape, where the rhythm of the waves and the whisper of the tropical breeze created a symphony of tranquillity. Here, every view was a picturesque scene, inviting you to step into a world where time slows down and nature's beauty takes centre stage.

CHAPTER TWENTY-ONE
Let it be

Over the coming months, we ignored the ego's game of seeing each other as combatants and dared to choose for love. Despite increasing his burdens, Yianni assumed more of the remote management of the resort, and traveled back and forth, predominantly by himself. Rather than marital divorce, I divorced myself from the day-to-day stresses of the resort business, so I could follow my destiny. I still supported him as I'd always done, providing backup and advice whenever needed, but my active participation declined, giving me the space, I needed. We both continued in the management of Capital Parking, and I carved out more time to write. While I followed my dream of writing, he dealt with selling his dream of the resort. Even with three consecutive Annual Trip Advisor Excellence Awards and steady growth, the resort's sale would take longer than he wanted. There awaited another sequence of events to transform challenge to opportunity before all would be concluded.

I lived by the poet Rumi's advice, "Let yourself be silently drawn by the strange pull of what you really love. It will not lead you astray."

I studied and attended writing conferences, workshops and festivals, honing my skills and absorbing as much as I could. I had found a space where I could express my creative essence, my *being*, just as I'd done when I began dancing over half a century before. However, unlike dancing, being a writer wasn't dependent on peak physical performance, nor was it age exclusive, so it was a career to last the rest of my life.

Because I knew the law of attraction to be true, I listened, looked and leaned into the omens. Daring to place my avid attention and intention into this new career, I advanced boldly in the direction of my dream, assured that the unfoldment of my *being* would lead me every step of the way. With faith that fulfillment and success would surely follow, I pressed on.

Despite my business obligations as General Manager in Capital Parking, in less than a year I completed my first manuscript. While another two stories swirled in my mind demanding to be written as part of this series, the strangest aspect of this blossoming creative expression was the content of my first works. Having succumbed to an associate's insistence to read *Fifty Shades of Grey*, I was inspired to write a counter book about a recently divorced woman in her forties who leaps into her newfound singledom with unbridled passion. I'd rarely read romance novels and the idea of writing erotic romance had never occurred to me.

Still, I was driven to give women a story which spoke to feminine worth, confidence and sexual power. With certain similarities to my own life, the first book flew from my fingers onto the page. Yet it was not all steamy sex or emotional angst. Woven into the story was the goddess—that divine feminine aspect within me with whom I'd been conversing and expressing all these years. Subtle messages of trust, faith, synchronicity, guidance and love of self, underpinned the story, elevating the erotic elements to a higher level. Having never understood why society found spirituality and sexuality mutually exclusive, I guess my erotic romance series matched my point of view. As a woman who dared to speak her truth, these stories were a perfect fit. I was living with a new mantra—*Every move I make, every step I take, aligns with the unfoldment of my being.*

We can never presume where inspiration may lead. Our role is to follow. Unless our dreams align with the unfoldment of our *being*, they will never manifest. There's no point resisting this unfoldment and guidance, for the resistance will manifest in our environment and bodies. The more we yield and align ourselves, the more inspired and glorious our lives become.

I love the synchronistic nature of life. How in hindsight, everything, every person and every event emerges as coherent, necessary and orchestrated to deliver us into the present moment. That is the magic and miracle of life—the transition, transformation and transcendence. Who we were, to who we are now, is really our past life; and we live many of them as we embody this particular human form.

Looking back wistfully to the "good old days when we were younger" lowers the resonance of our Consciousness, whereas the vision of a brighter future exudes enormous drawing power. It energizes our life and attracts to us that which is "the best yet to come." The present moment is the gift in which challenges and opportunities abound as offerings for us to master our destiny. When we become more conscious of being Consciousness in expression, the parts of our lives which appeared to be lacking are reversed, healed and changed.

In contrast to my expanding level of Consciousness, my mother's faded with her worsening dementia. Refusing to challenge her vehement tantrums to remain in her unit, I engaged more carers to assist with day-to-day duties. Since her heart attack, I'd intuited that she was leaving. Drifting from her human form, her Consciousness came and went, but her love of being here never faltered. She found great joy in the simple things—being escorted to the nearby shopping center, having coffee and caring for her beloved cat—activities with which she contentedly filled her days. Still capable of personal hygiene and taking her medication, she secured herself a few more months of independent living and fussed around in her unit on an endless mission of moving objects from place to place.

She had previously celebrated birthdays, Christmas, Easter and other milestones with untold enthusiasm, and it was sad to see her forget these dates. Even though we included her during these festivities, after a short time her awareness wandered, and she was swamped with a panic to return to her unit.

Over the next months, the decline hastened. The loss of her treasured cat and her growing fear of death took an enormous toll on her. While I watched her fade away, I sought for a deeper meaning to dementia. Perhaps it was merely a transition; not from life to death, but from one experience of Consciousness to another. Although her mind drifted in and out, Mum's palest-of-blue eyes still held their same intensity. Her *being* still existed, inseparable and eternal, reaching out and telling me all was right time, right place. Sometimes I wonder if dementia is nothing more than dipping one's toe into the truth of Consciousness and then returning to this lifetime, dazed and overwhelmed. A little like being caught in a dream when we sleep. There's a part of us that knows it's a dream, and we struggle to wake up from it.

Both dreaming and dementia have a sense of reality to them, but we choose not to stay in the dream. Dementia may well identify someone struggling to choose whether to stay in this lifetime or go to the next. Their love of this life and for their loved ones here is so strong they struggle to stay. When in fact, their Consciousness is bursting to move on from the human form it currently embodies. Hence the drift of dementia until eventually the human body can no longer contain the expression of Consciousness.

Throughout these months, Mum and I played a waiting game together, one she refused to discuss. I knew no matter how much she or I longed for her to leave in a peaceful sleep, her fear of death would be her last challenge.

On 13 March 2015, category-five Cyclone Pam hurled its vengeance across the South Pacific. On the south-east corner, our resort lay in its destructive path as it pummeled Vanuatu, decimating vegetation and razing buildings to the ground. It was the worst cyclone in recorded history for this poor, struggling country and one which would have long-term effects. With fifty-foot waves ripping out the beach, torrents of unending rain saturating the property and 198-miles-per-hour winds tearing off roofing and uprooting old-age trees, our little slice of paradise weathered a calamitous hammering. We remained in constant contact with our resort manager, who evacuated guests and staff until communication networks failed, and we lost contact. A few days after the cyclone, Yianni prepared to depart on the first available flight to Port Vila.

I smiled at him. "You do know this is exactly what you wanted, don't you?"

He groaned. "What do you mean?"

Taking his hands, I pulled him beside me on the bed. "You wanted to be rid of the resort. Now you have that chance. Maybe not the way you thought, but here it is. If you see this as an opportunity rather than a problem, Cyclone Pam could be the best thing for us. The resort is insured. So instead of rebuilding and going through all that pain, let's just sell it in whatever condition it is."

A heavy sigh escaped him. He rose and stood gazing out the window, pensive and still. "You're right." He paused and his shoulders dropped. "You're absolutely right."

It's right in the middle of these so-called catastrophes that the ego screams loudest about how unfair life is. *What are you going to do now? This is terrible and will cost more and more money.* But right in the middle of the apparent turmoil is the truth. Physically and metaphorically, when winds, tides and rain prevail, the truth is our anchor. When we dare to disregard the ego's ranting of disaster, loss, lack and separation, we can then lean into the truth with trust and faith.

On the other side of chaos always lies clarity. It doesn't mean that what's going on in the world around us doesn't exist. It means our interpretation of it changes. We experience life from a new frame of reference, a more conscious approach based on the truth that everything is the unfoldment of *being*, individually and collectively. It's not about giving up when life throws a curve ball. It's about giving in. When we give in and listen to the still, small voice within, we inevitably stretch further and catch the ball.

Amidst more workshops, courses and final edits, I prepared to submit my first manuscript to a range of publishers. Knowing that rejection was the "name of the game" and that I'd entered an industry notorious for unceremonious rejection amused me. None of this new career was accidental.

"Clearly there's an invisible force in the universe that handles everything. No exceptions," wrote Dr. Wayne W. Dyer in one of his last books. Confirming this fact and in a series of synchronistic events, I ended up in the audience of about five hundred people on Maui attending one of his last workshops, Writing from Your Soul 2015.

During this time, two offers arrived to publish my first book. Elated, I signed with the company whose business practices reflected more transparency and professionalism, and in doing so, my other books in the series were guaranteed publication. In less than a few weeks of submitting my first manuscript, I was about to be a published author. Magic and miracles manifested around me once more.

Some would say I was lucky to have my first submitted manuscript picked up by two offers of publication. It wasn't luck and neither was my manuscript a groundbreaking work of literature. But I dared to dream, I dared to lean into my *being*, and after setting a clear intention and resonating to the reality I wanted, the law of attraction worked through me. I had fulfilled one of my first writing goals, that of being published.

Within fourteen days of my return from Maui, my ninety-three-year-old mother suffered a stroke. Fortunately, she was having coffee with her carer, who rang an ambulance and rushed her to the hospital. A small window existed for me to authorize the use of a drug which would open her veins and allow the blood clot to dislodge. Advised it carried a fifty-fifty success rate and with Mum incapable of making a decision, I authorized the drug.

Over the course of the next eight hours, my frail mother fought like a warrior. She struggled out of bed, refusing to rest. She screamed and cried, pushing with the strength of a lion against the young male attendant and me. As I watched the terrified face of the young man, I felt like the priest from the *Exorcist* trying to hold Regan down while in the throes of demonic possession. A bit extreme I know, but the strength and ferocity my mother mustered through those hours was unbelievable.

I'd often heard stories of people finding superhuman strength in extraordinary circumstances. This was one such event in my mother's life. Weighing barely fifty kilos, she fought so valiantly that by the next day, all my dancer's muscles ached like they'd just completed a marathon rehearsal. The poor male attendant was replaced by a more experienced carer, and we awaited Mum's recovery.

When she awoke, she recalled nothing of the previous night's horrors and smiled weakly. Although her face looked wretched, her spirit was restored, and her blue eyes danced at me in relief. Within a couple of days, most of her speech and mobility returned with some of her cognitive ability. She played with her favorite fluffy toys and began reading the newspaper aloud. Her doctors shook their heads in disbelief, amazed that she had made such a strong and rapid recovery.

"My mother stood on a railway platform for the first four years of her marriage waving her new husband off to war, never knowing if he'd return. She's made of tough stuff," I told them. Small of stature she may have been, but she possessed a mighty spirit.

Since she needed twenty-four-hour care, I had no other recourse than to place Mum into a nursing home, one of her greatest fears. By now, her capacity to understand that she'd lived independently before was no longer an issue and she settled in, albeit with some confusion. Fortunately, the two resident cats took a liking to her, making the transition a little easier, as did surrounding her with familiar toys, knickknacks and photographs.

A month later when we arrived to bring her home for her weekly visit, she declined, saying she was too tired. Like a sick, little girl huddled under the quilt, she looked lost and forlorn. No matter how I tried, she wouldn't be persuaded. When I kissed her cheek to leave, I intuited that her struggle to cling to this world would end soon.

If only she believed what Buddha said, "You can only lose what you cling to." But she was a World War II bride, and she wasn't going without a fight.

I received a call that night from the nursing home saying Mum was in pain, and they were awaiting the ambulance to take her to hospital. On reaching her bedside, I knew she was in more than pain. My mother never complained about anything, but her cries and pleas to "make it stop" echoed down the corridor and pierced my heart. That we live in a society where medical staff watch an elderly woman shriek in agony rather than give her serious pain relief for fear of litigation is beyond me. How can we possibly call ourselves civilized? Most people aren't afraid of dying, they're afraid of the pain. Dying pain-free is everyone's birthright.

Had I known that the night nurse wouldn't dispense more than a couple of Panadols every few hours, I would've brought stronger painkillers with me from home and given them to her myself. To have Mum cling to my arm screaming shredded my heart. I tried to reassure her that the ambulance would arrive soon, but it didn't. Two hours and another two Panadols later, the paramedics finally strode into the room. Her body temperature had dropped to 95.1 Fahrenheit and her left leg was ice cold with no signs of life.

By the time she was wheeled into hospital emergency, I'd completed the paperwork and prayed there'd be relief for her soon. Dazed and still in pain, she disappeared down a corridor on the ambulance gurney. My heart sank. Clasping hands, Yianni and I steeled ourselves for what was to come. After enduring four hours of merciless pain and another two hours of tests and analysis, she was finally administered morphine. As she drifted away, I leaned close to her ear. "Don't worry, Mum. I'll take care of everything."

An uneasy churn began in my stomach, and knowing its message, I swallowed the lump of emotion in my throat. The bearer of bad news was the vascular specialist who arrived at dawn. A blood clot had lodged in Mum's left groin. She had no pulse in her left leg and minimal in her right. The options were limited. Operate and amputate her left leg, an operation from which she may or may not recover. Or place her in palliative care, manage her pain and allow her body to break down and die. When the nurses settled her into Ward 3E to manage her pain, I stood by in silence asking for guidance, listening for the still, small voice within. I was sure Mum wouldn't want to lose her leg, and yet the thought of forcing her body into protracted shutdown offered no solace.

From the limited, human perspective my mother was dying. From the truth of conscious *being*, we never die—as energy we only change form. I knew amputation was not her wish and that on some level, she'd chosen to leave this incarnation in this way. My role was to assist her as best I could. Supported by a terrific doctor and team of nurses, I authorized palliative care and prayed she would yield.

Shock and grief accompanied me over the next few days, scurrying around like puppies at my feet trying to get my attention. My heart cleaved open, filled with love and longing, but also with a deep sense of peace. Alternating between bouts of sobbing and quiet meditation, I set about funeral preparations.

That we cannot choose to end the last days of our life with one simple injection when we're already in palliative care is absurd. Our pets are afforded more dignity in death than we're allowed to give ourselves. Starving and dehydrating our loved ones while their bodies slowly wither away on morphine is mistreatment of the highest order. Why do we do this? What is the benefit? Why do we legislate for the torture of the dying?

Over the next few days I watched this horror unfold as my mother clung to this life while I encouraged her to let go. She hadn't regained consciousness since being admitted. On one early occasion, she had partially opened one eye as if questioning what was going on. When I explained her body was broken beyond repair, her brow creased in confusion and a sense of misery surrounded her. Poor darling, she was still there, she just couldn't talk. And she didn't want to leave. Her love of life and fear of death were equally strong. The battle had begun.

Her facial grimaces motivated my demand for regular top-ups to the continuous morphine feed, which the doctor authorized. Helping her transition be as pain-free and dignified as possible became my primary role. My warrior spirit stood vigil. Here was my precious mother needing my protection. I was up for the task.

Over the remaining days I read to her, played music, assured her of what was happening and provided as much comfort as I could. Although I knew, as Consciousness, she wasn't dying, the physicality of the event distressed me. Before my eyes, she shrank into a form I'd not seen in this lifetime. Like a death camp survivor from World War II, she was no more than a bag of skin and bones, and I was her torturer.

At home I couldn't control the grief, the guilt and the tears. I threw myself, wailing and inconsolable, into Yianni's arms. "Look what I'm doing to her? I can't save her."

My knees buckled with overwhelming emotion. Even though I knew I wasn't doing anything to her, and it certainly wasn't my job to save her, my mother's slow death provided a wondrous opportunity to expand my Consciousness and hers, if she so chose. Her departure signified another step up the stairway to paradise. The decision to dance was mine.

I spent those last days holding her hand, telling her how much I loved her and reminiscing. Seeing her struggle for breath with her mouth blackened from the shadow of death, I spoke to her of my gratitude, my everlasting love and the assurance that we'd be together again.

Locked behind the morphine wall, she never had a chance to respond, and we never shared a conscious goodbye. While she slipped further from this lifetime, I began reading to her.

With blissful meditation music playing, Yianni and I sat on either side of the bed holding her icy, skeletal hands. While I was reading, an enormous energy seared my left arm, reminding me of Reiki energy—hot, specific and empowering. I glanced at Yianni, who released Mum's hand and rubbed his arm.

"You felt it too?" I whispered; glad it wasn't just me.

He flexed his fingers. "Yes. What was it?"

"Maybe she's leaving…" I stared down at my sweet mother as her chest rose and fell. The dragging of breath eased slightly, but she still lingered. When the nurses arrived to administer another morphine injection, I heard "let it be" as clearly as if someone in the room had spoken it aloud.

After the nurses left, I leaned down and kissed my mother on the cheek. "Good night, Mum. See you tomorrow or in my dreams. I'll leave it to you."

She came to me at 2.30am the next morning.

Either everything is energy, or it isn't.
Either everything is Consciousness, or it isn't.
Either everything is the unfoldment of *being* or it isn't.

If everything is energy, Consciousness, the unfoldment of *being*, then everything is fulfilling itself completely.

The death of a loved one is one of the most confronting events to this truth. For those of us left behind, the sense of separation can feel both intimately real and intellectually surreal. The sense of loss can be acute and for some, chronic.

But isn't it the loss of the familiar which is really the issue as we begin a new life, seemingly alone and separated from the one we loved? It's in this state of misplaced separateness that we're likely to give our ego carte blanche to regurgitate every negative emotion. Heartache, grief, self-doubt, guilt, indecision, blame, worthlessness, anger, inadequacy, fear of the future—an endless litany of emotions creeps up like silent raiders in the night to distract us from the truth.

I'm not suggesting that we should stop the expression of this emotional energy. Any energy blocked at the moment of its initial expressive need leads to disease at some later stage. However, in the expression of our grief, we have the opportunity to witness our growth, knowing that as conscious *being*, we're in no way affected by death. Just because we can't physically see, hear, smell, taste or touch the one who has died, doesn't mean they don't exist as Consciousness. And since we're all the activity of Consciousness in expression, we are all one. We're of the one source, the one Consciousness which is ever-changing, ever-moving, and never dies.

So, in the expression of my grief, I included gratitude and gave thanks for the selfless love and devotion of my mother. In the expression of my loss, I experienced love. By being still and silent, I elevated myself above sadness to serenity. When the ego tried to make me feel guilty for not being a good enough daughter, I forgave myself. For every negative emotion that threatened to overwhelm me, I reached for a positive feeling to counteract its impact on my Consciousness. I let love be my intention, even in my mother's death. I chose for peace, poise, passion and purpose to guide me during these testing times. There was much power in these decisions.

Five days after being admitted to hospital, my mother's Consciousness left her body. For me, the relief was two-fold. Firstly, the struggle and suffering to remain had ended, but most importantly, she finally knew the truth.

Anita Moorjani wrote of her near-death experience in her autobiography, *Dying to Be Me*, "When we spill out of our bodies, we cross all time and space with awareness…we're pure consciousness."

Without reservation, I knew this to be true, and now so did my mother.

On completing arrangements at the hospital, I continued my day. Walking past a newsagent, I slowed at the card stand and spied a Perfect Mother plaque which eloquently reflected my feelings. When I clutched it to my chest, a strong whiff of Mum's favorite perfume, which I'd been buying her for years, wafted around me. Peering over the stand, I spotted a diminutive elderly woman with an angelic face and lips accented in bright red lipstick. Dressed in lavish colors and scarves just like my mother used to wear, she smiled up at me. She bustled to the counter, made her purchase and when she turned to exit, I stopped her.

"Excuse me, are you wearing Giorgio perfume?"

Her smile was sweet like my mother's. "No. I'm wearing Chanel 19."

Knowing Giorgio and Chanel 19 smelled nothing like each other, I offered a meek apology through misty eyes.

She reached out to me. "Whatever is wrong, dear?"

"My mother passed away this morning. You dress like her and when her perfume surrounded me just now, I thought you must be wearing Giorgio."

She hugged me close. "No, dear, that wasn't my perfume you smelled."

While I accepted comfort in the arms of a stranger, I knew it had been an omen from my mother, telling me she was fine.

I eased away. "Thank you so much for being here at this moment."

"That's perfectly all right, dear. I'm pleased I could help." Even her kind demeanor mirrored my mother's.

After I paid for my purchase and left the newsagent, I sent a silent thank-you for the experience. I'd been touched by my mother's *being* as proof of our eternal Consciousness. She was now *being* in the experience and connecting with me. Love lifted me like levitation. I wanted to dance through the shopping center and tell everyone what was really happening all around and within us.

Over the following days while writing a eulogy, sincerity cards, producing a DVD on Mum's life and general funeral preparation, I finalized details for my forthcoming writing events. Within two days of the funeral I had to be on a plane interstate to attend a major writing conference. Shortly after my return, I'd be hosting a writing panel at another festival. After which I'd be launching my first book. As my time-management and organizational skills took over, I wondered if all mothers lived and died with the best wishes of their children's future and welfare at heart. I knew they probably didn't, but mine did. The timing of her departure slipped perfectly into the few available dates in my busy schedule. The more I pondered that nothing ever happens by accident but by intention, the more love filled my heart.

Sorting through Mum's things, I appreciated the love even more. Tucked in dusty old boxes were documents that I never knew existed—adoption applications, correspondence from the Children's Department requesting medical certificates and X-rays as proof of the adopting couple's health, and the adoption order, still with its steel paper pin in the top corner. Wedged in the middle of this pile from a distant past was a square of yellowed paper, a letter from an unknown woman. Plucked out on an old typewriter, the crooked letters' message of love wrote:

> *Adopted*
> *Not flesh of my flesh*
> *Nor bone of my bone*
> *But still miraculously my own.*
> *Never forget for even one minute*
> *You did not grow under my heart—but in it.*

This simple verse spoke of my mother's love for me, the daughter she had longed for and finally found. Other letters from adopting couples and magazine articles of the same sentiment, "Explaining the truth to the adopted child," "Especially Chosen" and more, fluttered from the box and my tears flowed. Not from grief, but from *being*. My human passion to fulfil my destiny transformed to oceans of gratitude for the divine love of my parents. I had been special to them, so very special.

The journey of adoption they'd embarked on had been monumentally challenging and life-changing. Their entire focus had been me.

I now knew what loving unconditionally meant. That was how I was loved. Up until now, I'd never experienced the everlastingness of it. Even when I was eleven years of age, and I demanded not to be special any longer or discuss my adoption, they loved me so much, they honored my wishes. How they must have wanted me to believe I was special. How they must have wanted to discuss my adoption as I grew older, to share their feelings, their journey and their gratitude. How blessed I was to have had them as parents. Rivers of tears drenched my cheeks while I sobbed in gratitude for my mother and father who nurtured me so well, for my biological mother and father who gave me such a strong genetic nature and for the love—divine, unconditional love most of us never experience.

None of us are rejected or abandoned. We are all chosen. We're all special. We're all divine love. That's what unifies and defines us. For most of our lives, we allow ourselves to be distracted, and we miss the very essence of *being*. We go in search of it through careers, through parents, through children, through lovers in the hope of finding it in another or in something else, when all the time it dwells in our heart, waiting to be freed, to wrap us in its unconditional embrace. If we all dared to love and connect with our inner peace, we'd change the world.

Like John Lennon lamented, "Imagine…."

In the lead-up to the funeral, my daily meditations anchored me. For the first time in months, I turned to the Native American Indian cards for a message. In pulling the lizard card, I registered the double meaning of its message. The first most obvious message pertained to Mum feeding the lizards in her garden before she moved into the nursing home. Heartbroken over losing her treasured cat, she'd reverted to saving the lizards and birds by feeding them bread. She loved doing this even though the other residents of the village hated the swarm of creatures she attracted. The lizard card also signified a dream time where lizard has no fear; he sees all and knows all.

The next day a water dragon from our pond perched itself on our outdoor dog bed. Never had a lizard been so bold as to come and take up residence at the kitchen door. After an hour or so, it disappeared, but its message was clear. Everything is energy.

The day of the funeral arrived, and I had no tears, only a warm embracing sense of my mother *being* with me, not necessarily as I knew her, but as Consciousness. I spent time in my Zen room contemplating the day ahead, and in my meditation, requested an unmistakable omen.

"A lizard," I said aloud. "Not the lizard from the other day, but a great big lizard, no less than two feet long to cross my path today. It can happen at the funeral or cemetery or anywhere. But it must be obvious."

I sent out my intention and returned to the center of my *being*. I knew this day would be challenging. But it also offered me an opportunity to experience living consciously, to come from *being* all day, while the conditions and circumstances tried to convince me I had suffered enormous loss.

Who are you now? You have no mother or father. Everyone is gone. You're all alone. Just like when you were abandoned as a baby. The sinister thoughts of the ego tried to worm into my mind, but no, I wouldn't allow them entry. Today was my day to live with peace and truly *be*.

Throughout the service and burial, and while others dabbed their eyes, a quiet sense of joy filled me. I knew. My mother's body lay cold and lifeless in the coffin, but that wasn't her. Like me, she was pure Consciousness. We were one.

After the funeral and on our way home, I turned to Yianni. "Did you see any lizards? I felt sure there would be a lizard."

"No. No lizards, but the day's not over yet."

Good point.

With a massive floral arrangement in my arms, I walked into our house to prepare for the guests. When I rounded the corner, I froze. What should be lounging on the pool coping looking directly at me through the sliding glass door, but an enormous water dragon, at least two feet long. Never had a water dragon, and certainly not one this big, ventured up to the house. It held its gaze and position, even when I opened the door and the puppies padded over for a sniff. In absolute delight, we stood gazing at the first guest to Mum's wake. I immediately applied the female gender to the lizard and named her Beryl, after my mother.

"Now, don't you go being a nuisance. Just leave your grandmother alone," I warned the puppies while I moved through the house into the kitchen.

I glanced back to find that Beryl had followed me and stood watching from outside the kitchen sliding door. Around her sprawled our three dogs as if somehow sensing a familiarity. When I slid the door open, she didn't move and remained unperturbed until the guests arrived, at which time, she left. Later, when I went to the Zen room for a gratitude meditation, she reappeared on a large rock in the pond.

Am I crazy? Some may think so. Was the lizard my mother? No. But on some level, the specific intention I'd flung out into the Consciousness brought to me that which I desired. For me, there's no doubt that the Consciousness of my mother still resonated to me after her death. This was further confirmed over the coming weeks because Beryl the lizard appeared every day. Was it the same lizard? Yes, because she possessed a distinct pink underbelly, my mother's favorite color.

Beryl arrived each morning at the kitchen door when Yianni made mid-morning coffees—Mum's favorite time of the day because she loved a piping-hot cappuccino. Throughout these visits, none of the dogs bothered her. Impressed with the repeated scene, Yianni took numerous photos and film of the puppies and Beryl lying side by side around the pool. This ongoing daily omen lasted for close to two weeks after the funeral, then became more sporadic over the next six months.

Not long after, when I drifted to sleep, I called on Mum one last time. During that twilight space when we disassociate ourselves with our physical body, she came to me and hugged me so tight, I felt suffocated. I knew unquestioningly this was her, because that's how she loved me throughout my life with the same intense protection. She clung to me, wanting me to go with her. Struggling back awake, I said, "Not now. I'll see you soon." That was the last cuddle I received from my mother. The cuddles I still miss, but I know she's with me always.

The year 2015 rolled into the next with more wonderous changes. The cycle of life continued with the addition of four grandchildren whose consciousness compelled them to incarnate into this family grouping. With one of these *beings* I have a strong, supernatural connection. Valentina is my spirit child—Natalie's daughter of body and mine of spirit. Since they live overseas, she was thirteen months old before we first met, but we both registered an uncanny familiarity. Her chocolate-brown eyes locked on mine and a look of recognition settled onto her face.

Up until this time, I had no idea what I wanted my step-grandchildren to call me. Grandma, nana, nanny all felt wrong. However, Valentina solved the dilemma the moment she saw me and called me Nene. I'd never heard the term before, but she seemed quite insistent on the strange name. It wasn't until three years later that Natalie came across an Instagram image of Mother Theresa taken in Albania. It read Nene Theresa…Nene means mother. Was Valentina the one I'd terminated years ago? Was I supposed to have been her mother? Or had I been her mother before? Whatever the truth may be, when we met, we laughed like monkeys together, overjoyed at finally finding each other.

As far as Valentina was concerned, Natalie and I were interchangeable, and she called us both mummy as she grew into a toddler. I now eagerly wait for her vocabulary to improve so we can talk about Consciousness and what she remembers before this incarnation. The more I look, the more I see, and the more I adore this interwoven, congruent tapestry of life which is the demonstration of Consciousness in expression.

The resort sold, and after cutting our losses, Yianni breathed a sigh of relief to finally call Australia home for good. The second book in my erotic romance series was published, with the third not far behind it.

Where will it all lead? To my destiny, of course—there's no other possible conclusion. And what is my destiny? My destiny is that which I dare to choose. And what do I choose? To facilitate the evolution of human Consciousness in alignment with the unfolding of my *being* and keep dancing up the stairway to paradise. Simply, to let it, and me, *be*…

Insights…Be yielding, Be humble, Be honest, Be in a state of grace

To be the fullest expression of Consciousness and live each moment from this state of *being* is our ultimate purpose. We're all magnificent, powerful and immortal beings, resonating with Consciousness of love and light. It's in us, of us, around us, before and beyond us. All of who we are is eternally present, at every moment, regardless of what we do. Too often we misinterpret ourselves as finite, imperfect and decaying humans, rather than omnipresent, omniscient and omnipotent *being*. Too often we judge ourselves and others, and in doing so, we reject our inherent good and universal truth.

But when we come from conscious *being*, we can be in the world, but not of it. What is going on around us doesn't affect or distract us. Instead, we respond to it with honesty and truth. Honesty uplifts our energy. Truth quickens our influence. Being honest and telling the truth from *being* and not the ego's version of it, liberates us to express ourselves with dignity and congruence. It gives our words power. For when we dare to be humble and honest, we experience *being*.

We can never understand *being* from the ego's point of view, from our limited, human perspective. Even as you read this, the ego may be trying to confuse you, telling you this is all poppycock and where's the proof? It's all mumbo-jumbo because it doesn't make sense. But that's the addictive nature of the ego. It gives you another fix of confusion, doubt and indifference, hoping you'll disregard these words and the experience of them, rather than disregarding it. Let it *be*. Don't battle with the ego. Don't try to understand. Become undefended against the ego's endless negative chatter and dare to allow the peace inherent in the center of your *being* to guide you. "You will know the truth, and the truth will set you free."

The script of the ego never changes—same script, different actors, same drama, different stages. Our role is not to perform. We must turn down every part the ego offers. No matter how much we may hunger for the glittering illusion of life, we must decline the ego's proposal. Instead, we must direct and star in our own lives—consciously. We must come from Consciousness and focus on ourselves as conscious *being*. This is how we produce spectacular, fulfilling and successful lives.

Being is not intellectual, but rather experiential. It's the experience of yielding into something far greater than our limited, human perspective. It's not about thinking, believing, doing and having. When we live each day as an immortal *being*, all thought of death, lack, loss and separation slips from us, and we pass from fear to love, less to more, loss to miracle, separation to oneness. To come from *being*, we need to allow the energies of oneness and connectedness to permeate us and dare to lean into and yield to this experience.

Being is the humility of love. By asking for help from within and listening for the answer, we humble ourselves to the love which we are in expression. When we live as conscious *being*, as love, we're inspired to do great works, to move mountains. But, most importantly, when we're being humble, we don't move mountains, they move for us—subtle yet divergent frames of reference. One represents control of the mountains, which is grandstanding, while the other represents the mountains moving of their own volition due to our *being* and humility.

Being is living in a state of grace which requires no effort, skill or practice. Grace elicits beauty, dignity and elegance and is the conduit of our eventual transcendence. With grace, you know there's nothing for you to do, but everything to *be*. Many might say it's going with the flow. But going with the flow relative to the circumstances and conditions in our life relinquishes us from any responsibility of bringing these events to pass.

More correctly, grace is going with the flow of our unfolding *being*, our Consciousness. To go within to the center of our *being* from where the flow originates and to yield into it, is living with grace. The story of the ugly cygnet who turns into a beautiful swan through no manipulation of its own demonstrates grace's transformative and inspirational nature. It's living as a self-realized person with rapture, reverence and respect, knowing that no matter what's apparently going on, it too shall pass.

There is an inherent orderliness, harmony and principle to life. All life is Consciousness and is unfolding itself at every moment as a whole, not as an isolated part of the whole. We cannot by our intellectual processes alone impact this infinitely detailed and harmonious unfolding of *being*. Our role is to align our processes with Consciousness and not try to bring this unfoldment into line with our thoughts.

The dreams, desires and passions which empower us to reach for the stars originate from our *being*. We must dare to disregard the limited, human perspective and trust in the unfoldment of our *being*, the expansion of our Consciousness. In doing so, our dreams, desires and passions will spontaneously manifest. Harmony will always be the result if we come from the standpoint of *being* rather than from the standpoint of trying to manipulate and control. To align ourselves with the inherent intelligence of our unfolding *being*, is simply being conscious of Consciousness in expression, which is every one of us.

Little did I realize that back in 1971, The Beatles hit to which I became a sexual woman would become the underlying theme song for my life…"Let it Be." Over the years, this song has surfaced as repeated omens with Paul McCartney singing from my car radio or other device. "Let it be" was the phrase spoken numerous times in the stillness of my meditations and has been the predominant message in the tarot cards over the past thirty years. It was the instruction given to me at my mother's deathbed, to walk away, and in doing so, let her *be*. And it falls from my own mouth as words of wisdom whenever they're needed most. The meaning of the phrase is not to leave things alone, but to get out of the way and let it *be*. Let the conscious expression of *being*, be.

And therein lies not the secret, but the answer. Since we're all the activity of Consciousness in expression, we're all one. We are of the one source, the one Consciousness which is ever-changing, flowing, creating and eternal. You are, he is, she is, they are, we are, I am…one.

When we affirm, *I am healthy*, *I am successful*, *I am beautiful*, we use the adjective as a descriptor of ourselves. Yet this description is incorrect if we are one Consciousness. The Consciousness isn't healthy or successful or beautiful. The Consciousness is health, success, beauty and so forth.

Therefore, the more appropriate affirmation is, *I am health, I am success, I am beauty, I am abundance, I am intelligence, I am love, I am light, I am grace, I am gratitude, I am inspiration, I am life, I am.* It's when we associate ourselves with the *I am-ness* of Consciousness through these affirmations of indivisibility that we harmonize with the divine energies of our *being*.

In the final analysis, there is truly nothing for us to do. No steps to take, no processes to master, nothing to improve, no growth, nothing at all. We are already *being* the immaculate, unlimited expression of Consciousness expressing itself, whether we believe it or not.

We've been deluded into believing that what appears to be going on around us in the external world is all there is to life. Yet on a deep level, we know this isn't true. Once we dare to surrender these delusions and lean into our conscious experience of *being*, the illusion will pass. We won't cease to exist, but we will experience the truth which identifies us as Consciousness uniquely expressing itself fully every moment.

I am that I am…

At a remarkable 93 years, Mum's spirit remained as vibrant as ever, especially during the Christmas season. This year, wrapped in cherished memories, we celebrated our final Christmas together, a tender and precious moment in time.

On the day of Mum's funeral, our fur baby, Chanel paid no attention to the enormous water dragon waiting on the pool coping when we returned from the cemetery.

Everything is energy and that's all there is to it!

From our very first meeting, it was clear that Valentina and I were kindred spirits, connected by an unspoken bond that only love can weave. This cherished moment, captured forever, is a testament to the timeless love shared between us.

ENCORE

"All truth passes through three stages. First, it is ridiculed. Second, it is violently opposed. Third, it is accepted as being self-evident," wrote Arthur Schopenhauer. For those of us inspired to search for truth, we are just as inspired to share it. Many will say my story is subjective truth because it's my memoir. Nevertheless, there's a greater truth at work here. A universal truth that's been subjected to ridicule, violently opposed and is now for many people self-evident. It's the truth which illuminates the stairway to paradise on which I dance.

Even when I was young, I never saw the world as most other kids did. I had to find meaning. I needed to know. In retrospect, it was this urge to wake up and *be* which has directed every facet of my life. Despite everything else I wished, worked or strived for, it all faded into insignificance if it didn't constitute the evolution of my Consciousness and the unfoldment of my *being*.

Now, as I enter the third act of my life, I am at another beginning and what have I come to know?

I know we must stand up, speak universal truth, and let the chips fall where they may.

I know there's far more going on than the human experience. We must dare to live each day as immortal *being*, to lean into the omnipresence, omniscience and omnipotence of infinite mind, to trust universal Consciousness and have faith that *being* is all there is.

I know that meditation is the fastest, most direct route to the center of my *being*.

I know there's a divine spark within each of us that we cannot fully extinguish. No matter how hard we try, it will shine.

I know life isn't a dress rehearsal. It's show time, all the time. We're the writers, producers, directors, choreographers, dancers and actors in this grand production of life. Every day, we choose the part we play. Every person, prop, setting, costume, light, color, design, word spoken, note played, song sung, and step danced we've influenced in some way.

I know we must explore, energize and enjoy each day as if it was our first.

I know we must dare to go where our heart leads. For it's better to burn out in a blaze of passion than fade away.

I know success never manifests until the internal work is done. Each of us experiences exactly the amount of success and abundance we can justify receiving.

I know every decision we make moves us in the direction of our destiny. The more our Consciousness expands, and we align with the unfoldment of our *being*, the more congruent and powerful our decisions become.

I know, despite all else, that love matters. Never let a moment slip by that you don't reach out and hug the ones you love. A moment missed can never be redeemed. The love of self, family, friends and sentient beings across all universes stirs the evolution of human consciousness, uplifting us to higher resonances.

And I know that it's not just for the moment we live. We go on and on and on.

Now decades later, as I stand gazing at the night sky, no longer holding my father's hand, but feeling his and my mother's presence with me, I marvel at the matrix of possibilities which constitute our lives. Like the billions of stars, we resonate at different brightness and intensities, attracting to ourselves the unlimited options from which we can choose. Vast realms of opportunities and challenges likewise resonate, waiting to weave our destiny. It's not just for this current embodiment, but forever.

Our limited, human perspective can't even begin to comprehend the timeless incarnations and endless eternity we are, you are, I am. No matter our perceived age, gender, race, religion or morality, we're all luminescent, infinite *being*. When the world broadcasts situations of seeming horror we must be courageous, altruistic, hopeful, faithful, idealistic, loyal, unselfish, willing to seek the truth no matter where it leads and choose for love, not fear, individually and collectively.

Our planet, like the rest of the universes, transits and transforms itself on its orbit to transcendence, much as we do. We've all chosen to be here now, in order to yield into our Consciousness and be the fullest expression of *being*.

Still through Pollyanna eyes, I gaze upwards and know everything is unfolding infinitely in right time, right place. The dance of Consciousness is eternal and everlasting. It's a joyous, radiant routine, effervescing with energy in a never-ending celebration of life. Swirling and twirling, the dance beckons us to participate, to put on our dancing shoes and step up the stairway to paradise. Don't sit it out. Don't fear the fallout. Leap from your sideline seat of ignorance and command center stage. Dare to *be* the star of your own life. Dare to *be* you.

THE END

My first official publicity photograph as an author which marked the beginning of an extraordinary journey into the creative world of storytelling and literary exploration. A new adventure begins.

50 INSIGHTS TO BEING

Chapter 8 **Let go and lean in**	Be Decisive	Live with integrity and harness the power of your decisions
	Be Playful	Approach life with a childlike attitude
	Be Spontaneous	Live in a natural state of freedom
	Be Joyous	Sacrifice the negatives
Chapter 9 **Listen and look for omens**	Be Willing	See everything, everyone and every situation brand new
	Be Responsible	Be willing to respond rather than react
	Be Perceptive	Look for the omens
Chapter 10 **Stirrings of the soul**	Be Centered	Go within and connect to the center of your *being*
	Be Curious	Approach each day as if it were your first, not your last
	Be Receptive	Listen to the whispers
	Be in Communion	Open up to consciousness
Chapter 11 **Releasing my emotional past**	Be Love	Be love, loved and lovable through the giving and receiving of love
	Be Forgiving	Give forth love when it is the most challenging
	Be Present	Live in the moment by *being* in that moment
Chapter 12 **Fire of desire**	Be Focused	Set your vision, purpose and goals

	Be Committed	Commit to yourself and your growth
	Be Purposeful	Live life on purpose, with purpose and back it with action
Chapter 13 Passion is power	Be Passionate	Approach life with unstoppable enthusiasm
	Be Powerful	Disregard the ego and function with personal excellence
	Be Patient	Demonstrate faith by thinking right time, right place
	Be Fearless	Keep your eyes on the prize and go beyond fear
Chapter 14 Creating a brighter future	Be Peaceful	Value your peace above all else
	Be Healthy	Honor and value the five facets of yourself
	Be Disciplined	Practice makes perfect
	Be Driven	Energize your destiny
	Be Determined	Act as if it is already so
Chapter 15 Reaping the rewards	Be Persistent	Never, never, never give up
	Be Strong	Have the grit to stay the course
	Be Thankful	Practice gratitude
Chapter 16 Attention and intention	Be Intentional	Include purpose to your thoughts, words and actions
	Be Generous	Add value to yourself, your life and others
	Be Undefended	See the world as a friendly place, not a hostile one
	Be Courageous	Act from *being*, rather than conditioning
Chapter 17 Magic and miracles	Be Optimistic	Think abundance

	Be Open	Expect miracles
	Be Bold	Trust in your *being* and aim for stars
Chapter 18 A new role	Be Kind	Think, speak and act with kindness
	Be Intuitive	Let love guide your actions
	Be Flexible	Change your approach until you reach your goal
Chapter 19 Fulfillment and success	Be Inspired	Visualize victory
	Be Valuable	Aspire to be of service and help others
	Be Intelligent	Act from the infinite intelligence of your *being*
Chapter 20 Setting the trap	Be Gentle	Treat yourself and tread in the world with gentleness
	Be Intimate	Go within and become self-knowing
	Be Creative	Express yourself through creative pursuits
	Be Balanced	Live in harmony with your *being*
Chapter 21 Let it be	Be Yielding	Surrender conditioned thinking, past limitations and trust in *being*
	Be Humble	Ask for help from within
	Be Honest	Know and accept the inherent truth within everything
	Be in a State of Grace	Cultivate your inner beauty, dignity and elegance

Find out more about Diane's keynote speaking, interactive programs, executive coaching services, and books at:

dianedemetre.com

AWARD WINNING AUTHOR

"Dare to dream bigger than ever before, dare to forge your own path no matter how hard the challenges. But most of all, dare to be you and let the chips fall where they may. We are all warrior women with gossamer wings…It's time to soar!"

—Diane Demetre

Winner of 2019 SBAA International Women's Day Leader Award for Leadership in the Entertainment, Creative Arts and/or Media Industry.

Diane was nominated as a finalist in the ARRA Awards 2018 for Favourite Romantic Suspense, for her novel *Retribution*.

In 2017, Diane won the Romance Writers of Australia Emerald Pro Award for Best Unpublished Romance Manuscript, for her novel *Retribution*.

ALSO BY DIANE DEMETRE

NON-FICTION
Master Mindset

FICTION
The Diana Daniels Mysteries
Island of Secrets
Retribution
Take Me
Teach Me
Tempt Me

www.ingramcontent.com/pod-product-compliance
Lightning Source LLC
Chambersburg PA
CBHW071226080526
44587CB00013BA/1518